Mothers on the Job

Mothers on the Job

Maternity Policy in the U.S. Workplace

Lise Vogel

Rutgers University Press
New Brunswick, New Jersey

HD
6065.5
U6
D54
1993

Library of Congress Cataloging-in-Publication Data

Vogel, Lise.
    Mothers on the job : maternity policy in the U.S. workplace / by Lise Vogel.
        p.   cm.
    Includes bibliographical references and index.
    ISBN 0-8135-1918-7 (cloth)—ISBN 0-8135-1919-5 (pbk.)
    1. Maternity leave—United States.   2. Maternity leave—Government
policy—United States.   3. Pregnant women—Employment—United
States.   4. Pregnant women—Employment—Government policy—United
States.   I. Title.
HD6065.5.U6D54   1993
331.4'4—dc20   92-21874
                                                                                                  CIP

British Cataloging-in-Publication information available

Here she comes, running, out of prison and off pedestal; chains off, crown off, halo off, just a live woman.

Charlotte Perkins Gilman
"Is Feminism Really So Dreadful?" 1914

I am who I am, doing what I came to do, acting upon you like a drug or a chisel to remind you of your me-ness, as I discover you in myself.

Audre Lorde
"Eye to Eye," 1984

Contents

Acknowledgments

Many friends and colleagues contributed support and advice as I worked on this book. I am particularly indebted to Susan Reverby and Kathleen Daly for enthusiasm, conversation, and knowledgable critiques, provided over a number of years. I am fortunate to have been able to draw so frequently on their stores of wisdom and feminist savvy. At critical junctures and in various guises, Ruth Milkman, Judith Stacey, and Hester Eisenstein read the manuscript, sometimes more than once. Their comments and suggestions were invaluable, as was their warm encouragement. For patient explanations of the legal aspects of the issues and assessments of the political ones as well, my deepest appreciation goes to Joan Bertin, Donna Lenhoff, and Nadine Taub. I owe a special debt to Cynthia Harrison, who generously went over the entire manuscript with a feminist historian's fine-toothed comb. I am also grateful to many colleagues and friends for reading selected chapters or giving expert advice on particular points. For this much appreciated assistance I thank Eleanor Bader, Ava Baron, Renate Bridenthal, Nancy Cott, James Dickinson, Myra Marx Ferree, Martha Fineman, Jack Hammond, Terry Haywoode, Alice Kessler-Harris, Paul Montagna, Molly Nolan, Ellen Schrecker, Roberta Spalter-Roth, Ronnie Steinberg, and Carole Turbin. Marlie Wasserman, my editor at Rutgers University Press, offered steadfast support and astute commentary, for both of which I am deeply grateful. Thanks also to Kathryn Gohl for sharp copyediting of the manuscript. Grants from Rider College, the American Council of Learned Societies, and the National Endowment for the Humanities partially supported the research.

Mothers on the Job

1

The Dilemma of Pregnancy Policy

In the United States, questions about what kinds of measures best address women's needs have often been formulated in terms of women's equality to or difference from men. Policy-makers ask, for example, whether women are better served by emphasizing equality or recognizing difference. Does treating women and men the same always produce the fairest result? Or does real equality for women require that their special concerns and activities sometimes be acknowledged positively in public policy? With respect to pregnancy and motherhood, should women have access to female-specific benefits to accommodate the special burdens created by maternity? Can policies treating mothers in a special manner be reconciled with the norms of equality?

In this book I explore the puzzle of policy for women by looking at the treatment of pregnancy in the workplace. My inquiry has a double purpose. On the one hand I examine the evolution of pregnancy policy as a strategic dilemma. On the other I trace it as a problem in feminist thought. Together, these two investigations extend a critique of equality thinking already undertaken by feminist theorists and legal scholars.

Most industrialized countries address the needs of pregnant workers by means of explicitly articulated maternity and family policies. In contrast, the United States has always resisted such a deliberate approach. Indeed, it is often said that the United States has neither a maternity nor a family policy. While else-where mothers and their families can rely on a systematically developed social welfare system, in the United States they face a haphazard policy maze. Federal, state, and local programs operate with little coordination and offer barely a fraction of the substantive support available in, for example, Canada or Italy. As U.S. Representative Patricia Schroeder of Colorado puts it, "the United States has never been able to formulate a comprehensive policy directed to the needs of the family." The editors of a recent book on parental leave concur: "The United States stands alone among industrialized nations in its lack of a formal policy recognizing a social responsibility toward the well-being of the family."[1]

Few would deny that American mothers and their families receive remarkably little support from the state. Nonetheless, the chaotic array of programs and policies affecting them attains a certain policy coherence. That is, a maternity and family policy can be said to have long been in place in the United States—heterogeneous, uncodified, and stingy though its components are.[2] This policy has been embodied in legislation, court opinions, government regulations, and employer practices concerning pregnancy, motherhood, and family. Recent efforts to implement new measures affecting families—for example, parental leave, child care programs, divorce reform, joint custody mandates—therefore challenge a system already in existence. These new initiatives signal a shift, I argue, toward a different kind of maternity and family policy. Where the older approach anchored families to assumptions of irreducible sexual difference, the emerging one situates family life and gender specificity within a framework of equality.

The more public policy has assumed equality among persons, the more puzzling the questions posed by pregnancy in the workplace have become. The dilemma deepened in the 1980s, when the validity of state laws providing special benefits for pregnant workers became the object of litigation. In the best-known case, Lillian Garland, a Los Angeles bank receptionist, sought in 1982 to return to her job after taking a four-month disability leave for a difficult first pregnancy. California law required employers to provide unpaid job-protected disability leaves to their pregnant employees, but Garland's employer refused to rehire her. Instead, the bank brought suit to invalidate the statute, arguing it conflicted with federal antidiscrimination legislation that mandated equal treatment. Five years later the United States Supreme Court upheld the California pregnancy disability statute as not inconsistent with federal law and ordered the bank to reinstate Garland. The decision was widely welcomed as a victory for working women. Garland, now a single mother, spoke for many when she commented that "women should not have to choose between being a mother and having a job."[3]

The California case brought the dilemma of pregnancy policy to a head and divided the feminist legal community. Feminist attorneys and legal scholars argued over the merits and dangers of pregnancy disability leave statutes and took opposing positions in the litigation. On one side of the issue were advocates of policies identified by equality terms. On the other were critics who endorsed strategies associated with the vocabulary of difference. Equal treatment, same treatment, and gender-neutral treatment lined up against special treatment, different treatment, and female-specific treatment. Although the arguments in this equality-versus-difference debate sometimes seemed convoluted and arcane, they implicated long-standing problems of feminist strategy and theory.[4]

At the heart of much of the discussion was a developing skepticism about the value of using equality principles to shape policy for women. Feminist policy activists in the 1960s and 1970s had concentrated on eliminating practices that excluded women because they were different. Rejecting notions of gender difference that justified the unfavorable treatment of women, they represented women as the same as men. The limits of same treatment in the name of equality became increasingly obvious, however. Including women within society's institutional structures as if they were the same as men turned out to be no guarantee of a fair outcome. Ignoring difference, just like emphasizing it, could result in practices that harmed women. In the case of pregnancy in the workplace, for example, treating women and men the same apparently meant denying women's special needs as childbearers and mothers. Here, as in other policy arenas, gender-neutral legal rules could collide with the sex specificity of women's experience.

Equality-versus-difference paradoxes became an important

focus of feminist policy analysis in the 1980s.[5] The concerns of the participants in the policy debates converged, moreover, with those of contemporary feminist theorists. As feminist lawyers and policy activists argued about the wisdom of female-specific measures, feminist academics from many disciplines commented on the meaning of difference and its relationship to concepts of equality. Their theoretical efforts addressed questions similar to those emerging from the policy discussions.[6]

Discussion of equality-versus-difference issues appeared to be exhausted by the end of the 1980s. Once the Supreme Court in the Lillian Garland case affirmed the validity of state laws mandating disability leaves for pregnant employees, the legal matter seemed settled; policy activists moved on to other issues. Concurrently, efforts by feminist theorists to resolve the equality/difference dilemma proved frustrating, and many began challenging the terms in which the questions had been posed. The opposition of difference to equality came to be viewed as conceptually flawed. For example, legal scholar Lucinda Finley argued that despite the appearance of antagonism, equal-treatment and special-treatment advocates actually rely on the same conventions of equality analysis; to move forward, equality theory itself must be transcended. Such a transcendence was described by many as a move away from the liberal tradition of competitive individualism and toward values of caring, community, and interpersonal responsibility. Others reframed the critique of equality in terms of a poststructuralist refusal of fixed oppositions and totalizing scholarly practices. Historian Joan Wallach Scott suggested, for instance, that the dichotomous formulations employed in the equality-versus-difference debates be deconstructed. Legal scholar Martha Minow likewise rejected bipolar oppositions; in her portrayal, the "dilemma of difference" is inherently unstable and without solution. All agreed that the reduction of complex issues of policy and theory to the equality/difference antithesis foreclosed discussion of structural constraints, political context, and alternative options.[7]

In the chapters that follow I look at the evolution of the pregnancy policy puzzle with attention, once again, to the play of equality/difference issues. Given the current disillusionment with equality, my choice of topic and approach may seem contrary, even backward. But I return to these supposedly settled problems because I do not think they have been resolved. Declaring a dichotomous opposition to be an "illusion" or "intellectual trap" that must be transcended is one thing; actually doing so, another. Moreover, it is probably not possible to arrive at a single conclusion—once and for all, in practice or in theory—about such questions. As literary critic Ann Snitow shows, feminism moves in complex and unsystematic ways among commitments to equality and difference, sameness and specificity, essence and diversity. "A common divide keeps forming in both feminist thought and action between the need to build the identity 'woman' and give it solid political meaning and the need to tear down the very category 'woman' and dismantle its all-too-solid history."[8] "Woman" may be constituted for a time in terms of a unitary collectivity, whose sisterhood provides a basis for action; then, the self-evident solidarity of womanhood somehow dissolves, as other allegiances and specificities become more salient. In the individual, moreover, these positions are not even temporarily secured, for consciousness involves an endless negotiation along multiple axes. That is, entangled in the equality-versus-difference dilemma are problems of the construction of subjectivity and identity.

The feminist divide described by Snitow continually returns in new guises and cannot, she argues, be permanently transcended. A position may be chosen, but the choice is never final. However frustrating the lesson, feminism must learn to "embrace the paradox," for "there is no transcendence, no third course."[9] To which it should be added that the content and structure of the divide are not fixed. As the poles repeatedly reconstitute themselves, the corridor between them now thickens with layers of meaning, now empties out into chasms of unexplored depth. The effort to embrace the paradox is historically specific.

In *Mothers on the Job*, I examine how pregnancy policy has traveled the equality/difference divide—a divide that is itself constantly in transformation. Others have already documented the pervasiveness of equality-versus-difference issues across the policy spectrum, for example, in studies of affirmative action, divorce and child custody law, military service, surrogacy, or sexuality.[10] Here I look at a single trajectory traced along the chameleon divide: the construction of the problem of pregnancy in the American workplace. Such an intensive exploration—pursued on the twin terrains of policy and theory—provides a case study of the evolution of the equality/difference conundrum.

The book begins with a consideration of the historical background to current debates about pregnancy policy. Programs in support of working mothers have been central to the evolution of family policy elsewhere, but they have largely been absent in the United States. Chapter 2, "Woman's Place," shows how discourse about gender difference was mobilized and reworked in the United States during the nineteenth and early twentieth centuries. In particular, I distinguish the arguments used by turn-of-the-century reformers supporting female-specific labor legislation from the reasoning put forth by the Supreme Court in its 1908 *Muller v. Oregon* decision. Not surprisingly, it was the Supreme Court's rationale that was incorporated into dominant ideology about woman's place. Chapter 3, "Mothers at Work," suggests, contrary to popular opinion, that the United States has had a maternity policy in place for most of the twentieth century. The policy is dual, offering distinct tracks. On one, white women are constructed as different and receive special but sometimes disadvantageous treatment. On the other, the female specificity of women workers of color is disregarded.[11] Either way, U.S. public policy has provided virtually no support for women's needs as mothers; the contrast with social welfare systems established in Europe during the same years is stark.

Having delineated the two tiers of what may be called traditional maternity policy, I turn to recent policy initiatives in the area of motherhood and employment. Chapter 4, "Feminism and Equality," shows how American feminist strategy shifted in the 1960s to the equality side of the equality/difference divide. After World War I, a deep split polarized activists on behalf of women. On the one hand, reformers represented women as essentially unlike men; on the other, equal rights feminists campaigned for same treatment. In the 1960s, the equality position prevailed, and efforts to improve women's position in the labor market began to target female-specific practices as discriminatory. Sex was analogized to race, and both were regarded as differences that should not make a difference. With some success, women activists attempted in the early 1970s to extend the equality framework to include childbearing and child rearing. In effect, they were mobilizing the conventions of U.S. legal argument to propose a new kind of maternity policy, framed in terms of equality rather than difference.

Feminists were not alone in their interest in reshaping workplace maternity policy in terms of equality. Employers, for example, had much to gain. From a feminist point of view, the extension of equality strategies to cover the female-specific phenomenon of pregnancy turned out to be problematic, for equality in the workplace could be interpreted in a variety of ways, some of which would harm women. Chapter 5, "Difference in Court," looks at how these various interpretations took shape within the constraints of the U.S. legal system. Responding to several Supreme Court decisions in the 1970s, feminists supported the 1978 Pregnancy Discrimination Act (PDA), which prohibited employers from discriminating against pregnant workers. Almost immediately, the PDA clashed with pregnancy disability statutes which provided benefits that seemed at least as important. The result was debate, a series of lawsuits, and the Supreme Court ruling in the Lillian Garland case. The litigation defined maternity policy as a sphere of struggle and split the feminist legal community.

With chapter 6, "Questioning Equality," I move to a series of difficult questions that have emerged in the course of the pregnancy policy controversy. I begin by examining how ideological commitments and confusions obfuscate efforts to move beyond the polarization of the debate. Chapters 7–9 then explore strategic and theoretical issues. Chapter 7, "The Equality Framework Extended," evaluates current gender-neutral measures that seek to address the needs of pregnant workers. It considers the disputed question of whether the Pregnancy Discrimination Act has helped or harmed women workers, and explores more recent concerns about the limits and possibilities of gender neutrality in such measures as the Family and Medical Leave Act. Chapter 8, "Difference as Strategy," situates the controversy over pregnancy policy in a larger strategic context. It argues that given the peculiarities of the U.S. legal system and the increasingly conservative political climate, the equality framework continues to offer a strong practical basis for developing pregnancy policy.

Arguments in favor of equality-based pregnancy strategies are, in my view, generally persuasive, but they need a firmer theoretical foundation than their defenders have provided. Chapter 9, "Beyond Equality versus Difference," considers some theoretical issues implicated in discussions about pregnancy policy. The chapter surveys the theoretical models articulated in the debate over pregnancy policy and then looks at attempts that have been made to theorize gender specificity in a way that transcends the equality/difference opposition. Despite strengths, these efforts share a set of difficulties; in particular, they continue to deploy dichotomous conceptualizations, and they fail to encompass diversity.

In chapter 10, "Different but Not Unequal," I draw the threads of *Mothers on the Job* together. At the end of the twentieth century, U.S. pregnancy policy is assuming a new position on a reshaped equality/difference divide. From many quarters, attempts are being made to construct women as both different and equal and to affirm the female specificity of childbearing alongside universalist principles of equal opportunity. Not all such constructions are benign from a feminist point of view. I maintain that in the current political context, women will best be served by an equality-based approach to pregnancy policy, specifically that taken in family and medical leave legislation. But I also argue, paradoxical though it may seem, that policies framed in terms of equality jurisprudence can be consistent with the contemporary questioning of equality. Such policies, conceptualized in terms of what I call differential consideration, can incorporate maternity within a framework that respects a range of human specificities. Offering a feminist response for the 1990s to the pregnancy policy dilemma, they resist the equality/difference opposition without abandoning the equality strategy.

2

Woman's Place

The Domestic Code

The notion that women require and deserve special treatment has a long history. In the nineteenth century, sex-differentiated policies were justified by a particular ideology or discourse about woman and her place. Known today as the domestic code or the doctrine of separate spheres, this ideology constructed women as inhabitants of a distinct realm of experience. Within their sphere, women were to conform to specified social roles and to engage in appropriate womanly activities. The domestic code circumscribed the scope of women's legitimate activity, but it also seemed to offer a level of autonomy as well as the community of a supposedly universal sisterhood. Confined within the domestic bounds of the family unit, women could develop their special strengths and capabilities and even have socially approved access to certain kinds of power.[1]

The domestic code arose in the early nineteenth century, replacing several earlier conceptualizations of woman's proper place. Among them was the common law doctrine of coverture, which incorporated the legal identity of the feme covert within that of her father or husband. Coverture presumed that the man represented the family household and denied other family members—for example, wives and daughters—social existence as independent persons. Imported from England, the doctrine of coverture was at some variance with the reality of life in the American colonies, even among those groups to whom it might most be expected to apply. Some women were, in fact, quite independent—those who were heads of propertied households, or whose husbands were away, for example. With the coming of the Revolution, the issue of women's independence as citizens or dependence as wives and daughters was broached and then resolved in favor of the latter. Not long after, the consolidation of the domestic code largely silenced the competing voices of the revolutionary era.[2]

At the core of the domestic code was the notion that women who bear children have special experiences and needs. As in other times and places, the phenomenon that childbearing creates particular demands on women was universalized into a global female identity. Normative notions that woman's proper place is in the home—meaning that her identity and activities ought to derive from her role as wife or daughter within the household of a heterosexually bonded family unit—have lasted into the late twentieth century.

Presumed to apply to all, the domestic code shaped and reinforced social relations. That is, the domestic code was a dominant ideology, and its power obscured the ways in which it was in fact highly race, class, and region specific. Separate-spheres prescriptions drew mainly on the experience of women in the upper layers of the New England class structure. Most American women were not members of these sectors, and their lives differed sharply from those lived by the "true women" of the eastern bourgeoisie. Separate-spheres doctrine therefore defined the experience of most women as, to a greater or lesser extent, abnormal. Although hegemonic, it could not entirely obliterate the existence of other versions of womanhood, however. In historian Nancy Hewitt's summary:

> Evidence from the lives of slaves, mill operatives, miners' wives, immigrants, and southern industrial workers as well as from "true women" indicates that there was no single woman's culture or sphere. There was a culturally dominant definition of sexual spheres promulgated by an economically, politically, and socially dominant group. That definition was firmly grounded in the sexual division of labor appropriate to that class, just as other definitions developed based on the sexual division of labor in other class and racial groups.[3]

The majority of women were participants in particular cultures sometimes only dimly related to the doctrine of domesticity. Farthest from its canons was the experience of black women, constituted from their African history, on the one hand, and the demands of slavery, on the other. Even the women of the urban bourgeoisie were not homogeneous in culture and outlook. Thus the domestic code rendered the rich diversity of women's experience almost invisible.

Not only was the domestic code actually race, class, and region specific, it was also time bound. Dominant ideology can be stubbornly persistent and at the same time remarkably malleable. For example, the canons of domesticity that emerged in the early 1800s assumed new forms less than a century later. In the sections that follow, I show how the 1908 Supreme Court decision in *Muller v. Oregon* exemplified the shift. My inquiry suggests that the Court's was not the only voice on the matter, moreover; the construction of normative notions of gender is always contested.

Equal Rights and Special Treatment

Separate-spheres doctrine received its paradigmatic nineteenth-century jurisprudential form in an opinion written by Supreme Court Justice Joseph Bradley, concurring in *Bradwell v. Illinois* (1873). The case concerned the right of Myra Colby Bradwell, "a woman of learning, genius, industry and high character," to practice the profession of law. Active in the suffrage movement and in efforts to reform Illinois laws that disadvantaged women, Bradwell was the founding editor of an important weekly, the *Chicago Legal News*. When she applied for admission to the Illinois bar in 1869, Bradwell was refused admission because of her sex. The Illinois Supreme Court and then the United States Supreme Court supported the state bar.[4] In agreeing to deny Bradwell the right to pursue her chosen profession, Justice Bradley articulated a fully elaborated view of the eternal and divinely ordained distinction between the sexes:

Civil law, as well as nature herself, has always recognized a wide difference in the respective spheres and destinies of man and woman. . . . The constitution of the family organization, which is founded in the divine ordinance, as well as in the nature of things, indicates the domestic sphere as that which properly belongs to the domain and functions of womanhood. . . . The paramount destiny and mission of woman are to fulfill the noble and benign offices of wife and mother. This is the law of the Creator.

Conjuring up the tradition of coverture, Bradley suggested that woman's independence is dangerous. "The harmony, not to say identity, of interests and views which belong, or should belong, to the family institution is repugnant to the idea of a woman adopting a distinct and independent career from that of her husband." Although some women are not married, "the rules of civil society must be adapted to the general constitution of things," not to "exceptional cases." Bradley not only assumed the separation between the two spheres to be God-given and for all time, he regarded it as all-pervasive. No aspect of woman's experience could escape gender assignment. Being a woman entailed being a wife, and being a wife meant remaining within the domestic sphere.[5]

When Myra Bradwell applied to the Illinois bar, she sought the same right to practice law that men in her state enjoyed. That is, her demand for equality took the form of a request for same treatment. Bradwell's efforts were part of a larger campaign challenging state laws and practices that constituted women as by nature different from men. The movement pushed current liberal theories of natural rights to their limits by seeking to extend them to women. As the 1848 Seneca Falls Declaration, modeled on the Declaration of Independence, put it:

All laws which prevent woman from occupying such a station in society as her conscience shall dictate, or which place her in a position inferior to that of a man, are contrary to the great precept of nature and therefore of no force or authority. . . . Woman is man's equal—was intended to be so by the Creator and the highest good of the race demands that she be recognized as such.[6]

For woman-movement activists in the middle of the nineteenth century, campaigning for same treatment as citizens seemed an obvious way to bring women within the norms of equality.[7]

A quarter of a century later, activist women continued to seek same treatment in a number of areas, and they also worked vigorously for passage of labor legislation treating some women differently from men. Social transformations wrought by industrialization, urbanization, and immigration had put the legal argument from difference onto the reform agenda. At the end of the nineteenth century, large numbers of working-class women were employed outside the home for wages. Usually occupying low-level positions in industry or as domestic servants, these were the approximately 25 percent of American women who worked in the paid labor force at the time. Although most women workers left their jobs when they married, 10 percent of married women worked for wages, not an insubstantial number in absolute terms. The statistics changed over time and varied according to race, ethnicity, and region. In industrial towns and cities with large immigrant populations, for example, as many as a third of the women working in the mills were married. The labor-force participation of African-American women, whether married or not, was always several times that of white women. Pay for women was low. Crowded into a few occupations in a sex- and race-segregated labor market, they earned 60 percent or less what men earned. On this amount, it was impossible for most women workers to live, even meagerly, apart from a family setting. Working conditions in shops, factories, and households were often brutal and hours extremely long. The labor movement, weak and craft-oriented, addressed the needs of women members even less adequately than it did those of men.[8] Increasingly alarmed at the deteriorating conditions of working-class women's lives, activists campaigned for the passage of industrial legislation regulating the work of women but not men.

A strategy that singled out women for special treatment could not rely on natural rights reasoning. The general argument for women's labor legislation—initiated in Europe and advanced wherever industrialization penetrated—started from the assumption that woman's distinct physiology creates special needs.[9] Given these needs and given, furthermore, working-class women's role as the bearers of future citizen-workers, it was concluded that society had an interest in assuring their well-being. In the campaign for protective labor legislation, woman's difference, projected as physically based and scientifically verifiable, became the major theme.

Laws regulating women's work were first enacted in the United States in the middle of the nineteenth century. In 1853, for example, Massachusetts limited women's working day to eleven hours; in 1874, it reduced the maximum to ten. Most female-specific industrial legislation was put in place at the turn of the twentieth century. States limited hours, restricted night work, and excluded women from occupations viewed as physically or morally dangerous. Such occupations as metal grinder, underground miner, elevator operator, letter carrier, meter reader, or bartender were closed to women on the grounds that they might be exposed to physical or moral dangers inappropriate to their sphere.[10]

Passage of legislation affecting female but not male workers soon resulted in legal challenges.[11] Lower courts did not always agree on the validity of statutes mandating special provisions for women workers. Some used natural rights language to claim that protective labor laws were an improper limitation on the equal rights of all to control their destiny. For example, in 1907 a New York court struck down a law that prohibited night work for women, declaring:

> An adult woman is not to be regarded as a ward of the state, or in any other light than the man is regarded, when the question relates to the business, pursuit or calling. She is entitled to enjoy unmolested her liberty of person and her freedom to work for whom she pleases, where she pleases, and as long as she pleases, within the general limitations operative on all persons alike.[12]

Like contemporary court decisions on labor legislation affecting men, such opinions assumed that women workers and their employers were equally powerful actors in the marketplace for labor. Ironically, the affirmation of woman's equal rights with respect to her "business, pursuit or calling" was precisely what activist and would-be lawyer Myra Bradwell had sought thirty years earlier.

While some courts invalidated female-specific labor laws by emphasizing equal rights and freedom of contract, others upheld the laws on the basis of woman's difference. For example, the Nebraska Supreme Court cited a range of political, physical, and familial disabilities special to women in an opinion affirming Nebraska's ten-hour law in 1902:

> Women and children have always to a certain extent been wards of the state. Women in recent years have been partly emancipated from their common-law disabilities. But they have no voice in the enactment of the laws by which they are governed, and can take no part in municipal affairs. They are unable, by reason of their physical limitations, to endure the same hours of exhaustive labor as may be endured by adult males. Certain kinds of work, which may be performed by men without injury to their health, would wreck the constitutions and destroy the health of women, and render them incapable of bearing their share of the burdens of the family and the home.[13]

In this interpretation, female-specific legislation is justified because it compensates for women's political powerlessness and preserves women's health, and thereby contributes to family and social welfare.

Woman's role as mother was sometimes invoked more directly to defend protective laws. In 1900 the Pennsylvania Superior Court worried about the threat posed by unregulated working conditions to the health and safety of future generations: "Surely an act which prevents the mothers of our race from being tempted to endanger their life and health by exhaustive employment can be condemned by none save those who expect to profit by it."[14] After all, seconded the Washington Supreme Court in 1902, "that which would deleteriously affect any great number of women who are the mothers of succeeding generations must necessarily affect the public welfare and the public morals."[15] Here, the concern shifted away from women as citizens with special needs requiring special provisions. Because women are mothers and hence entrusted with the well-being "of our race," the court reasoned, they need protective labor legislation.

Lower courts remained divided over the validity of female-specific industrial legislation. Over a period of thirty-two years, state supreme courts decided seven cases concerning legislation limiting women's hours or night work, upholding four female-specific statutes and invalidating three. In its 1908 decision in *Muller v. Oregon*, the United States Supreme Court tried to settle the dispute.

The Facts of Common Knowledge

On Labor Day of 1905, Curt Muller, owner of the Grand Laundry in Portland, Oregon, required a female employee to work beyond the legally limited working day. Convicted and fined under a 1903 state statute prohibiting the employment of women for more than ten hours per day, Muller challenged the law. He argued that the hours limitation unconstitutionally restricted women's freedom to contract to work as long as they desired. When the Oregon Supreme Court upheld his conviction, Muller, supported by other local laundrymen, appealed to the United States Supreme Court. The Court's ruling in the test case was expected to determine whether or not women workers were to be treated as free agents in the labor market.[16]

Freedom of contract had just been firmly endorsed by the United States Supreme Court in *Lochner v. New York*, decided in 1905. That decision invalidated New York's law limiting hours worked in bakeries on the basis that it interfered with workers' constitutionally guaranteed freedom to bargain with their employers. The Court noted that states had the right to limit this Fourteenth Amendment freedom through exercise of their "police powers [in the areas of] safety, health, morals and general welfare of the public." But it determined that the New York law was not a valid exercise of such powers. Rather, statutes that limit "the hours in which grown and intelligent men may labor to earn their living are mere meddlesome interferences with the rights of the individual."[17] Conveniently ignoring the reality that workers participate in the labor market with considerably less power than their bosses, the Court deprived New York's bakers of state protection. Might it not do the same should it have to decide a case involving industrial legislation applying only to women? This was the fear that haunted advocates of protectionism as *Muller v. Oregon* reached the United States Supreme Court.

In an effort to influence the decision in *Muller,* the reformers joined with the state of Oregon to present a brief to the Supreme Court. The brief, prepared by Louis Brandeis and Josephine Goldmark, offered the legal argument that female-specific hours laws are rational. It therefore had to distinguish the Oregon ten-hour statute from the New York law struck down in *Lochner.*[18] At stake in Oregon but not in New York, the brief claimed, were the "public health, safety, morals, or welfare"—precisely the categories acknowledged by the Court in *Lochner* and other precedents as falling within the scope of a state's police powers. The "facts of common knowledge" concerning sexual difference show that if women's working day is not limited, "there is material danger [to] public health, safety, morals, or welfare."[19] Because women differ from men in certain factually verifiable ways pertaining to the relevant categories, advised the brief, the state may depart from the principle of freedom of contract endorsed in *Lochner.* In other words, sexual difference justifies making an exception to the doctrine of liberty of contract. Unlike the "grown and intelligent men" whose individual rights were endorsed in *Lochner,* women need the protection of the state and Oregon's law is valid. Sexual difference establishes women as a distinct class whose special treatment is constitutionally justifiable.

This legal argument was made in a scant two pages of the Brandeis/Goldmark brief. It turned on establishing the "facts of common knowledge," in the prescribed areas of health, safety, morals, and the general welfare. These were presented in the brief's remaining hundred-odd pages, organized in two unevenly sized parts. A short part 1 overviewed legislation limiting working women's hours in Europe and in twenty U.S. states. These laws, enacted "for the protection of [women's] health and safety and the public welfare," were presented as a kind of precedent.[20] Part 2, "The World's Experience upon

Which the Legislation Limiting the Hours of Labor for Women Is Based," contained the bulk of the reformers' exposition of "facts." Here, Brandeis and Goldmark amassed dozens of short citations from European as well as U.S. legislative, governmental, medical, and scholarly reports. The citations exhibit a mix of empirical observations and interpretation that makes it difficult, by modern standards, to see them as facts.[21] At the time, however, the introduction of such data into a legal brief was a radical innovation, seemingly executed in scientific fashion. Brandeis and Goldmark provided a one- or two-paragraph preface to each group of citations, indicating for the Justices the point to be drawn.

The first section of part 2, "The Dangers of Long Hours," argued that long hours are particularly dangerous for women "because of their special physical organization," and also because of the intensification of labor due to technological change.[22] The section then considered the effects of long hours on, in turn, health, safety, morals, and general welfare. The longest subsection documented the impact of overwork on women's health. "The fatigue which follows long hours of labor becomes chronic and results in general deterioration of health. Often ignored, since it does not result in immediate disease, this weakness and anaemia undermines the whole system; it destroys the nervous energy most necessary for steady work, and effectually predisposes to other illness."[23] Medical commissioners observed neurasthenia, insomnia, headache, ulcers, swelling, varicose veins, constipation, lassitude, reduced lung capacity, pulmonary disease, and "general torpidity of functions." A Massachusetts government committee noted that "in the cotton mills of Fitchburg the women and children are pale, crooked, and sickly-looking." One in Maine found that "many saleswomen are so worn out, when their week's work is ended, that a good part of their Sundays is spent in bed, recuperating for the next week's demands."[24]

In addition to the generally harmful impact of long hours on women's health, Brandeis and Goldmark enumerated "Specific Evil Effects on Childbirth and Female Functions," among them pelvic disease, premature birth, and menstrual problems. According to a printshop foreman, for example, "female compositors, as a rule, are sickly, suffering much from backache, headache, weak limbs, and general 'female weakness.' "[25] A short subsection on safety documented that fatigue increases the chances of injury due to accidents. Another, equally short, considered morals, claiming that long hours produce a tendency to drink and referring darkly to "other excesses."[26]

Brandeis and Goldmark devoted the concluding pages of the brief's section on long hours to describing how overwork endangers the general welfare. "When the health of women has been injured by long hours, not only is the working efficiency of the community impaired, but the deterioration is handed down to succeeding generations. . . . The overwork of future mothers thus directly attacks the welfare of the nation."[27] The state therefore had an interest in protecting women.

After surveying the dangers of long hours, the brief moved on to the advantages of short hours, considering health and general welfare in turn. Succeeding sections then reassured the Court that the economic effects of shortened hours would not be harmful and that physicians, employees, employers, and officials affirmed the positive impact of hours limitation. A final section presented data on conditions in the laundry industry—described as one of the "dangerous trades" whose employees are "worn out while still young."[28]

In a one-paragraph conclusion, Brandeis and Goldmark returned to the legal argument. "In view of the facts above set forth," they observed, "it cannot be said that the Legislature of Oregon had no reasonable ground for believing that the public health, safety, or welfare did not require a legal limitation on women's work . . . to ten hours in one day."[29] That is, the Oregon law ought to be declared valid.

Implicit in the "facts of common knowledge" assembled by Brandeis and Goldmark are several distinct rationales for restricting the hours of women but not men. First and most prominent, overwork is harder on women physically, because they have a "more delicate physical organization."[30] While the citations documented the harmful impact of long hours on male as well as female workers, the brief argued at length that women have a physiologically greater need for the reduction in hours. In general, "disease makes greater inroads upon them, . . . industrial labor is more injurious to women than to men."[31] The second rationale, briefly mentioned, pointed to the pressures created by women's differential responsibilities in the household. "Desirable . . . would be a reduction of the working hours which should give to married women more time for their housework and family life, and to the younger unmarried women the opportunity to learn the art of home-making, because upon this the health, welfare, and prosperity of her whole family will depend."[32] Physical makeup and social role together make women more vulnerable than men to the damaging effects of overwork. Such "facts" suggested that working-class women as individuals needed the protection of a law restricting hours.

The brief also offered a third reason to limit women's working hours, based not on individual but general welfare. Women must be protected because they make an indispensable contribution to society as mothers. The "efficiency and value" of "future generations [depend] upon the protection of working women and girls."[33] Such arguments, which represent working-class women as vehicles for the biological and social perpetuation of society, were common by the end of the nineteenth century. They justified shorter hours for women on the instrumentalist basis that "the State has a vital interest in securing for itself future generations capable of living and maintaining it."[34]

Throughout the brief, inspectors, physicians, officials, and legislative committees, as well as Brandeis and Goldmark themselves, made comments that strike many modern readers as sexist. Women are "fundamentally weaker than men in all that makes for endurance: in muscular strength, in nervous energy, in the powers of persistent attention and application."[35] Their "physical inferiority" makes them vulnerable.[36] Legislators should "protect and preserve the health of the women in their character as wives and as the mothers of future generations."[37] Taken in isolation, such extracts portray women workers as needing state protection mainly so their extraordinary physical fragility will not obstruct their socially central functions as wives and mothers. Absent from this picture, but not from the brief, is the reformers' emphasis on the well-being of women as persons in their own right.

The paternalism and, indeed, patriarchalism of many formula-

tions in the Brandeis/Goldmark brief have been particularly gall-
ing to contemporary feminist sensibilities. The brief is generally
believed to have not only provided legal logic but also shaped
the motherhood-based argument that is at the core of the Supreme Court opinion.[38] Two observations must, however, be
made. First, such references were in part necessitated by the
legal argument adopted by the reformers, which had to show
that unlike the New York law overturned in *Lochner,* the preserva-
tion of public morals and the general welfare as well as of health
and safety required hours limitations. Second and more important, a fair reading of the entire brief discloses that its emphasis
is, in fact, on the threat to women's health and physical well-
being constituted by long hours. Modern readings of the
Brandeis/Goldmark brief have, in short, been selective, filtering
out the greater part of what it contains. By projecting the conclusions reached by the Supreme Court in *Muller* back onto the
Brandeis/Goldmark brief, contemporary scholars often obscure
the critical tension between the two documents.

A Class by Herself

In its unanimous decision in *Muller v. Oregon,* the Supreme
Court endorsed the legal argument in the Brandeis/Goldmark
brief, concluding that "[woman] is properly placed in a class
by herself, and legislation designed for her protection may be
sustained, even when like legislation is not necessary for men
and could not be sustained."[39] But the Court's rationale for the
decision departed from that presented in the reformers' brief.
The Justices had, it turned out, their own way of reading the
"facts." And it was of course the Court's rendering that became institutionalized within dominant discourse concerning
woman's place.

The Court's opinion in *Muller,* written by Justice David J.
Brewer, begins by affirming the principle of equality as embodied in Oregon state law. "In the matter of personal and contractual rights [women] stand on the same plane as the other
sex."[40] But in the matter of the labor market, it would be in-
correct, said the Court, to apply the reasoning of *Lochner* to

Oregon's women workers. The "copious collection" of facts cited in the Brandeis/Goldmark brief suggested, rather, that "woman's physical structure, and the functions she performs in consequence thereof, justify special legislation restricting or qualifying the conditions under which she should be permitted to toil."[41] What are these facts? The Justices offered their summary in a footnote:

> Perhaps the general scope and character of all these reports may be summed up in what an inspector for Hanover says: "The reasons for the reduction of the working day to ten hours—(a) the physical organization of woman, (b) her maternal functions, (c) the rearing and education of the children, (d) the maintenance of the home—are all so important and so far-reaching that the need for such reduction need hardly be discussed."[42]

Although Brandeis and Goldmark had presented a range of evidence pertaining to women as workers and individuals, three out of the four items in the inspector's list concern women in their roles as mothers.

The Justices cited the Hanover factory inspector's remarks because they, like he, focused on motherhood. In the rest of its opinion, the Court conceptualized women workers virtually entirely in terms of the maternal role. Barely mentioning the advantages of reduced hours to women as persons, it asserted that the primary purpose of the Oregon law was to protect mothers and thereby benefit families and society as a whole:

> As healthy mothers are essential to vigorous offspring, the physical well-being of woman becomes an object of public interest and care in order to preserve the strength and vigor of the race. . . . [Woman's] physical structure and a proper discharge of her maternal functions—having in view not merely her own health, but the well-being of the race—justify legislation to protect her from the greed as well as the passion of man. The limitations which this statute places upon her contractual powers, upon her right to agree with her employer as to the time she shall labor, are not imposed solely for her benefit, but also largely for the benefit of all. Many words cannot make this plainer.[43]

Many words indeed could not make it plainer that the Supreme Court was not particularly interested in ensuring the welfare of women. The Justices would surely have agreed with the French politician who declaimed, "When we ask . . . for a lessening of the daily toil of women, it is not only of the women that we think; it is not principally of the women, it is of the whole human race. It is of the father, it is of the child, it is of society."[44]

According to the Court's opinion in *Muller*, sexual difference and woman's consequent inequality are rooted in biology. "That woman's physical structure and the performance of maternal functions place her at a disadvantage in the struggle for subsistence is obvious."[45] Female dependence is a permanent feature of social life, and "history discloses the fact that woman has always been dependent upon man."[46] For women, same treatment before the law can therefore provide only the illusion of independence. "It is impossible to close one's eyes to the fact that [woman] still looks to her brother and depends upon him. Even though all restrictions on political, personal, and contractual rights were taken away, and she stood, so far as statutes are concerned, upon an absolutely equal plane with him, it would still be true that she is so constituted that she will rest upon and look to him for protection."[47] Sexual difference is, in other words, an irreducible obstacle to the kind of equality projected in natural rights theory:

> Though limitations upon personal and contractual rights may be removed by legislation, there is that in [woman's] disposition and habits of life which will operate against a full assertion of those rights. She will still be where some legislation to protect her seems necessary to secure a real equality of right. . . . Looking at it from the viewpoint of the effort to maintain an independent position in life, she is not upon an equality.[48]

"Real equality" requires, indeed, appropriate state-mandated special treatment.

With its opinion in *Muller*, the Supreme Court consolidated what may be seen as a modified version of the domestic code. As in its earlier decision in *Bradwell*, the Court declared that women are sufficiently different from men that they must come under different employment rules. At the same time, it recast the terms within which it thought about sexual difference and woman's place. In *Bradwell*, Justice Bradley projected distinctions between women and men to be all-encompassing, eternally fixed, and divinely ordained. The Court in *Muller* instead referred to evidence concerning physical and social differences between the sexes; scientific rationalism replaced religious belief as justification. Sexual difference was still viewed as fundamental and universal, but it now rested on what appeared to be a sound foundation of scientific documentation.

Women were represented as an undifferentiated class in both *Bradwell* and *Muller*. Not articulated but nevertheless present in the opinions was the question of who the women affected by the decision in each case were. Whereas *Bradwell* concerned women belonging to the native-born urban elite, *Muller* addressed the situation of women working in industry and commerce. In Justice Bradley's words, the problem in *Bradwell* was women who as "exceptions to the general rule" go against "the general constitution of things" and wish a career—particularly one that might "require highly special qualifications and demanding special responsibilities." When Myra Bradwell, a member of the urban middle class, challenged her exclusion from the profession of law, she was thus stepping out of what was quintessentially her place. The Supreme Court decision in the case attempted to keep Bradwell, along with any others of her class who might likewise try to become "exceptions," in the domestic place deemed appropriate by prevailing ideology. For these women, Justice Bradley scolded, the supposedly golden age of coverture and family unity was only barely past, and they would do better to think of themselves as femes coverts. In *Muller* the Supreme Court considered a quite different category of women, those who engaged in the "struggle for subsistence." These were the masses of working-class women, most of them European immigrants and many foreign-speaking, who flooded into industrial communities across the United States at the turn of the century. As workers they were already "exceptions" to the rules of the Yankee-based domestic code, and as mothers they were responsible for producing the next generation of industrial workers. Thirty-odd years after *Brad-*

well, the *Muller* Court faced a twentieth century in which increasing numbers of women from diverse backgrounds could never live lives even remotely related to the prescriptions of the domestic code.[49]

In *Muller* the Supreme Court extended the domestic code by redefining the meaning of woman's place to be, above all, fulfilling "her maternal function." In so doing it endorsed a shift already under way in dominant ideology. As historian Anna Davin suggests for Britain, the late nineteenth and early twentieth century saw an important redefinition of the role of women. Women came to be seen primarily as mothers rather than as wives or daughters, and motherhood became an increasingly pressing concern of the state. "The family remained the basic institution of society, and woman's domestic role remained supreme, but gradually it was her function as mother that was being most stressed, rather than her function as wife. . . . Child-rearing was becoming a national duty not just a moral one; if it was done badly the state could intervene."[50] Where Justice Bradley had fussed over the threat to a middle-class woman's wifely duties should she follow a career, the *Muller* Court worried about working-class motherhood and its effects on the "well-being of the race."

After *Muller*

The unanimous decision in *Muller v. Oregon* was a powerful victory for the reform coalition that backed protective labor legislation. Few noticed or cared that the Supreme Court's opinion showed more concern for the well-being "of the race" than for that of women workers. After all, the Court had adopted the Brandeis/Goldmark brief's legal argument and upheld the female-specific legislation thought to be in working women's interests.

Here and there, some could sense danger in the Court's decision and voiced their misgivings. For example, economist and labor activist Sophonisba Breckinridge observed that "it is obviously not the women who are protected. For them, some of this legislation may be a distinct limitation. For example, the prohibition against work in mines or against night work may very well limit the opportunities of women." She suggested that protective labor legislation was intended to serve the interests of the state. "No one should lose sight of the fact that such legislation is not enacted exclusively, or even primarily, for the benefit of the women themselves. . . . The object of such control is the protection of the physical well-being of the community."[51] Others also worried about the short- and long-term consequences of protection. For instance, a New York women's group protested the *Muller* decision in the pages of the *Woman's Journal*. "The recent decision of Justice Brewer is not in accordance with facts or with equity. . . . [It must be condemned] as unjust and humiliating to women; as tending to sex slavery; as opposed to economic freedom; and as inimical to the best interests of present and future generations."[52]

Most reformers welcomed *Muller* as an opportunity to move forward on behalf of working-class women. The decision opened the way, they believed, to immediate passage of more female-specific protective legislation. Many thought it could eventually be used to extend protection to men as well as women. "Henceforth both men and women need only show a clear relation between their working hours and their good or bad health in order to have statutory restrictions upon their working day sustained by the Supreme Court of the United States."[53] In such formulations, the reformers ignored the gap between their interest in the well-being of women as industrial workers and family members and the Supreme Court's focus on women as mothers. But it was of course the Court's definition of woman's nature that became institutionalized.

Over the years, judicial opinions concerning women workers relied heavily on *Muller*, almost regardless of the matter at hand. In 1910 the Illinois Supreme Court parroted *Muller* to uphold a recently passed hours law; significantly, it elevated to the center of its reasoning the *Muller* footnote quoting the anonymous Hanover inspector.[54] Court decisions upholding the exclusion of women from certain occupations and from jury duty, and denying them access to state-supported colleges, cited *Muller* as precedent. Whether or not *Muller* was itself cited, courts referred to the well-known "facts" of women's physical weakness, maternal function, and dependence in cases involving their differential treatment. As late as 1968, a court quoted as reasonable the way the *Muller* Court "took account of the differences in physical structure, strength and endurance of women, as well as the importance of their health to the future well being of the race."[55]

From the vantage point of the 1990s it is hard to imagine activists in the cause of women enthusiastically supporting the paternalistic verbiage generated by the *Muller* opinion. In the context of the period, however, protective legislation appeared to many to be the best bargain that could be struck to alleviate the burden of working-class women's double day and to defend them against their employers' greed. Not only would it provide a certain amount of immediate protection for women, it was also expected to set a precedent for a future campaign for sex-neutral labor policies that would "remove the evils of industry as they affect either men or women workers."[56]

A surge of new state labor legislation followed the ruling in *Muller v. Oregon*. Within five years of the Supreme Court decision, twelve states had enacted laws limiting women's working hours in certain industries, and others had renewed or strengthened existing legislation. By 1924, forty-three states had put some kind of limitation on the maximum hours women could work, coupled in some instances with restrictions on night work.[57] Over the years, regulation applying only to women expanded to include caps on daily and weekly hours and on night work, mandatory meal and/or rest periods, occupational limitations, weight-lifting restrictions, and a variety of employment standards requiring seats, washrooms, dressing and rest rooms, or toilet facilities. Several states enacted legislation prohibiting the employment of women immediately before or after childbirth.[58]

On their face, female-specific labor laws seem to fall into two categories, some regulating women's working conditions and others restricting their occupational choice. This neat classification does not adequately predict the laws' actual effects, however, for regulatory legislation could prove as restrictive of occupational opportunities as explicit exclusion. As historian Alice Kessler-Harris observes, "no rigid lines existed. Laws that regulated lighting, seating, and ventilation arrangements under which women could work often served in fact to prevent women from being offered certain kinds of jobs."[59]

Protective legislation in principle forced employers to put a ceiling on their demands for women's time and energy and to provide minimum standards in the workplace. Coverage and enforcement varied greatly from state to state and from industry to industry within each state.[60] Large numbers of women workers, perhaps the majority, were not covered. Women employed as domestic servants or in agriculture, for example, were generally exempted; among them were virtually all black, Asian, and Chicana women workers. For the many whose work was covered, the laws often protected in ways that were critically important. Connecticut women working ten or more hours at night in 1917 enthusiastically welcomed a law limiting women's night work. "You can't imagine how good it is. . . . Five to one [o'clock] is ideal. Whoever put that up did something good. . . . It is better than a 10 hour day for married women and single ones too."[61] Working-class men sometimes benefited as well, as when industries to which protectionist legislation applied reduced hours or improved conditions for all employees. But enactment of protective laws could also lead to the loss of employment opportunities. Women printers in New York, for example, discovered that a 1913 law restricting night work threatened their livelihood. Women polishers and grinders in the New York machine tool industry had already been pushed out of their jobs by an 1899 statute. Women workers hired to replace men during World War I likewise lost skilled and relatively well-paying jobs as a result of night work prohibitions. For such women, same treatment had been beneficial. A woman streetcar conductor reported that it was the "lightest work I ever did and best pay. . . . Do you wonder I appreciate[d] being treated as well and paid just the same as a man?"[62]

In short, protective labor laws benefited many women while simultaneously excluding some from jobs they wanted and were qualified for. Exemptions to the protective labor laws enabled women cleaners, nightclub dancers, and cloakroom attendants to work at night, but they were generally not granted for women in the skilled and highly paid trades. The contradictions inherent in the protectionist strategy she supported worried economist Elizabeth Baker, writing in 1924:

> While some special laws for women—whether or not they are based upon false sex physiology—have tended to improve the working conditions of both men and women, other laws have tended to penalize women. The penalty falls more sharply on those significant minorities who have emerged from the mass into a more self-reliant position. Since it appears to be no longer doubted that women are in industry to stay, warning must again be sounded lest the progress of these minorities—the economic standard bearers in the progress of women—be thwarted.[63]

It is difficult to evaluate the impact of female-specific labor legislation in the United States.[64] Strange as it may seem to some to concede today, evidence suggests that passage of protective laws was, at least initially, a generally positive step for women. At the time, and in the context of the development of American industry, labor, and law, protection was virtually the only route left unblocked to those seeking amelioration of conditions for women in the industrial workplace. Practically speaking, more women workers experienced and appreciated the benefits of protective legislation in its first several decades than suffered from its exclusionary effects.

In the long run, however, a high price was paid for the immediate benefits of women's labor legislation. In return for a modicum of protection for some female workers against a hostile economic environment, the domestic code was revalidated and forcefully extended to working-class women. Women industrial workers were constructed not just as weaker and less capable than men, but as primarily defined by their role as mothers. Sexual difference was enshrined in the doctrine of separate spheres more firmly than ever, and it now enjoyed the blessings of reformers, the labor movement, and many women activists, as well as of the state. Willy-nilly, the ideological foundations for the structural inequality of women in the modern labor market and in society at large were reinforced.

3

Mothers at Work

Maternity Benefits

Early twentieth-century reformers had hoped to establish a social welfare system that would broadly address the needs of
women workers and their children. Protective legislation remained, however, a hodgepodge of limited and poorly enforced measures. The maternalism of dominant discourse never
translated into comprehensive programs to address women
workers' needs as mothers. At the end of the twentieth century
as at its start, American women live in a country that is unique
in the stinginess of its support for maternity and parenting.
Despite an entrenched public ideology venerating motherhood
and family, remarkably few benefits are available to assist
women workers who bear children. Recent studies document
the continuing absence of even the most basic components of
an adequate maternity policy: health insurance, a job- and
benefit-protected leave, and some income replacement during
the leave.[1]

Having a baby is an expensive undertaking, as a 1987 study
by the Alan Guttmacher Institute documented.[2] For a normal
delivery and birth, costs average about $2,900 (1985 dollars);
hospital charges for mother and newborn make up about 60
percent of the expense, and physician and laboratory fees the
rest. If there are complications, the bills are much higher. A
caesarean birth costs about $4,860 if the baby has no problems,
and $6,250 if there are complications. Premature births and
major complications push medical bills to $12,000 and more.[3]
Health insurance can cover some of the high medical costs of

pregnancy and childbirth. In 1985, private insurance plans paid at least some of the maternity expenses for approximately 64 percent of the women who gave birth. But not all private insurance policies cover maternity care: 9 percent of women aged fifteen through forty-four are covered by private plans that exclude maternity.[4] Most policies impose waiting periods, and some exclude those who are already pregnant. Moreover, 17 percent of women aged fifteen through forty-four have no insurance coverage whatsoever for their medical expenses.[5] Not unexpectedly, the 26 percent of women of childbearing age who have no maternity coverage at all tend to be younger, poorer, and less likely to be married than the general population; they are also more likely to be unemployed or to work part time, to work in smaller firms, and to be black or Latina.[6] For those whose insurance policies cover maternity, having a baby still costs money. Most plans do not reimburse all the medical costs of pregnancy and childbirth. Deductibles, copayments, and maximums ordinarily limit the reimbursement for medical bills associated with delivery and care of the newborn; essential costs of prenatal care may also be restricted or excluded.[7]

In addition to coverage of their medical expenses, women workers who bear children need job- and benefit-protected leaves, together with some replacement of their income during the leave. In the United States, most women workers have not enjoyed such benefits, although some progress is beginning to be made. In the 1970s, many firms started to provide a short unpaid job- and benefit-protected childbirth leave. A study of the private sector conducted in 1981 suggests that perhaps 75 percent of medium and large companies offer this option to employees. Small firms, which are less likely to provide good benefits, were not included in the study, however. A national study of working mothers sponsored by the Center for the Child presents data comparing maternity benefits in small firms (fewer than twenty workers) to those available in larger firms (twenty or more workers). Seventy-two percent of those working for larger employers and 51 percent working for small employers receive at least eight weeks of pregnancy disability leave; health insurance and income replacement are less frequently available in small than in larger firms. In general, maternity leave policies in American workplaces are informal and inconsistent. Because the leave policies are understood to be a childbirth benefit, they are not ordinarily available to fathers or adoptive parents.[8]

Maternity leaves in the United States are usually unpaid. No more than 20 percent of women workers—those in the better jobs or at larger companies—have the option of even two months of partially paid childbearing leave, followed by several months of unpaid job- and benefit-protected leave. Some income replacement may be available through paid sick leave, but sick leave benefits are usually low and tied to length of service. Moreover, a new mother returning to work who has used up her sick pay may have the same need for sick leave as other employees. Some workers are covered by temporary disability insurance; this ties maternity benefits to proof of inability to work, but may provide perhaps six weeks of income replacement. About half the medium and large firms surveyed in the 1981 study offered temporary disability benefits.

The absence of even minimally adequate support for maternity and parenting is particularly distressing in a country that has long had the highest divorce rate in the world as well as a substantial proportion of mothers in the paid workforce. Where the pressures on women workers are exceptionally severe, support is paradoxically least available. Economist Sylvia Ann Hewlett surveys the difficulties in *A Lesser Life*, her popular account of work and motherhood in the United States. Infuriated by her own failure as a young professional to combine career and family, she offers a devastating picture of the obstacles American women workers face. And she yearns for the comprehensive benefits provided by European policies that regard motherhood as "a social function similar to military service for men."[9]

Hewlett celebrates the European tradition of state support for motherhood, but she does not grasp the distinctive historical path taken by the United States in developing social welfare policy, and she ignores the complex dynamics of social change. Instead, she blames the startling lack of societal support for maternity on feminists. According to Hewlett, "hostility towards mothers and children permeates the American women's movement," which therefore pursues strategies that disregard women's special needs as mothers.[10] Feminists, she claims, emphasize equal rights when they should be campaigning for the kinds of substantive social benefits that materially support maternity in Europe. But her analysis misreads feminist activism, overestimates the power of reform movements in the United States, and ignores current strategic possibilities. In particular, the contemporary women's movement has never had the power to effect change that Hewlett ascribes to it. Her implication that many American feminists would hesitate to import European-style social welfare policy is, however, correct. To see why, it is necessary to look briefly at how European and U.S. policy traditions differ in their approach to motherhood.

Motherhood as a Social Function

By the turn of the twentieth century, European countries had developed social welfare policies that are extremely comprehensive by American standards. Germany pioneered sickness insurance for industrial workers in 1883, adding accident insurance the following year; old age and disability insurance were put in place in 1889. Between 1906 and 1911, Britain initiated an old age pension system, unemployment and national health insurance, and a spectrum of welfare services. Other European countries followed suit in the next decades.[11] To address the particular situation of women workers, governments generally adopted a female-specific approach. Labor legislation excluded women from dangerous occupations, limited their working hours, and restricted night work. In Britain, for example, the Factory Act of 1844 was the first to restrict the working day of women as well as prohibit night work altogether; daytime hours and a shorter working day were justified on the basis of women's special responsibilities as wives and mothers. European social welfare policies assumed that women's needs and responsibilities were wholly different from those of men, especially in the area of childbearing and child raising. Germany first legislated maternity benefits in the 1880s; paid maternity leaves were mandated in 1911. By the eve of World War I, several European countries had some form of government support for maternity on the job. In France, for instance, women teachers and post office employees obtained paid maternity leave in 1910, and in subsequent years the right was extended to other women workers.[12] European welfare policies thus singled out women workers in a manner analogous to U.S. protective labor legislation but with a substantially different outcome, for they provided a range and depth of benefits unknown in the United States.[13]

In 1919 the International Labor Organization (ILO) adopted the first set of international standards covering childbirth and maternity as well as protecting pregnant women in the workplace. The 1919 Maternity Protection Convention applied to women working in public or private industrial or commercial settings other than family enterprises. It mandated that a covered woman worker not be permitted to work for six weeks after childbirth; in addition to this compulsory leave, a pregnant worker had the right to stop work up to six weeks prior to her confinement. While on leave, the worker was to be paid benefits "sufficient for the full and healthy maintenance of herself and her child." Her medical care and income replacement were to be paid out of public funds or through a system of insurance. A worker who was absent from work for maternity leave could not be dismissed by her employer. Once returned to her job, she was to be allowed to interrupt her work twice daily for half an hour in order to nurse the infant.[14]

To the extent that countries implemented the ILO recommendations concerning maternity, women workers who bore children obtained important benefits. At the same time, the 1919 Maternity Protection Convention reflected a politics of motherhood that reinforced separate-spheres ideology and justified women's secondary status.[15] In the early decades of the twentieth century, the need to maintain adequate supplies of industrial and military manpower had become a source of anxiety throughout Europe. Contemporary commentators often linked the well-being of the state to maternity. "The history of nations is determined not on the battlefield but in the nursery," worried a British physician. But "there is no State womb, there are no State breasts, there is no real substitute for the beautiful reality of individual motherhood."[16] The state therefore has a compelling interest in the well-being of women insofar as they are, or may become, mothers. "The pregnant woman is a national asset," argued a French legislator on behalf of state-funded maternity homes; "the State is disappointed by the loss of a child."[17] Likewise, a British politician appealed for the enactment of special provisions for mothers and infants: "Give us good motherhood, and good pre-natal conditions, and I have no despair for the future of this or any other country."[18] A similar emphasis on motherhood and future generations permeated American domestic ideology of the period—evidenced, for example, in the 1908 Supreme Court opinion in *Muller v. Oregon*. The assumption that the State would actually assume responsibility for the protection of motherhood was, however, a distinctly European characteristic. As a British report put it, "the children of the State are the business of the State."[19]

The 1919 ILO Maternity Protection Convention functioned as the international standard for maternity policy until 1952, when it was amended. In the revised Convention, coverage now extends to many more women, including agricultural and domestic workers. Job-protected maternity leave is increased to twelve weeks. Six of the twelve weeks must be taken as a compulsory postnatal leave; the rest may be distributed before or after childbirth. Additional leave is to be available for the woman worker should a pregnancy- or childbirth-related medical condition require it. Income replacement and medical benefits must be "sufficient for the full and healthy maintenance of herself and her child in accordance with a suitable standard of living." Where based on previous earnings, income is to be replaced at not less than two-thirds the worker's earnings. Medical care is to be free and comprehensive. A nursing mother is to have breaks during normal working hours to nurse her child; these breaks are to be counted as working hours and paid. Costs of maternity benefits are not to unduly burden the individual employer.[20]

The comprehensive system of substantive rights and benefits for working women who become mothers that is in place today in virtually all industrialized nations originates in this history. Considerable state intervention ensures more or less universally available maternity benefits and rights. Financing is often directly from the government, sometimes supplemented by employer and employee contribution. In all European countries, as well as in Canada and many developing nations, women workers receive pregnancy and parenting benefits that meet or exceed current ILO minimum standards and that certainly go beyond most plans available in the United States. Working mothers and their children enjoy broad health care coverage, including hospital and physician expenses during pregnancy, for childbirth, and for postnatal care; the coverage is generally provided through a national health care system. A new mother has the right to a paid leave of absence no shorter than fourteen weeks, and often considerably longer. While on paid leave, she receives cash benefits amounting to as much as 90 percent to 100 percent of her pay. Additional unpaid leave is usually available. Not only are women workers able to return from their leaves to the same or a comparable job, but seniority, pensions, and other benefits are preserved. Once a mother is back at work, child care is often available.[21]

In short, public policy in most industrialized countries envisions childbearing as a social responsibility and offers substantial benefits to women workers and their children. The discourse that traditionally accompanies these maternity policies singles out women as different and emphasizes the important societal role of motherhood.[22] It thereby establishes an ideological foundation for sexual stratification in the workplace and the disadvantageous treatment of women workers. But unlike American labor legislation and social welfare provisions, European-style maternity policies have provided much of what women workers need.

Motherhood as a Private Responsibility

While European countries developed their extensive social benefits programs in the early twentieth century, the United States trailed far behind. Unable or unwilling to achieve the passage of labor legislation covering all workers, reformers and organized labor concentrated on female-specific measures. The protective laws that were enacted represented a step forward, and at first they functioned generally to the benefit of those women workers who were covered. The comparatively weak set of substantive supports they put in place never came close to meeting working women's special needs, however, nor was it ever possible to notably expand their scope. Many women workers, perhaps the majority, had no access to even the meager protection offered by labor legislation. Domestic service and agriculture, major sources of female employment, were generally exempt from regulation; other occupations often escaped as well, for example, work in hotels, restaurants, and cabarets. Many workplaces were too small to be covered, and many employers ignored the regulations. Social insurance—for example, protection against loss of income due to unemployment or temporary disability—was virtually unknown until the 1930s. Once enacted, only workers in certain occupations and industries were covered; in any case, benefits were usually denied to pregnant women. Health care remained private, with maternity reimbursed skimpily, if at all.[23]

As in Europe, female-specific labor laws often restricted women at the same time that they protected them. Over the decades, U.S. protectionist legislation played a more and more ambiguous role, for the limits a statute placed on women's employment opportunities and benefits could outweigh the tangible help it provided. The principle that women's special needs should be met through special treatment became increasingly vulnerable to interpretations that might harm women workers. Female-specific labor laws seemed to license employers to treat women in a not only separate but also unequal manner, and male workers appeared to benefit from the lack of competition from women. By the middle decades of the century, gender-specific practices in most American workplaces treated male and female workers differently, often with severely unfavorable consequences for the women workers. The special needs of women, presumed rooted in physiological and social role differences, had been converted into a justification for what was effectively disadvantageous treatment in the labor market.

Policies with respect to pregnancy were typical in the unfavorable ways they could sometimes "protect" women. As late as the

1970s, an employer could put a pregnant worker on mandatory maternity leave, with neither benefits nor job rights. Alternatively, the employer could fire her. Maternity leave was implicitly conceptualized as a combined pregnancy, childbirth, and parental leave and could be imposed regardless of the employee's desire and ability to work. Most employers required pregnant workers to stop working three to six months after conception. Employers could not only force a woman onto maternity leave, they could also determine the point at which she was fit to return; a new mother ready to go back to work might have to wait. Employers could also refuse to hire a female applicant on the basis of pregnancy. Such practices had long- as well as short-term consequences, for they ordinarily entailed loss of seniority, promotions, and accrued retirement benefits.[24]

Alongside practices that negatively affected pregnant women's access to and tenure in employment were health plans that provided unequal coverage. Health insurance policies often excluded from coverage normal and caesarean deliveries, or even childbirth altogether; the rationale was that pregnancy is a normal condition, not an illness. When covered, pregnancy-related expenses were usually reimbursed at a much lower rate than other medical costs. A 1976 survey showed that 60 percent of workers whose health plans included maternity benefits received less for the expenses of a normal delivery than for expenses incurred due to other conditions. That is, the plans covered pregnancy-related needs in a different and less adequate manner. Higher deductibles, reduced hospital coverage, limited surgical benefits, and lump-sum payments were among the devices that resulted in smaller benefits for maternity than for other covered conditions. In addition—and especially infuriating—employers often provided better medical coverage for the wives of their male employees than they made available to their female employees.[25]

A woman worker on maternity leave not only had to cover substantial portions of her medical costs herself, she also could not expect to have her lost income replaced. Most states explicitly excluded pregnant women and those recovering from childbirth from eligibility for unemployment or temporary disability benefits; private disability plans also excluded disability by reason of pregnancy. Some employers would not allow pregnant workers to use accumulated sick leave for childbirth-related absences. Once again, the justification for these exclusions was that pregnancy is a normal condition, not an illness. Maternity leave generally had to be taken without income replacement, and without extension of benefits, retention of seniority, or rights to reinstatement. In many companies, seniority and pension benefits were frozen for the duration of the maternity leave. Seniority could also be taken away entirely, reducing a returning worker to the status of a new hire. Where employees enjoyed relatively good maternity benefits—the minority of cases—these were usually the product of either collective bargaining or employer good will, the latter not necessarily extended to all female employees. For example, some employers provided benefits only if the employee was married.

A Two-Tier Policy

Special but less favorable treatment of pregnant workers remained the legally permissible norm until quite recently. The United States never ratified the ILO Maternity Protection Convention, and it has seemed to lack a policy consensus. Nonetheless, a national maternity policy has been implicit in the generally disadvantageous ways that pregnant workers have been treated on the job. This treatment has not been the same for all groups. Rather, twentieth-century U.S. maternity policy has been constituted with two tiers. On the one hand, it constructs women workers of European origin—"white" women—as essentially different and therefore deserving of special treatment. On the other hand, it largely ignores black, Asian, Chicana, and other women workers of color, leaving them outside the ambiguous protection of female-specific treatment.

Within the practices and programs directed at white women who become mothers, a consistent policy can be discerned. Four principles, presented here in schematic form, guide the framing of this implicit policy. Together, they prescribe the proper articulation of motherhood, family, and employment.

- Motherhood is to be regarded as morally and practically incompatible with labor-force participation. Because most women are or will become mothers, employers can assume women workers to be only temporarily in the workforce.
- Pregnancy is to be given a special status in the workplace as a condition that is simultaneously normal and unique. The fact that pregnancy is a normal condition justifies denying pregnant workers benefits. However expensive and disabling pregnancy may be, it is not a sickness and employers need not include pregnancy-related problems in their health and disability plans. The fact that pregnancy is unique justifies employment policies treating pregnant workers differently than other workers.
- Mothers and fathers are to be assigned distinct family responsibilities; the sexual division of parental duties generates their respective involvement in paid employment. Mothers are to make a full-time commitment to raising children and maintaining the heterosexual family household. Fathers are to bear the financial costs of child rearing and family life by being employed. The boundary between work and family is regarded as fixed, defining two distinct spheres of activity.
- Maternity and child rearing are to be considered the private responsibility of individual family members. The state should not provide benefits in support of family life, nor should it directly intervene.

These principles underpin an effectively race-specific maternity policy that originated in the early decades of the century, when masses of European immigrants were entering the industrializing labor market. Unspoken but well institutionalized, they have endured into the late twentieth century. For women workers who are white, pregnancy and motherhood have made a fundamental difference. To the extent that all women are viewed as potential mothers, furthermore, these assumptions have provided a basis for treating white women workers categorically as special.

By contrast, black, Asian, Chicana, and other women workers of color have generally been denied the special status deemed appropriate for white women. African-American women in particular have historically participated in the paid labor force in high numbers, suggesting distinct assumptions about the relationship between motherhood and employment, the treatment of pregnancy in the workplace, and the division of family responsibilities. In addition, the state has often taken an openly interventionist role with respect to family life in communities of color. In the case of black and other women workers of color, then, the principles governing maternity policy assume a different shape:

- Motherhood is to be regarded as irrelevant to employment status. If a woman of color holds a job, her employer can expect her to place the job's requirements ahead of the needs of her own family.[26]
- Pregnancy is to receive no special status in the workplace. Pregnant workers who cannot do their work should get no special protection.
- Although mothers and fathers are presumed to have different family responsibilities, it is normal for mothers to participate in the financial support of the family.
- Maternity and child rearing are in general to be considered the responsibility of individual family members. However, the state may, at its discretion, intervene.

Public policy has embodied these principles in various ways. For example, agriculture and domestic service—the two main occupations of women workers of color for most of the twentieth century—have generally been exempted from regulation. Firms that employ women workers of color are often below the minimum size for regulatory coverage. Bureaucrats look the other way when employers with large numbers of low-wage workers of color evade regulations. To the extent that female-specific measures have offered an element of protection, however problematic, to working women, such support has not been available to most African-American and other women workers of color. The state leaves women workers of color to fend for themselves in the workplace. At the same time it shows no respect for the boundaries of "privacy" that conventionally veil family life. If the state finds it advisable, children can be removed from the care of their parents and women can be sterilized without their consent.[27]

A maternity policy that is race- as well as gender-driven has, in sum, long been in place in the United States. Its racialism has been complex and changing, moreover. As political scientist Gwendolyn Mink documents, early twentieth-century welfare policy focused on the "lesser races"—the working-class European immigrants—seeking to assimilate their otherness while maintaining their subordination.[28] In subsequent decades, the diversity of the European immigrants was subsumed within an increasingly homogeneous notion of "white"-ness. Simultaneously, African-American and other non-European peoples came to be constructed as "nonwhite." In accordance with the consolidating white/nonwhite racial hierarchy, U.S. maternity policy by midcentury construed only some mothers as worthy: those white women who stayed in their place as full-time wives and homemakers, caring for children. These women probably made up the majority of mothers of children under eighteen until the 1960s, but large numbers of mothers did not conform to this standard—mothers who worked, women workers who became pregnant, and all women of color. They were thus by definition unworthy, as were single, lesbian, or divorced mothers. White wives who conformed to the norm by leaving the labor force could not look to the state for assistance. Despite the rhetoric glorifying motherhood, U.S. public policy has treated maternity as a private matter, not a basis for entitlement.

Women who become pregnant on the job have thus faced, in the United States, a peculiarly inhospitable situation. As in most European countries, a maternalist ideology has been the justification for gender-specific policies that purport to assist women yet simultaneously contribute to occupational sex-segregation and a secondary position for women in the labor market. But European maternity policies have provided a great deal of practical help to women workers, and they have always been embedded in universalistic social welfare packages that over the decades have been reasonably well enforced and even expanded.[29] By contrast, U.S. policies have been designed within a very different historical context. The few substantive programs that exist, largely aimed at white women, have been stingy and often worked to women workers' disadvantage. Constituted on a race-based two-tier foundation, U.S. maternity policy has offered shamefully little support for pregnancy and child rearing to anyone.

4

Feminism and Equality

True Equality and Real Protection

In the 1960s, a new wave of women's activism emerged in the United States. Its focus was on equality, and it moved away from earlier reform efforts to emulate European social welfare legislation. To underscore motherhood as woman's essential function and seek sex-specific protection from the state now seemed neither practical as a legislative strategy nor promising from a reform perspective. State intervention on behalf of women workers had been weak as well as often dangerous to women's interests. Labor reformers had never been able to expand the scope of protective legislation. Broadening protection might, moreover, further entrench the system of occupational sex-segregation that already so harmed women. Instead of looking to European precedents, women's movement strategists took another path. For a number of reasons the emphasis shifted from difference to equality.

The shift to equality did not come easily. Liberals, women reformers, and labor activists had for decades championed protective labor legislation and other female-specific measures. Their efforts relied on a dichotomous construction of gender difference that was a precipitate of the restructuring of women's activism after World War I. In contrast, the feminism of the 1960s posited women, even mothers, as more like than unlike men. It entailed not only a change of strategic direction but also a transformation in the representation of women. This section reviews the evolution of discourse about women, showing how gender became a polarized terrain in the third decade of the twentieth century. It thereby provides the background necessary to understand the emergence of the equality framework as the hegemonic feminist strategy in the 1960s. And it tells a story that has certain parallels to recent debates about gender difference.

Woman-movement thinking in the later nineteenth and early twentieth centuries constituted women as both different and equal. Deploying a flexible view of sexual difference, activists offered two kinds of argument to advance their cause. As historian Nancy Cott summarizes:

> On the one hand women claimed that they had the same intellectual and spiritual endowment as men—were human beings equally with men—and therefore deserved equal or the same opportunities men had, to advance and develop themselves. On the other hand, women argued that their sex differed from the male—that whether through natural endowment, environment or training, human females were nurturant, pacific and philosophically disinterested, where males were competitive, aggrandizing, belligerent and self-interested; and that it therefore served the best interests of both sexes for women to have equal access to education, work and citizenship in order to represent themselves and balance society with their characteristic contribution.[1]

Notions of human commonality and assumptions about women's and men's different roles thus coexisted within the woman movement. Moreover, arguments from difference and from equality could be made on behalf of either same treatment or special treatment of women. Suffragists, for example, sought the vote on the basis of both claims for women's equal rights as citizens and suggestions that the vote would bring a special feminine influence to bear in public life. And reformers supported female-specific labor laws as necessary extra measures to make women truly equal competitors in the marketplace and as justifiably special treatment for women's unique needs.

Underpinning the equality argument was the traditional reasoning of natural rights: because women and men are essentially alike, they should have the same rights as citizens. The argument from difference rested on the notion that woman's distinct nature, experience, and responsibilities, especially as homemaker and mother, can make a special contribution to society. "The interests of the home, protection of the children, and the morals and behavior of the community make the standard of even unlettered women one notch higher than that of their ignorant husbands." Women's special experience as mothers was said to give them a differential interest in universal peace. "Let us do our utmost to hasten the day when the wishes of the mothers shall have their weight in public affairs, knowing that by so doing, we hasten the day when wars shall be no more." Indeed, "this war should be a good argument for suffrage."[2]

Arguments from difference were sometimes particularized even more narrowly in terms of women's special concerns as members of distinct sectors. Black suffragists hoped the ballot would help in the struggle for racial justice.[3] Women industrial workers said it would assist them to counterbalance the power of their employers. "Working women must use the ballot in order to bring about conditions where all may be able to live and grow because they work. The ballot used as we mean to use it will abolish the burning and crushing of our bodies for the profit of a very few."[4] These positions acknowledged no contradiction in asserting the special character of the lives of black women or of female industrial workers in order to demand equality.

Suffragists were not alone in their ability to mobilize sexual difference and the ideology of domesticity on behalf of equality. Historian Susan Levine documents an analogous complexity in late nineteenth-century working-class circles, when the Knights of Labor reworked the doctrine of separate spheres into what she calls a "labor feminism." The Knights supported equal pay, women's suffrage, and equal participation by women in the organization. At the same time, they celebrated working-class women as wives and mothers who brought a special female sensibility to the home, the factory, and the public world. For a brief time, the Knights managed to project equal rights for women and female domesticity simultaneously as noncontradictory ideals.[5]

For activist women at the end of the nineteenth century, sexual difference did not have to have a fixed meaning. Arguments for suffrage in particular could be framed around either equality or difference, depending on the context in which woman's cause was being forwarded. Arguments for protective legislation relied more wholeheartedly on difference, but could easily be voiced by those supporting suffrage on the basis of equal rights. Women reformers followed a dual reform strategy, seeking simultaneously to have women treated the same as and differently from men. In the campaigns for the ballot and for protective legislation, traditional equal rights notions rested more or less comfortably alongside claims of woman's difference. Both natural rights theory and the domestic code had been radically co-opted in the cause of women.

Among women activists, the tension between focusing on women's special needs and insisting on the common humanity of women and men remained latent and unexamined for decades. Once suffrage was achieved, however, contradictions surfaced. In the course of regrouping into new organizational forms and shaping new programmatic agendas, activists in the 1920s found they could no longer endorse both kinds of strategies.

The dispute over proposed equal rights legislation triggered a polarization in woman-movement discourse. In 1921, the National Woman's Party (NWP), a small organization of militant suffragists, initiated a campaign to further woman's cause by seeking legal equality defined strictly as same treatment before the law.[6] The next step beyond suffrage should be, they argued, state laws and a constitutional amendment mandating equal rights—the Equal Rights Amendment (ERA). According to the NWP, such legislation would remove women's remaining legal disabilities by eliminating all laws that treated women differently from men.

From the start, the NWP's equal rights strategy collided with the gender-specific approach embodied in protective labor legislation. Woman's Party members argued that special legislation restricted women's opportunities in the sphere of employment. "In many highly paid trades women have been pushed into the lower grades of work, limited in earning capacity, if not shut out of the trade entirely by these so-called protective laws." And they pointed to the ways protective legislation reinforced sex-segregated occupational structures that put women in poorly paid dead-end jobs. "Whatever the effects on women of sex legislation aimed to protect them, it has been a real protection to men by slowing down the competition of women for their jobs." Women industrial workers would be better served, the NWP insisted, by equal rights legislation, which would remove the discriminations against them that protection legitimated. The party also expected that its equality strategy would eventually establish the principle that labor legislation should apply to both men and women. In support of its views, it mobilized a handful of women workers—no doubt the skilled workers whom economist Elizabeth Baker described as the female vanguard of the working class. "Do you think women workers want special protective legislation?" asked NWP member and socialist Crystal Eastman of one such woman. "No," the worker replied, "we don't want it! You can't protect women without handicapping them in competition with men. If you demand equality you must accept equality. Women can't have it both ways."[7]

Tiny but persistent, the National Woman's Party projected itself as truly feminist in its dedication to eliminating "all remaining forms of the subjection of women."[8] It drew a picture of women industrial workers as independent individuals capable of taking care of themselves. And it derided representations of women as weak, vulnerable, and enmeshed in family obligations. In particular, the party ridiculed reformers for supporting laws that grouped women with children as wards of the state. Reformers were not feminists at all, according to the NWP, for their interests lay more in motherhood and the future of the race than in the well-being of women. The "real protection" they sought was not, in the NWP's view, intended for women.

Reformers regarded the proposed equal rights legislation with alarm. They questioned the NWP's claim that protectionist statutes hurt women workers. They doubted that the benefits of protection would actually be extended to men. And they criticized the party's class and race bias, noting the ominous convergence of the NWP's support for equality with laissez-faire arguments against protective legislation. With good reason reformers feared that mandates of equal rights for women and men would lead not to the extension of protection to men but, rather, to the wholesale invalidation of female-specific labor legislation. Thus physician and reform activist Alice Hamilton pleaded in 1922 with a prominent member of the NWP to reconsider:

> The liberation of women from disabilities due to sex is desirable and I think a feminist organization such as yours should undertake it. But if you carry it through in the way you have started, it will be as if you began to drain a swamp by first taking down the frail bridge we have thrown over it. . . . You will have harmed a far larger number of women than you will have benefited and the harm done to them will be more disastrous.[9]

Efforts to bring the two sides in the dispute together, including attempts to design wording that would enable equal rights legislation to guarantee extension of protective provisions to all, failed. The National Woman's Party resisted the reformers' pleas, and supporters of protection could not hear the feminists' warnings. An exceptionally bitter split developed among women active on behalf of women, lasting nearly a half century. Under the pressure of tensions among feminists, reformers, and unionists over equal rights legislation, the complex but fragile representations of sexual difference constructed in earlier years were abandoned. Arguments made on behalf of women bifurcated into two strongly held, mutually exclusive, and simplistically delineated views of gender difference. On the one hand, the "pure feminists" of the National Woman's Party insisted on the substantive identity of women and men as citizens, due exactly the same rights, treatment, and opportunities. On the other, women reformers focused on women's distinctive biological and social roles. "The working mother is handicapped by her own nature," they argued. "The inherent differences are permanent. Women will always need many laws different from those needed by men."[10]

Reformers arguing for protective legislation sometimes appropriated the concept of equality, perhaps echoing the Supreme Court's declaration in *Muller* that women need special laws in order "to secure a real equality of right." Thus a representative of the League of Women Voters spoke of the need "to secure for women a true equality" in testimony at the 1931

Senate Hearings on the Equal Rights Amendment. "The end we are seeking is not equality in the sense of identity but justice and human happiness and opportunities for the most useful development of citizens of the country regardless of sex—an end to which equality is only a means."[11] In her formulation, protection does not diminish women's equality because women are so different from men—biologically, socially, and occupationally—that myriad special measures are required. The earnest words of the League representative displace equality into a jumble of differences and vague goals that barely recalls the fluent amalgams of the presuffrage era. The term equality becomes virtually meaningless.

Defenders of protective legislation—frustrated, and extremely angry at the National Woman's Party—could no longer project a delicately balanced vision of difference as integral to women's "true equality." Florence Kelley, for example, a former NWP member and proponent of extending protective legislation to men, now observed that "so long as men cannot be mothers, so long legislation adequate for them can never be adequate for wage-earning women; and the cry Equality, Equality, where Nature has created Inequality, is as stupid and as deadly as the cry Peace, Peace, where there is no Peace." By focusing on motherhood and female specificity, reformers mobilized the domestic code in a manner less and less responsive to earlier woman-movement visions of a human equality that could incorporate difference. Eventually, it was hard to distinguish their formulations from the Supreme Court's delineation of a dominant ideology that focused on women as mothers. Thus a suffragist turned League of Women Voters leader claimed in 1926 that "the most important function of woman in the world is motherhood, that the welfare of the child should be the first consideration, and that because of their maternal functions women should be protected against undue strain."[12]

In short, the subtle representations of gender difference that woman-movement activists had earlier maintained splintered apart after World War I. Advocates on behalf of women divided into two opposing forces. On the one side of the staunchly defended barricades was a small band of feminists who saw women as strong and independent individuals, more like than different from men. On the other were large numbers of reformers, regrouped within a spectrum of advocacy organizations, who increasingly emphasized the ways women were encumbered as mothers and family members, hence fundamentally unlike men. In this atmosphere, the gap between the maternalist canon projected by the nation's courts and the representations of sexual difference utilized by women reformers gradually closed. The meaning of the fact that such a gap had once existed was never seriously explored.

Sex, Race, and the Equality Framework

The notion that equality would best serve the interests of women returned to center stage in the 1960s. Hardly more than a decade after World War II, the ability of the domestic code to represent existing family relations and underpin U.S. policy with respect to women was under pressure. The massive entry of white women into wage labor constituted perhaps the most important challenge to dominant ideology. Women had of course never been absent from the paid labor force; between 1890 and 1940, the percentage of women who worked hovered around 25 percent. But most of these women were young and unmarried, many were women of color, and the doctrine of domesticity rendered the labor-force participation of the wives among them largely invisible. In the 1950s the numbers of women, especially wives and mothers, who worked accelerated rapidly. More than a third of all wives were in the labor force by 1970, and most women workers were married.[13] The double shift, with its accompanying stress on women and family life, was becoming a norm across society. Large numbers of wives and mothers—not just those in the bottom layers of the working class—were in the labor force on a more or less permanent basis. With these developments, conventional notions of woman's difference were becoming less and less able to encompass the experience of American families.

The election of John F. Kennedy to the presidency in 1960 brought to Washington a liberal administration and demands to address the problems of women.[14] Encouraged by Esther

Peterson, his appointee to head the Women's Bureau, Kennedy issued Executive Order 10980 in 1961, establishing the President's Commission on the Status of Women (PCSW). Peterson, long active in the labor movement and a firm supporter of protective legislation, hoped to use the commission to move beyond the long-standing stalemate between liberal reformers and the National Woman's Party (NWP) over the Equal Rights Amendment (ERA). Decades after the NWP first proposed the ERA in the 1920s, the controversy endured. The NWP continued to promote the ERA as the best means to improve women's status, and reformers just as persistently opposed their efforts. What particularly enraged liberals and organized labor was the NWP's insistence that an ERA would do away with the supposed evils of protective labor legislation. Peterson sought a way to meld protectionist concern that women's labor legislation be preserved with the NWP's commitment to establishing the constitutional equality of women.

The President's Commission on the Status of Women operated with a contradictory view of woman's place. Executive Order 10980 condemned "prejudices and outmoded customs [that] act as barriers to the full realization of women's basic rights," noting that "women should be assured the opportunity to develop their capacities and fulfill their aspirations." At the same time, it mandated that the PCSW develop recommendations to "enable women to continue their roles as wives and mothers while making a maximum contribution to the world around them."[15] In general, the commission espoused the traditional view that a woman's first duty was to her husband and children, but it also saw women as independent persons deserving equal rights. Its 1963 report recommended measures that would reduce barriers to social participation and enhance personal development, but it did not support the ERA. Likewise, the commission rejected its Employment Committee's proposal that a study be made of whether the antidiscrimination provisions in fair employment practices legislation should be extended to women. The PCSW "preferred not to link discrimination because of sex with discrimination because of race."[16]

The ERA and fair employment practices legislation made commission members nervous for two reasons. In the first place, most liberals still saw the ERA and antidiscrimination policies as threats to the protective labor laws they claimed helped women. And in the second, liberals made a sharp distinction between the issues of race and sex, arguing that race and sex were not comparable bases for discrimination and that racial issues were far more serious as well as more difficult to overcome. The commission thus drew back from an endorsement of the ERA and of the extension of antidiscrimination legislation to cover women. It did, however, accept black feminist activist and civil rights attorney Pauli Murray's suggestion of an alternate strategy to achieve women's equality before the law: litigation could force the courts to recognize that the Fourteenth Amendment already guarantees equal rights for men and women. Adopting Murray's reasoning, the 1963 report recommended that "interested groups" initiate court suits in order to obtain an "early and definite court pronouncement, particularly by the United States Supreme Court . . . to the end that the principle of equality become firmly established in constitutional doctrine."[17]

Protectionism—the cornerstone of liberal policy with respect to women—came under cautious examination in the PCSW's 1963 report. The commission noted that certain gender-specific laws and practices "do not appear to be reasonable in the light of the multiple activities of women in present-day society." It recommended that officials "scrutinize carefully" such measures, in order to remove "archaic standards which today operate as discriminatory." Not surprisingly, the PCSW report remained particularly ambivalent on the subject of female-specific labor laws. Legislation limiting women's hours did not function all that well, it suggested, but where it "represents the best so far attained it should be maintained and stengthened." Other protective statutes—weight-lifting limitations, night work restrictions, prohibitions on homework—were "originally intended to protect women workers, [but] have sometimes proved impracticable in their actual operation [and] may work to the disadvantage of women in some circumstances."[18] In sum, the President's Commission skirted an endorsement of the ERA and full equal rights while simultaneously acknowledging growing criticism of the damaging effects of female-specific legislation. The debate between equality and protection was not resolved, but the work of the PCSW brought the two sides closer.

Several other important governmental initiatives pertaining to women were taken during the Kennedy administration. Congress enacted the Equal Pay Act, endorsed by Kennedy and strongly supported by the Women's Bureau, in 1963. The act, which was the first federal law against sex discrimination in employment, barred employers from paying women less than men for equal work. Between 1963 and 1965, thirty-six governors established Commissions on the Status of Women to investigate and make recommendations on the state level.[19]

Publication of Betty Friedan's *The Feminine Mystique* in 1963 played an important role in moving questions concerning woman's place and the possibility of equality into public consciousness. According to Friedan, American women were afflicted with a "problem that has no name." Looking mainly at upper-middle-class women, Friedan described lives trapped in suburban meaninglessness. Her subjects suffered from having never been permitted to develop "their full human capacities." In order to solve this problem without a name, obstacles to equality had be overcome. "Every woman who fights the remaining barriers to full equality which are masked by the feminine mystique makes it easier for the next woman." Friedan praised the President's Commission on the Status of Women for creating "a climate where it is possible to recognize and do something about discrimination against women, in terms not only of pay but of the subtle barriers to opportunity." And she cautioned against traditional preferential treatment. "A girl should not expect special privileges because of her sex, but neither should she 'adjust' to prejudice and discrimination. She must learn to compete then, not as a woman, but as a human being."[20] While the President's Commission had clung to the traditional assumption that women's family ties are their first responsibility, Friedan emphasized women's identity as independent persons. *The Feminine Mystique* shot rapidly to the top of the bestseller lists.

A new vision of woman was being broached. Formulated at first in the language of equal rights, it went beyond the narrow legal equality that had come to be associated with the feminists of the National Woman's Party. The women activists of the early sixties were suggesting a view of women as persons whose development had been stunted by a hostile social structure and whose human capacities needed to be allowed full scope. And they were, albeit often in ladylike manner, moving toward a critique of the society that permitted these and other injustices.

The new stream of feminism emerged onto a social landscape shaped by contemporary civil rights struggles. Early feminists operated as an isolated handful of elite lobbyists and organizers, but their efforts drew on the strategies and rhetoric elaborated by the civil rights movement in the South. Seeking equal rights and speaking a passionate language of justice and human liberation, the black movement challenged all who observed it to think about the meaning of equality.

During the mid-1960s, women activists forged a new strategy, focused on rights and equality. Activists viewed women and men as more alike than different, and they made an analogy between sex and race inequality.[21] To achieve equality, they argued, women, like blacks, need access to the same opportunities, facilities, and benefits that white men have. At the same time, the women's movement, like the increasingly militant civil rights movement, often looked beyond equality to a future society characterized in terms of human rights and just social relations. For many, equality meant more than merely formal rights with respect to the existing status quo.[22]

A consensus that transcended the dispute over the ERA was at last emerging. The new feminists took aim at practices that used women's childbearing role to justify a globally secondary status for women. And they often relied on the analogy between race and sex discrimination. When Congress inserted the word sex alongside race, color, religion, and national origin in Title VII of the 1964 Civil Rights Act, it set the seal on subsequent developments. In the next years, the analogy between sex and race moved to the center of feminist strategic thinking.

The inclusion of sex as a category in Title VII, which prohibited discrimination in private employment, is often presented as having been an accident or a male chauvinist joke. No hearings were held to consider it, and the little discussion that took place occurred in an atmosphere of hilarity and ridicule. In reality, the addition of sex to the list of prohibited categories reflected the changing climate for women's issues as well as years of lobbying by National Woman's Party feminists. Together with the National Federation of Business and Professional Women's Clubs, the NWP had not only persistently promoted the Equal Rights Amendment among government officials and legislators, but also worked for the inclusion of sex in earlier fair employment practices measures. These efforts had generally been blocked by women reformers and organized labor, who insisted that sex discrimination reflected "problems sufficiently different" from race discrimination "to make separate treatment preferable."[23] This traditional scenario, product of a forty-year impasse between supporters and opponents of protection, had a different outcome in the 1964 effort to write sex into the new civil rights legislation. Conservative Southern Democrats bent on defeating the omnibus civil rights bill joined longtime supporters of the ERA to endorse a hastily introduced amendment making sex one of the prohibited bases of employment discrimination. On the other side, the Women's Bureau opposed inclusion, arguing as usual that race and sex discrimination were substantively different and required different remedial measures. For the first time at the federal level, the supporters of gender specificity lost out. When the civil rights bill went to the House and Senate for final approval, the sex provision was still intact. The prohibited categories of employment discrimination included sex, although Congress provided little evidence of legislative intent.

Enactment of Title VII shifted the terms of the debate between equality and protection in the sphere of employment. The President's Commission on the Status of Women had been dominated by the protectionists, but now the principle of equality was suddenly the focus of attention and activity. Title VII seemed to offer a powerful set of legal tools. Henceforward, efforts to remedy women's secondary employment status would most easily be formulated in terms of an antidiscrimination framework.

Immediately following passage of the 1964 Civil Rights Act, activists maneuvered to redefine their positions. As always, protective legislation constituted a central issue. Like the ERA,

Title VII threatened to invalidate female-specific labor statutes. On its face, protective legislation discriminated by treating women as a class, but it was still widely viewed as beneficial to women. The analogy between race and sex, however, undermined assumptions that protection helped women in the workplace. Like policies singling out blacks for special treatment, female-specific labor legislation encouraged negative stereotypes, fostered segregation in the labor market, and contributed to women's permanent status as second-class citizens. To the extent that it actually helped women, protection came at a high price. Because Title VII focused just on employment and because liberals could refer to their fairly well-developed critique of racial discrimination, it was becoming easier to see how protection could harm women. It now seemed clear to many that, as policy activists Pauli Murray and Mary Eastwood put it in an influential article, "the rights of women and the rights of Negroes are only different phases of the fundamental and indivisible issue of human rights."[24]

The years 1965 and 1966 saw the first shaping of government policy with respect to women's equal employment opportunity under Title VII. On the sensitive question of protection, the Women's Bureau, the Department of Labor, mainstream women's organizations, and the AFL-CIO continued to argue that female-specific labor laws were somehow not in conflict with Title VII. But a number of key women activists had reversed their positions. Esther Peterson, for example, enthusiastically welcomed Title VII as a "great opportunity" to convert labor legislation to a single standard; unusually difficult working conditions could be dealt with, she suggested, by extending protective legislation to men. Likewise, Pauli Murray and Mary Eastwood, along with many of the state Commissions on the Status of Women, now believed the principle of protectionism had to be left behind. State protective laws had "waning utility," they argued, and could not be "harmonized" with Title VII.[25] State legislatures had already begun to revise legal codes, and some were moving to repeal protective legislation or extend its provisions to men.[26]

Activists were ready for a major policy debate over the meaning of equality for women, but the government body charged with implementing Title VII was not. The Equal Employment Opportunity Commission (EEOC) was barely paying attention to the many cases of sex discrimination being brought before it. Headed by officials who regarded the inclusion of sex as a fluke without significant legislative history, the EEOC had decided to proceed slowly on sex discrimination. It deferred to the tradition of support for state protective laws by determining that their distinction between women and men was a valid exception to Title VII; being a woman, in the EEOC's earliest considerations, was a bona fide occupational qualification which legitimated virtually any female-specific employment practice. Most irritating to many observers, the commission ruled that employers could continue to place help-wanted ads in sex-segregated, but not race-segregated, listings. It was clear that the commission considered issues of sex discrimination to be diversionary. As a spokesman told a reporter, the EEOC "did not want this area to interfere with its main concern, racial discrimination."[27]

The EEOC's foot-dragging angered activists, many of whom had been working together in Status of Women organizations at the state level. Nearly a third of cases brought before the EEOC during its first year concerned sex discrimination, but still it refused to develop a forthright policy to further women's equal employment opportunity. Women, some began to argue, needed a civil rights movement. In October of 1966 the National Organization for Women (NOW) held its founding conference. Although members still differed on the question of protective labor legislation, NOW's Statement of Purpose spoke forcefully against paternalistic special treatment: "We are . . . opposed to all policies and practices—in church, state, college, factory, or office—which, in the guise of protectiveness, not only deny opportunities but also foster in women self-denigration, dependence, and evasion of responsibility, undermine their confidence in their own abilities and foster contempt for women."[28] With its membership growing rapidly, NOW picketed newspapers, integrated male-only bars, and made sure that government officials knew the issue of sex discrimination was being monitored. In May of 1967 the EEOC at last held hearings on issues of concern to NOW members: protective labor legislation, sex-segregated newspaper advertising, pension inequalities, and discrimination against airline stewardesses. In October President Lyndon B. Johnson issued Executive Order 11375, adding a ban on sex discrimination to an earlier directive that prohibited discrimination in federal employment and by federal contractors on the basis of race, creed, color, or national origin. At the end of the year, NOW picketed EEOC offices across the country, demanding that it change its position on sex-segregated want ads. In February 1968, NOW filed formal suit against the EEOC to force it to comply with its own regulations. A week later the commission issued a new set of guidelines, declaring it would decide on a case-by-case basis whether a particular protective labor law conflicted with Title VII's ban on sex discrimination. In August the EEOC reversed itself on newspaper advertising.

The signing of Executive Order 11375 and the changes in EEOC rulings and guidelines signaled that federal policy had finally acknowledged that it was possible to make an analogy between sex and race discrimination. In the course of the next decade, the assumption that race and sex could be paralleled as essentially comparable phenomena began to shape government policy with respect to women. Many of the efforts of the new women's movement proceeded within the same framework. It now seemed obvious that women, like blacks, had long been denied full participation in society as persons and citizens, and that the barriers must be removed. No more than race, sex was not a valid basis for differential treatment.

The Pregnancy Policy Puzzle

By the late 1960s, the rudiments of an equality policy for women were in place. Within the constraints of American jurisprudence, the new women's movement sought to articulate its implications. In particular, feminism had to confront the difficult theoretical and strategic problem of motherhood. How was the female-specific phenomenon of maternity to be incorporated within the equality framework?

Feminist legal strategists quickly developed a general

approach that could be used to think about women's equality regardless of the specific legal setting.[29] Whether considering the Fourteenth Amendment, Title VII, or the proposed Equal Rights Amendment—which most mainstream women's organizations now supported—the premises were the same. A lengthy 1971 article published in the *Yale Law Journal* surveyed the new legal terrain through an analysis of the ERA. Written by three students and a professor—Barbara Brown, Gail Falk, Ann Freedman, and Thomas Emerson—the article started from the basic principle that "sex is not a permissible factor in determining the legal rights of women, or of men." Differences between women and men, whether physically or socially based, should not be allowed to matter, and "sex is a prohibited classification."[30]

If classification by sex is no longer permissible, then "the law must deal with particular attributes of individuals."[31] Classifications can be made, but they must be based on realistic "functional" distinctions, not stereotypical generalizations. For example, strength, not maleness, might be required for certain jobs; the fact that women on average are not as physically strong as men could not be used to exclude a particularly strong woman from a job requiring heavy lifting. Similarly, years out of the labor market, not femaleness, might be the criterion for entry into a job retraining program; the fact that widows and divorcees are more likely to need such retraining could not be used to exclude a man from the program.

Experience in the area of racial discrimination had already shown that eliminating sex as a basis for classification would probably not be enough, for not all discrimination is overt. A law or policy that appears neutral can actually have a disproportionately negative impact on a particular group. Given the history of discrimination in education, for example, impartially administered literacy tests for voters in practice fell more heavily on blacks than others, denying them the vote. Likewise a minimum height requirement for prison guards is not on its face sex-specific, but it would effectively exclude most women from the job. Such practices are "fair in form but discriminatory in operation," as the Supreme Court determined in 1971. Where a neutral rule has a disparate impact on members of one group, it may constitute an evasion of laws attempting to eradicate discrimination. Feminists wanted the party defending a formally sex-neutral rule with a discriminatory impact on women to have to justify it in court under strict standards. The minimum height requirement for prison guards, for instance, would have to be shown to be a business necessity that could not be satisfied by less discriminatory means. Otherwise, a truly gender-neutral rule would have to be developed, one more functionally related to the work of guarding prisoners. Disparate impact analysis would provide a way to attack formally equal treatment that in fact substantively disadvantaged women. It would therefore enable feminists to confront not only overt discrimination but also a facially neutral social structure that in reality favored men.[32]

Feminist legal strategy with respect to pregnancy in the workplace took shape within the new equality framework. For decades, differential and often disadvantageous treatment of women workers had rested on the implicit basis that all women are, or may become, mothers, and that mothers have no legitimate place in the labor market. The women's movement developed a critique of such undifferentiated notions of woman's vocation to mother and of motherhood's relation to labor-force participation. As early as 1966, NOW's Statement of Purpose questioned the inevitability of sex divisions of labor in family life by pointing to the need for "a different concept of marriage [and] an equitable sharing of the responsibilities of home and children." Feminists were soon suggesting more clearly that childbearing should be distinguished from child rearing. As Elizabeth Koontz, director of the Women's Bureau, put it in 1971 in what was widely cited as a pathbreaking article, "only women can bear children, but both men and women are capable of rearing children. The conceptual framework of childbearing and child rearing fits both present and future reality better than a conceptual framework that assumes that childbearing and child rearing are both solely the responsibility of women."[33] Thus disentangled from global conceptions of mothering, pregnancy emerged as one of only a handful of physical characteristics unique to one sex.

It was now clear—apparently for the first time—that what had traditionally been called maternity policy entailed policies to address two distinct kinds of needs. Only those associated with the unique physical characteristics of childbearing seemed to pose theoretical questions for the equality framework. Feminist legal activists believed that laws acknowledging such sex-specific characteristics—by providing a benefit or imposing a restriction—would not necessarily violate the principle of equality. As the 1971 article on the ERA suggested, the law could pay attention to some sex-specific characteristics by recognizing a "subsidiary principle" alongside the fundamental principle that sex is a prohibited classification. The subsidiary principle— "limited to *physical* characteristics and [not extending] to psychological, social or other characteristics of the sexes"—would enable a small list of sex differences to be acknowledged in the law. Thus legislation concerning wet nurses and sperm donors and, more relevantly, some laws pertaining to maternity, would be permissible. The authors cautioned that such sex-specific laws "introduce elements of a dual system of rights" that might be interpreted in too broad a manner. The subsidiary principle must be understood to be "strictly limited to situations where the regulation is closely, directly and narrowly confined to the unique physical characteristic." Courts would have to guard against attempts to use it to justify laws "that in overall effect seriously discriminate against one sex."[34]

Consistent with the argument that a subsidiary principle permitted sex-specific classifications where appropriate, the Citizens' Advisory Council on the Status of Women, a committee of private citizens appointed by the president, asserted in 1970 that the proposed Equal Rights Amendment would not affect "laws providing maternity benefits." Feminist legal scholars were more precise in considering the impact of the ERA: "Laws establishing medical leave for childbearing" would be permissible, "though leave for child*rearing* would have to apply to both sexes."[35]

While allowing that narrowly drawn laws providing maternity benefits could be harmonized with the equality framework, feminist legal strategists generally pursued a different approach to address the needs of pregnant and parenting workers. Rather than accommodate pregnancy as a physical characteristic unique to women, they sought ways to make pregnant employees analytically comparable to their nonpregnant co-workers. By the late 1960s, the approach that was adopted had been articulated. The 1970 Citizens' Advisory Council report, for example, made two recommendations concerning maternity benefits. The first suggested that pregnancy-related medical problems and childbirth be defined and treated, in the employment context, as temporary disabilities:

> Childbirth and complications of pregnancy are, for all *job-related purposes*, temporary disabilities and should be treated as such under any health insurance, temporary disability insurance, or sick leave plan of an employer, union, or fraternal society. Any policies or practices of an employer or union, written or unwritten, applied to instances of temporary disability other than pregnancy should be applied to incapacity due to pregnancy or childbirth, including policies or practices relating to leave of absence, restoration or recall to duty, and seniority.

The council noted that employers and state temporary disability systems often denied women benefits explicitly because pregnancy is a "normal physiological condition." Better, it concluded, to treat pregnancy as a temporary disability. "Economically it makes no difference whether an employee is unable to work at his [*sic*] regular job because of pregnancy or because of hernia, ulcers, or any other illness or accident; in any case he or she suffers loss of pay and has extra medical expenses." A redefinition of pregnancy as a temporary disability would prevent the normalcy of childbearing from serving as a pretext to disadvantage women.[36]

The second recommendation made by the Citizens' Advisory Council was that policymakers eschew all pregnancy-specific practices and benefits, even those that seemed to treat women preferentially:

> No additional or different benefits or restrictions should be applied to disability because of pregnancy or childbirth, and no pregnant woman employee should be in a better position in relation to job-related practices or benefits than an employee similarly situated suffering from other disability.

Of course, observed the council, women are subject to "all the other disabilities of mankind," and it could therefore be maintained that they require additional benefits for pregnancy. But to treat women as a class in this manner would be both unfair and counterproductive. "Giving special treatment for pregnancy will inevitably lead to situations in which men and other women who are suffering from disabilities other than pregnancy will have less benefits than pregnant women. This is not sociologically or economically justified and would be divisive. In addition, . . . such policies could very well result in reluctance to hire women of childbearing age."[37]

In sum, although feminist strategists acknowledged the validity of narrowly drawn policies targeting the female-specific physiological uniqueness of pregnancy, they preferred to analogize the situation of the pregnant worker to that of other workers. Insofar as pregnancy and childbirth affected a woman employee's ability to work, the conditions were to be included in benefit plans as if they were temporary disabilities. Much of the discussion concerned the disabling aspects of pregnancy, but the approach had implications that were at least as important for pregnant women who were able and willing to work. Insofar as pregnancy and childbearing did not affect women's ability to work, employers and the state would have to treat them like other workers. Such employment policies as mandatory maternity leaves or denial of eligibility for unemployment benefits would be redefined as discriminatory and illegal.

Feminist lawyers had their work cut out for them. As of the late 1960s, the Supreme Court had not yet issued a ruling banning sex discrimination and only a little progress had been made toward achieving the feminist equality agenda. On the question of pregnancy at work, federal policies generally reinforced the traditional view of maternity still embodied in state protective legislation and employer practices. That is, employers were still free, within limits established by protective laws, to treat the condition of pregnancy as they deemed appropriate. In 1966, for example, a company asked the Equal Employment Opportunity Commission whether exclusion of pregnancy and related conditions from coverage by its disability plan would be construed as sex discrimination under Title VII of the Civil Rights Act of 1964.

The EEOC assured the firm it had nothing to fear because pregnancy is both unique and normal:

> Commission policy in this area does not seek to compare an employer's treatment of illness or injury with his treatment of maternity since maternity is a temporary disability unique to the female sex and more or less to be anticipated during the working life of most women employees. Therefore, it is our opinion that . . . a company's group insurance program which covers hospital and medical expenses for the delivery of employees' children, but excludes from its long-term salary continuation program those disabilities which result from pregnancy and childbirth would not be in violation of Title VII.

The EEOC also made it clear that employers did not have to cover pregnancy-related medical expenses at all: "An insurance or other benefit plan may simply exclude maternity as a covered risk, as such an exclusion would not in our view be discriminatory."[38] And it ruled that employers could provide paid sick leave but unpaid maternity leave, and that they had the right to decide at what point in an employee's pregnancy her employment could be suspended.[39]

The EEOC made no effort, in short, to require employers to develop benefit policies covering pregnancy disability on a basis comparable to other temporarily disabling conditions. It simply permitted employers to continue to use the normalcy of pregnancy as a justification for special treatment that was in reality grossly disadvantageous. In the EEOC's view, pregnancy was a natural event, not a sickness, and it could therefore be excluded from benefit plans.

Federal policy on women began to change in the 1970s. The Supreme Court invalidated a sex-based classification on constitutional grounds for the first time in 1971.[40] Shortly thereafter, the EEOC—pressured by women's groups and perhaps influenced by the tumultuous social movements of the period—revised its position on pregnancy. In new guidelines issued in 1972, the commission explicitly discussed discrimination on the basis of pregnancy as a violation of Title VII and specified appropriate nondiscriminatory practices in three areas. First, pregnancy could no longer be a reason for denying women access to work. An employer who fired or refused to hire a pregnant woman would be violating Title VII.[41] Second, pregnancy-related disability was defined as a temporary disability "for all job-related purposes." Here, the EEOC closely followed the language used in the Citizens' Advisory Council report.[42] Third, employers were warned that an employment policy which provided "insufficient or no leave," and which resulted in the firing of pregnant employees, might constitute a violation of Title VII's ban on neutral rules with disparate impact.[43]

The 1972 EEOC Guidelines laid a foundation for substantive changes. Employers and courts started to establish a record of treating pregnant workers as comparable to other workers whose ability to work was similarly affected. Practices that had been customary only a decade earlier were redefined as discriminatory and unacceptable. Job security and benefits for pregnant workers, especially in the areas of health, disability, and unemployment insurance, improved. Increasingly it seemed acceptable practice that a woman work until as late into her pregnancy as she wished and that she receive childbirth leave with some job protection. The provision of paid leave became somewhat less unusual. By the late 1970s, the treatment of pregnant women workers in the American workplace had been transformed, although it remained pitifully below minimum ILO recommendations.[44] The widespread view of pregnancy as a unique but normal condition which employers could treat in a special—but, as it turned out, generally inferior—way began to fade.

A New Solution

Changes in the treatment of pregnancy at work over the past two decades suggest that a new kind of maternity policy is being shaped.[45] Modest and indeed peculiar by European standards, it does not center on specific substantive benefits for mothers, nor does it define its goals in terms of social welfare. Instead, its touchstone is an antidiscrimination principle: maternity cannot be the basis for unequal treatment of a woman. Each of the two distinguishable components of motherhood—

childbearing and child rearing—is to be treated in a gender-neutral manner. In order to address the sex-specific aspects of maternity, pregnancy and childbirth are at times to be analogized to temporary medical disability.

Necessary to the development of the revised maternity policy is the transformation of old assumptions about motherhood, family, and employment. A new set of policy principles, framed in terms of equality, has been challenging traditional notions of women as different and maternity as special. Where the older emphasis on difference and special treatment effectively pertained only to white women, the turn to equality to some extent reflects the convergence of white women's labor-market experience with that of women of color. Thus the revision promises to disavow difference in two ways. First, it constructs motherhood on the basis of equality rather than difference. Second, it threatens to dissolve the distinction between the two tiers of traditional maternity policy. In schematic form, the principles underlying the new policy approach can be outlined as follows:

- Motherhood is to be regarded as compatible with labor-force participation. Employers should expect women workers to remain permanently in the labor force.
- Pregnancy can be regarded as comparable to other conditions that affect or do not affect workers. Pregnant employees do not have a special status and should not be treated differently than other employees.
- The responsibilities of child rearing and family life are to be shared by fathers and mothers. The boundary between work and family is seen as changing and sometimes permeable.
- Maternity and child rearing are still, in general, private obligations. However, the state may provide some benefits and at times intervene.

These revised principles construct pregnant and mothering workers as more like than unlike other workers. Launched in the 1960s and 1970s, their import for policy remains in many ways unspecified, and they are still in contention with traditional assumptions. For example, the meaning of the principle that child-rearing responsibilities are to be shared is contested. Feminists suggest that mothers and fathers have identical obligations toward their children, emphasizing that fathers as well as mothers should do the actual work of child rearing. Much more common in public policy—as evidenced, for example, in family law reform and the transformation of divorce practices—is a version of the parental sharing principle that leaves primary responsibility for the work of raising children with mothers while imposing equal financial obligations on divorced spouses. The practical effect of this interpretation has been to greatly increase, not equalize, the burdens of women. Yet another approach to sharing child-rearing responsibilities is advanced by the men's rights movement, which adopts the language of equality in an effort to reassert the power of fathers.[46] Implicit and therefore invisible though U.S. maternity policy still is, it has become a site of intense struggle.

As white mothers, many with preschool children, join mothers of color in the labor force, maternity policy is being redefined. In certain ways, the new framework seems to extend to white women the assumptions underlying workplace practices encountered by women of color. That is, the principles guiding the new maternity policy recall those traditionally applied to women of color: motherhood is no longer viewed as a bar to employment, pregnancy loses its special status, mothers and fathers have joint responsibilities, and the state sometimes intervenes. The context is, however, importantly different, and the outcomes are yet to be determined. Affirming the compatibility of motherhood with employment does not necessarily entail denying the existence of special needs. Treating pregnant workers comparably to other workers can improve job security and preserve benefits. Sharing family responsibilities should enhance sex equality. Where traditional maternity policies offered black women a stingy and motherhood-denying equality, these principles could imply a different sort of egalitarianism. In the intentions of feminist proponents, indeed, they suggest policies that can be beneficial to women. Nonetheless, the potential for equality to cut another way remains. The representation of pregnant and mothering workers as essentially the same as other workers turns out to have a pernicious underside.

5

Difference in Court

Pregnancy Discrimination and the Supreme Court

By the early 1970s the beginnings of a new approach to treating pregnancy at work had been delineated, based on assumptions of equality and the permanence of female labor-force participation. With input from the women's movement, a national policy consensus on maternity seemed to be developing. Into this process stepped a disruptive United States Supreme Court, staunchly resisting the notion that pregnancy could be brought within the equality framework. Led by Justices Potter Stewart and William H. Rehnquist, the Court delivered two opinions endorsing the traditional view of pregnancy as normal but unique and not comparable to other conditions. The decisions had the practical impact of denying employment benefits to women. In *Geduldig v. Aiello* (1974) the Court determined that a temporary disability insurance plan that excluded pregnancy-related disabilities did not violate Fourteenth Amendment guarantees of equal protection. In *General Electric Company v. Gilbert* (1976) it ruled that denial of sickness and accident benefits to women disabled by pregnancy did not violate the equality mandate of Title VII.[1]

The Supreme Court majority opinions in *Geduldig* and *Gilbert* insisted on the fundamental difference that pregnancy makes. Of course, the Justices noted, insofar as women and men are alike they must be treated the same. But women's normal biological capacity to become pregnant is unique—sui generis— and insofar as pregnancy is a unique condition, the situations of men and women cannot be viewed as comparable. Different treatment of pregnant workers is therefore not necessarily un-equal treatment. In legal terms, the sexes are not similarly situ-ated in this respect, and special treatment of pregnant women does not constitute discrimination. The difference between the sexes simply represents an extra burden—an *"additional* risk, unique to women."[2]

In effect, the Court was declaring that for the purposes of equality analysis, men are the standard against which women are to be measured. Burdens created by characteristics not shared by men are extra and need not be picked up by em-ployers. "Lawmakers are constitutionally free to include or ex-clude pregnancy from the coverage of legislation . . . on any reasonable basis." To a lower court's assertion that the inclu-sion of pregnancy in benefit plans, even if expensive, would validly compensate for "women's biologically more burden-some place," the Supreme Court replied that Title VII need not cover women's and men's "differing roles in 'the scheme of human existence.' "[3] The specter of *Muller v. Oregon* haunted the Court's reasoning, as it returned to earlier views of preg-nancy as a unique condition, and dependent motherhood as woman's place. In the Justices' view, the pregnant worker was still essentially an abnormal presence in the workplace.

The Supreme Court's pregnancy decisions were widely con-demned. On the theory that woman's childbearing capacity marks her as globally different, the Court had denied benefits to pregnant workers. Its understanding of sexual difference recalled old doctrines of separate spheres and female subordi-nation. Feminists and progressives had good grounds to mis-trust the Court's reasoning, for it threatened to give new life to supposedly separate-but-equal arrangements that in reality disadvantaged women.

Outraged by the Supreme Court's attempt to reimpose tradi-tional notions of woman's proper place on public policy, a large coalition of over three hundred feminist, labor, civil rights, church, and even antiabortion groups mobilized as the Cam-paign to End Discrimination Against Pregnant Workers.[4] The coalition pressured Congress to make Title VII of the 1964 Civil Rights Act consistent with the 1972 EEOC Guidelines banning discrimination on the basis of pregnancy. Congress could not change the Supreme Court's opinion in *Geduldig* that a classification based on pregnancy does not involve an unconstitutional denial of equal protection under the Fourteenth Amendment. Ominously, the Justices' broad interpretation of how physiological and social-role sex differences justify special treatment of pregnancy remains part of constitutional doctrine today. But Congress could and did enact legislation that would nullify the Supreme Court opinion in *Gilbert*, which concerned Title VII. Despite strenuous opposition from business and conservative interests, Congress passed the Pregnancy Discrimination Act (PDA) of 1978, outlawing employment discrimination on the basis of pregnancy. Generally regarded as a victory in the struggle to achieve equitable treatment for women, the PDA represented a rejection of the Supreme Court's effort to turn back the clock on sex equality. Its enactment confirmed the policy directions initiated in the early 1970s.

Congress's intent in passing the Pregnancy Discrimination Act was to set aside the Supreme Court's rulings on pregnancy and Title VII in order "to ensure that working women are protected against all forms of employment discrimination based on sex."[5] The PDA specified that the terms "because of sex" or "on the basis of sex" in Title VII of the 1964 Civil Rights Act "include, but are not limited to, because of or on the basis of pregnancy, childbirth, or related medical conditions." The act also prescribed how employers were to treat the covered conditions: "Women affected by pregnancy, childbirth, or related medical conditions shall be treated the same for all employment-related purposes, including receipt of benefits under fringe benefit programs, as other persons not so affected but similar in their ability or inability to work."[6] Thus, the PDA did two things. It made sure that the preexisting Title VII bans on sex discrimination in employment would be understood to cover pregnancy discrimination. And it provided a standard for evaluating employer practices with respect to pregnant workers. While the case that prompted the *Gilbert* decision concerned pregnancy disability benefits, the PDA had a far broader scope, for it would "apply to all aspects of employment—hiring, reinstatement, termination, disability benefits, sick leave, medical benefits, seniority and other conditions of employment currently covered by Title VII."[7]

The Pregnancy Discrimination Act sought to reconcile women's unique capacities as childbearers with their status as members of the workforce by incorporating pregnancy into the equality framework. A notion of comparability was to be used to evaluate employer practices. In the words of the Senate committee report on the PDA, "the bill rejects the view that employers may treat pregnancy and its incidents as *sui generis*, without regard to its functional comparability to other conditions." Gender equality was to be enhanced by focusing "not on [pregnant employees'] condition alone but on the actual effects of that condition on their ability to work."[8] Given the Supreme Court's willingness to permit disadvantageous special treatment of pregnant workers, supporters of the PDA believed that women workers could best be protected by establishing comparability, "for all employment-related purposes," between pregnant workers and others similarly able or unable to work. Where earlier EEOC policy tended simply to identify pregnancy with disability— asserting in 1966 that "maternity is a temporary disability" and in 1972 that pregnancy-related disabilities "are, for all job-related purposes, temporary disabilities"[9]—the Pregnancy Discrimination Act adopted a different approach. The issue was no longer disability per se but the creation of a standard of comparability that would encompass both pregnant employees and their nonpregnant co-workers.

Compliance with the Pregnancy Discrimination Act entails the kinds of workplace policies already mandated by the 1972 EEOC Guidelines. Employers must generally make decisions about pregnant workers based on their capacity to work, just as such decisions would be made about other employees. For example, if able to work, a pregnant worker cannot be fired or forced to take a leave of absence. If not able to work, a pregnant worker must be treated no differently than other workers similar in their inability to work. An employer who ordinarily permits temporarily disabled workers to return to their old jobs, for instance, must provide the same option to pregnant workers.

An employer who treats pregnant and nonpregnant workers the same is not automatically in compliance with the Pregnancy Discrimination Act, for such same treatment may sometimes have disadvantageous effects on women. Title VII of the 1964 Civil Rights Act prohibits formally neutral rules that have substantively negative consequences for the equal employment opportunity of a covered group. The proper remedy in such a situation would be a new rule that affects all employees in a truly neutral manner, not one that applies only to adversely impacted employees. For example, despite the PDA's language directing that pregnant women "be treated the same," inadequate leave provided identically to all employees may be a violation of the PDA where it is tantamount to a policy of dismissal for pregnant workers. The courts might require an employer with inadequate leave policies to offer minimally adequate leave to all employees who need it. This solution to the problem of inadequate leave for childbearing is thus quite different from that provided by traditional maternity legislation, which limits leave to pregnant employees.

Like the EEOC Guidelines before it, the Pregnancy Discrimination Act does not shape the substantive content of the pregnant worker's rights and benefits. Rather, the treatment a pregnant worker might receive under the Pregnancy Discrimination Act largely depends on her employer's particular policies. It is this peculiarity that caused the PDA to become the focus of debate. While its passage represented a clear victory for the principle of women's equality, the act was soon at odds with state legislation also designed to help pregnant women.

Pregnancy Disability Legislation

In the 1970s, pregnancy in the workplace was an object of concern at the state as well as national level. Between 1972 and 1981, five states—Massachusetts, Connecticut, Montana, California, and Wisconsin—enacted maternity statutes.[10] The new laws generally mandated that an employer provide unpaid leave and a measure of employment security and benefit protection to eligible women workers. Massachusetts' 1972 childbirth leave statute was the first such provision in the country; somewhat vaguely, it required employers to provide leave "for the purpose of giving birth." Connecticut, Montana, California, and Wisconsin specified more explicitly that pregnancy leave must be based on disability. All but Massachusetts developed pregnancy disability legislation in the context of broader equal rights initiatives, such as state equal rights amendments or fair employment laws. For example, Connecticut included a pregnancy disability provision in its Fair Employment Practices Act in 1973, responding to court decisions holding that the exclusion of pregnancy from benefit plans is discriminatory. Similarly, Montana adopted an Equal Rights Amendment in 1972 and then reviewed existing state legislation in order to decide "what changes should be made . . . to achieve true legal equality of the sexes."[11] Lawmakers were particularly concerned that the new legislation preserve what they called traditional family values.

Massachusetts, Connecticut, and Montana put their pregnancy legislation in place before the Supreme Court rendered its decisions in *Geduldig* and *Gilbert*—the two opinions that permitted classifications based on pregnancy to be used to deny women workers benefits. California and Wisconsin enacted pregnancy statutes after Congress had passed the Pregnancy Discrimination Act, which attempted to ban such practices.[12] Although pregnancy disability laws were patently sex-specific, legislators believed them consistent with the equality framework. A public policy that implicitly constructed women as both different and equal seemed reasonable and was beginning to be institutionalized. No advocates noticed, apparently, that the new laws contravened the 1970 Citizens' Advisory Council recommendation against providing special pregnancy benefits. Nor did anyone anticipate that the conflict between their female-specific approach and current notions of equality could be used in an effort by employers to deny women benefits. But that is precisely what happened.

The Montana Maternity Leave Act (MMLA), which required employers to provide unpaid job- and benefit-protected leave for a "reasonable" period to women workers disabled by pregnancy, became the focus of litigation in the courts in 1980.[13] The case concerned Tamara Buley, hired by the Miller-Wohl Company to work in its Great Falls clothing store. Buley missed two and one-half days in her first week due to morning sickness, and she continued to miss work, take extra breaks, and spend a great deal of time in the bathroom in subsequent weeks. Less than a month after they hired her, Miller-Wohl fired Buley, in accordance with a personnel policy that denied sick leave to workers during their first year of employment. Buley filed a complaint with the Montana commissioner of labor and industry, charging that Miller-Wohl's stingy no-leave policy constituted a violation of the state pregnancy disability statute. In response, Miller-Wohl sought to have the MMLA declared invalid. The state statute, it claimed, forced it to violate the recently enacted Pregnancy Discrimination Act by treating pregnant women better than other temporarily disabled employees. That is, Miller-Wohl argued it could not simultaneously provide the special treatment mandated by the Montana Maternity Leave Act and the equal treatment required by the PDA. Under the supremacy clause of the United States Constitution, concluded the company, the federal Pregnancy Discrimination Act should take precedence over the state Maternity Leave Act.

Montana courts disagreed with Miller-Wohl's arguments, holding that the company had violated both the Maternity Leave Act and the Pregnancy Discrimination Act. The PDA does not preempt the MMLA, the courts declared, and the two laws are not in conflict. In mandating benefits for women temporarily disabled by pregnancy, the Montana Maternity Leave Act in fact enhances equal employment opportunity, for "by removing pregnancy-related disabilities as a legal ground for discharge from employment, the MMLA places men and women on more equal terms."[14] The Montana Supreme Court noted that the appearance of a contradiction would disappear were the legislature to extend the MMLA's benefits equally to all temporarily disabled workers and recommended that it do so.[15] The United States Supreme Court refused to hear the case, and the Maternity Leave Act remains in force in Montana.

Meanwhile, in California, a similar case was developing. A 1978 provision of the California Fair Employment and Housing Act required employers to provide pregnant employees up to four months unpaid disability leave with job security. Lillian Garland had been working as a receptionist in a Los Angeles branch of a large bank, California Federal Savings and Loan Association, when her difficult first pregnancy and delivery necessitated several months disability leave in early 1982. She attempted to return to her job at the end of the leave, but the bank claimed no receptionist or similar positions were available. Like Tamara Buley in Montana, Garland then sought her rights under the state pregnancy disability statute. In response, California Federal Savings, joined by the California Chamber of Commerce and the Merchants and Manufacturers Association, initiated a suit to invalidate the state law, arguing that it was preempted by the Pregnancy Discrimination Act. As in Montana, the employers pointed to the apparent conflict between the state law's requirement that pregnant employees be treated in a favorable manner and the federal law's mandate that they be treated equally. California Federal Savings did not provide job-protected leaves to employees temporarily disabled by conditions other than pregnancy, and it wished to treat its pregnant employees in the same niggardly way. The California case reached the U.S. Supreme Court in 1986, and a decision leaving the state law on the books was rendered in January 1987. According to the Court, the two statutes are not in conflict, and special treatment of pregnancy in the workplace does not necessarily contradict the imperatives of equality.[16]

The outcome of these two cases was of great importance to women workers. In both, employers were attempting to use the federal Pregnancy Discrimination Act to invalidate state pregnancy disability laws. If successful, their efforts threatened women workers with loss of important benefits. The equality framework that had seemed unequivocally on the side of women was revealing hidden ambiguities. At one level, the court cases pitted mean-spirited employers against pregnant workers needing job-protected disability leave. At another, they posed difficult questions for feminist strategy and theory.

Controversy in the Feminist Legal Community

The state pregnancy disability legislation departed from the strategic approach embodied in the 1972 EEOC Guidelines and the Pregnancy Discrimination Act by addressing directly pregnant workers' need for job-protected leave. Rather than provide benefits on a gender-neutral basis, the state laws openly acknowledged the female-specific character of pregnancy. As the Montana litigation moved through the courts, feminist lawyers across the country began to discuss the implications of the contradiction between the two strategies with more than a little consternation. Until then, their litigious attention had mainly been focused on the equality campaigns of the previous decade. Hardly three years earlier they had mobilized to circumvent the infamous Supreme Court decision in *Gilbert* through passage of the Pregnancy Discrimination Act. Feminist legal activists were ill prepared for an assault on women in the very name of equality. Yet here was the startling phenomenon that Miller-Wohl, Buley's employer, was seeking to invalidate the Montana maternity law by citing the equality mandate of the PDA. Worse, the scenario was repeating itself in California, where a malevolent coalition of banks and businesses was attempting to overturn California's pregnancy disability leave statute.

The problems posed by the Montana and California cases were debated at meetings and conferences, and it proved impossible to prevent a split in the feminist legal community. Participants conceptualized the problem as a choice between two approaches to the treatment of pregnancy in the workplace: special treatment and equal treatment.[17] Advocates of both positions supported the rights of Tamara Buley and Lillian Garland to have a pregnancy disability leave, and they maintained an employer could and should comply with both the federal Pregnancy Discrimination Act and the state pregnancy statutes. Within this shared framework, feminist litigators followed different reasoning and suggested different remedies. Proponents of special treatment argued that compliance with state statutes would automatically meet the requirements of the

Pregnancy Discrimination Act, because both laws were intended to promote equal employment opportunity. Advocates of equal treatment wanted employers to make unpaid job-protected leave available to all temporarily disabled employees and thereby eliminate the apparent conflict between the state and federal laws. From the special-treatment perspective, then, narrowly drawn laws providing benefits to pregnant workers to accommodate the specific physical burdens of pregnancy were consistent with the equality mandate of the Pregnancy Discrimination Act. From the equal-treatment perspective, however, consistency with the PDA required that the benefits provided by such laws be extended to all temporarily disabled workers.

In sum, three distinct positions were argued in the Montana and California litigation. The employers claimed that the state pregnancy disability statutes were invalid because the federal Pregnancy Discrimination Act preempted them. The states, together with some feminists, maintained that the statutes were consistent with the PDA and should be upheld. Other feminists suggested that the federal and state laws could be harmonized by extending special benefits to all temporarily disabled workers. While the employers wished to avoid having to provide disability benefits to pregnant workers, feminists on both sides of the developing dispute were seeking to make sure they got them.

As the cases proceeded through the courts, divisions among feminist attorneys hardened, and the controversy flowed beyond the boundaries of the feminist legal community. Feminists and progressives mobilized to represent plaintiffs, file amicus briefs, and participate in support coalitions. Most of the major organizations litigating women's rights and developing policy for women—for example, the National Organization for Women (NOW), the American Civil Liberties Union (ACLU), the League of Women Voters, and the National Women's Political Caucus—backed the equal-treatment position. Activists as well as organizations in the women's, labor, health, and gay movements frequently sided with the special-treatment position. In California, strong support developed for the state's defense of its pregnancy disability leave statute. Indeed, members of the ACLU of southern California endorsed an amicus brief in opposition to that written and submitted by the national organization.[18]

Feminist legal scholarship articulated the competing positions in a series of articles published in the early 1980s.[19] These established the terms of an increasingly bitter debate over special versus equal treatment of pregnant workers and, indeed, of women. Subsequent exchanges refined and amplified the arguments, producing several versions of each position, but the parameters of discussion remained the same. Participants in the debate distinguished the immediate needs of childbearing from the demands of child rearing, and they generally agreed that the legal system could address the needs of workers as parents through gender-neutral policies. The dispute centered on childbearing. Although each side recognized that equal employment opportunity requires that woman's childbearing experience be acknowledged in the workplace, they differed on the appropriate means. Each accused the other, moreover, of positing the worker as normatively male.

Advocates of special treatment emphasized the uniqueness of pregnancy and the special burdens it places on women in the workplace. In the presence of real physiological differences, they argued, equal treatment can yield unequal results. Equality denies sexual difference, and the supposedly gender-free norm turns out to be male. A pregnancy disability statute thus provides real equality, for it "places women on an *equal* footing with men and permits males and females to compete *equally* in the labor market."[20] Special-treatment proponents castigated advocates of equal treatment as liberal assimilationists whose middle-class individualism blinded them to the dangers of patriarchal power.

Those who supported equal treatment cautioned that special treatment in the law has traditionally translated into disadvantageous treatment of the targeted group. In their view, the special demands of pregnancy should be addressed by continued use of equality analysis, with sensitivity to adverse impacts of seemingly neutral rules. Pregnancy disability can best be acknowledged by analogy to temporary disability caused by other burdensome physiological conditions. Equal-treatment advocates belittled conceptions of sexual difference that constitute women as uniquely needy and argued that to regard pregnancy-related disability as special simply makes male experience the norm.

Feminist Friends of the Court

Feminist legal activists crystallized their positions in a series of amicus briefs, offering a spectrum of representations of pregnancy and sexual difference in the workplace. The briefs had the potential to influence judicial thinking about the treatment of women generally. Reasoning developed for one situation could even become legal doctrine, laying the ground for a more feminist understanding of women within the law. That same doctrine might also be subject to reinterpretation by an obtuse and misogynist judiciary. Legal opinions could influence legislators and other policymakers. In addition, court decisions have an impact on media and popular views. An amicus brief's impact might therefore extend well beyond the specific litigation for which it was prepared.

By the time the California case reached the United States Supreme Court, feminists on both sides of the debate had presented amicus briefs to courts at several levels in two states. The feminist briefs submitted to the Supreme Court as it considered the California case therefore represented the most distilled versions of the various legal views. Two, submitted by Equal Rights Advocates and the Coalition for Reproductive Equality in the Workplace (CREW), offered the special-treatment argument to justify the California pregnancy disability statute. Two others, authored by the American Civil Liberties Union (ACLU) and the National Organization for Women (NOW), presented the equal-treatment position.[21] Contrary to some popular accounts of the controversy, NOW and the ACLU did not support California Federal Savings in its effort to deny Lillian Garland her pregnancy disability leave.[22] Rather, their briefs stipulated that they were filed "in support of neither party"; signers took a position in opposition to both the bank's attempt to void the

California disability statute and the state's effort to defend it as a law validly applying only to pregnant women.

The ACLU and NOW argued that the proper remedy to the dilemma posed by the contradiction between the state law and the federal Pregnancy Discrimination Act would be to extend the benefits offered by the statute to all temporarily disabled workers. Although they shared a basic analysis of the case, ACLU and NOW emphasized different points in their briefs. The ACLU brief—written by Joan E. Bertin of the ACLU's Women's Rights Project and cosigned by the League of Women Voters of the United States, the League of Women Voters of California, the National Women's Political Caucus, and the Coal Employment Project—devoted nearly half its space to an interpretation of California's pregnancy disability statute as a modern example of protective legislation. According to the brief, early twentieth-century protective legislation harmed women, and decades later, female-specific classifications, including those meant to provide advantages, are still inherently dangerous. Hence, the ACLU argued, even where it may appear rational to draw such distinctions, as with pregnancy, the potential for stereotyping and for the use of difference to disadvantage women remains. The ideology of separate spheres that underpins protectionist maternity statutes such as the California law generates concealed costs which will later have to be paid. Indeed, the ACLU pointed out, the Pregnancy Discrimination Act—with its express requirement that pregnant employees be treated like other employees similar in their ability or inability to work—was enacted precisely to deal with the Supreme Court's supposedly reasonable but actually harmful differentiation of pregnant and nonpregnant persons.

According to the ACLU brief, the California pregnancy disability statute, like all protective legislation, reflects stereotypical assumptions about women workers as unreliable, prone to sickness, and needing extra help. The workplace issue is more likely to be one of discrimination, however, than of pregnant women's disproportionate need for extra benefits. "If pregnant women are disadvantaged because employers do not guarantee disability leave, it is not because they are disproportionately disabled, but more likely because their requests to return are discriminatorily refused."[23] Pregnancy disability statutes purport to solve women's problems through preferential treatment, but they do not address their more pressing needs; even less do they meet the needs of all workers for job- and benefit-protected leaves in case of temporary disability and for care of dependents. The ACLU concluded that the policy approach that would best serve the majority of women workers is the strict equality standard embodied in Title VII and the PDA, complemented by disability, parenting, and caretaking benefits available on a gender-neutral basis.

The NOW amicus brief—written by Susan Deller Ross of the Georgetown University Law Center and cosigned by the NOW Legal Defense and Education Fund, the National Women's Law Center, the Women's Law Project, the Women's Legal Defense Fund, and the National Bar Association, Women Lawyers' Division, Washington Area Chapter—hardly discussed protective legislation and the ideology of separate spheres. Instead, it focused squarely on the conflict at the core of the litigation. Although the state and federal statutes both seek to address the needs of pregnant workers, it argued, their "philosophies and approaches . . . are diametrically opposed."[24] On the one hand, California's pregnancy disability law conceptualizes pregnancy as a condition that is unique—sui generis—and requires special preferential treatment. On the other, the federal Pregnancy Discrimination Act mandates equal treatment of pregnancy, which it views as a condition that can be analogized to other conditions affecting workers. These two models are inherently opposed to one another but they can be made to operate jointly. NOW recommended that the Supreme Court require California employers to obey both by extending leave benefits to all temporarily disabled workers. In this way, temporarily disabled nonpregnant as well as pregnant employees would receive unpaid job-protected leaves.

Like the ACLU, NOW emphasized that the California litigation could be resolved in a manner that preserved both the equality framework and the state pregnancy disability law. At the same time, the NOW brief underscored the ultimate incompatibility of the two approaches to pregnancy policy as well as the dangers inherent in special-treatment jurisprudence. Its examination of the legislative history of each statute emphasized the fragility of recent gains for women. Within the state and federal record of legislative and judicial action, even in recent instances of supposedly preferential treatment, lurks the ancient ideology of separate spheres. Female-specific statutes have the potential to "undo the PDA by resurrecting the *Gilbert* rationale that pregnancy is *sui generis*, thus encouraging the reinstitution of pregnancy-based classifications expressly harmful to pregnant workers."[25]

Two coalitions of organizations and individuals filed amicus briefs that supported on feminist grounds California's defense of its pregnancy disability law. Both argued that the provision of pregnancy disability leave is fully consistent with the Pregnancy Discrimination Act, and both emphasized "the real biological sex differences in the reproductive roles of men and women."[26] Following somewhat divergent lines of inquiry, each considered how workplace policies intersect with the supposedly nonemployment issue of women's and men's differential involvement in childbearing.

The brief submitted by Equal Rights Advocates, a feminist law firm in San Francisco—written by Judith E. Kurtz and cosigned by the Northwest Women's Law Center, the San Francisco Women Lawyers Alliance, and the California Teachers Association—presented an "episodic" analysis of gender difference. Developed by legal scholar Herma Hill Kay, episodic analysis takes biological sex differences to be "legally significant only when they are being utilized for reproductive purposes." In evaluating whether pregnancy discrimination has occurred in the workplace, the groups that should be compared are neither pregnant and nonpregnant persons nor women and men; these categories are too broad. Instead, the focus must more narrowly be on those women and men who have engaged in "reproductive behavior," that is, in sexual intercourse resulting in pregnancy. In more everyday terms, working women who bear children must be compared with working men who become biological fathers.[27]

Episodic analysis suggests that sex differences should be regarded as inconsequential except for the relatively brief time when pregnancy results from sexual intercourse. Having engaged in reproductive behavior, women and men are similarly situated, but "real biological differences" mean that as the pregnancy advances the sexes "are affected differently in their capacity to work." Only the women develop special physical needs, and only the women risk losing their jobs because of pregnancy. California's pregnancy disability statute therefore enhances equal employment opportunity. The statute addresses the special needs generated by the limited and episodic effects of real biological differences but in no way resembles traditional protective legislation. Where protection "fosters inequality in the absence of true difference, [California's law] promotes equality in the presence of a genuine physical distinction."[28]

The Equal Rights Advocates brief claimed that an employer who has an inadequate leave policy violates not only any special state pregnancy disability law that may pertain but also the Pregnancy Discrimination Act. Such a leave policy "has an adverse impact on women who engage in reproductive conduct while men who engage in the same conduct are not so disadvantaged."[29] In this interpretation of disparate impact theory, Title VII itself makes California Federal Savings's stingy leave policy illegal, for the latter is a facially neutral rule with disproportionate impact on women; California's special-treatment law in effect provides a permanent remedy for the discriminatory impact of inadequate disability policies. The brief cited the PDA's legislative history as evidence that the federal statute was never intended to conflict with state laws granting pregnant employees reasonable leaves of absence. States are free, it argued, to enact such laws.

A large coalition calling itself the Coalition for Reproductive Equality (CREW) submitted the second feminist amicus brief in support of the state of California's case. Headed by Betty Friedan, CREW included the International Ladies' Garment Workers Union; 9 to 5, National Association of Working Women; Planned Parenthood Federation of America; a long list of state and local labor unions, women's organizations, Mexican-American groups, and lawyers associations; and prominent activists and legislators such as Dolores Huerta, Maxine Waters, Howard Berman, and Verna Dauterive. In its brief, written by Christine

Anne Littleton of the UCLA School of Law, CREW presented many of the same arguments made by Equal Rights Advocates. The California law is said to be narrowly drawn and entirely distinct from discriminatory and normative protective legislation. It "does not 'protect' women from the workplace, but instead *enables* women to be in the workplace."[30] Like the Pregnancy Discrimination Act, it is intended to enhance equal employment opportunity and correct sex discrimination. CREW's brief interpreted the California pregnancy disability statute not only as a permanent Title VII remedy for the disparate impact of inadequate leave policies, but also as a sort of affirmative action program. It read the legislative history of the PDA as having been thoroughly in support of its interpretation.

The core of CREW's position, and its most distinctive contribution, was its particular emphasis on procreative choice. According to CREW, the equality issue that must be resolved concerns women's lack of procreative freedom. Unlike men, women have to choose between their jobs and their constitutionally guaranteed right to have children. The Supreme Court has recognized procreation as a fundamental right, declaring that "the decision whether or not to beget or bear a child is at the very heart of [a] cluster of constitutionally protected choices."[31] An inadequate leave policy, in the CREW brief's formulation, has a disparate impact on working women and men with respect to procreative choice. Women but not men have to choose between their jobs and their wish to procreate. A law such as the California statute protects women workers' right to carry a pregnancy to term, and complements Title VII by remedying the adverse effect of inadequate leave policies on women workers who decide to bear and parent a child. "Title VII requires employers to remove disparate impact on the terms and conditions of women's employment, while the California statute requires employers to remove disparate impact on working women's right to exercise procreative choice."[32]

The CREW brief justified special benefits for pregnant workers on the basis of rights accorded in a nonemployment area. Alongside equal rights on the job, the equal right to bear children becomes a key issue. By shifting the domain of equality concerns away from the workplace and into the sphere of family formation, the brief challenged the traditional demarcation between work and family life. Motherhood rather than equal employment opportunity became the centerpiece of the analysis, as CREW spoke compellingly for a gender-neutral right to procreative freedom. Workplace policies, it argued, should enable "male employees who become fathers and female employees who become mothers . . . to combine procreation and employment to the same extent."[33] CREW here suggested a fundamental shift in the terms of the feminist debate over special treatment as it had developed. In place of equal employment opportunity, CREW depicted procreative freedom—the right to be a mother—as the heart of the controversy.

CREW's argument, measuring equality in terms of procreative rights, was never extensively developed in the scholarly literature associated with the debate in the feminist legal community. Earlier commentators occasionally referred to procreative freedom, but the CREW brief and several articles by its author, Littleton, remain the only arguments that base special treatment of pregnant workers on it.[34] Notwithstanding, the notion that women, like men, should not have to choose between work and parenthood remains a powerful theme in popular understandings of the issues.

In sum, feminist amicus briefs offered a variety of rationales to the Supreme Court in support of Lillian Garland's right to a pregnancy disability leave. At the practical level, Equal Rights Advocates and CREW defended the validity of statutes mandating special benefits for pregnant workers, while NOW and ACLU argued that benefits must be extended equally to all employees with comparable needs. Distinct feminist representations of pregnancy and sexual difference were implicit in the briefs. Equal Rights Advocates and CREW both portrayed pregnancy as unique. Disability caused by pregnancy, they maintained, requires special attention if equal employment opportunity standards are to be met, and if women are not to be disadvantaged as workers. Equal Rights Advocates focused on the episodic consequences of sexual difference in the workplace. CREW sought more explicitly to transcend the work/family boundary by emphasizing procreative choice. In sharp contrast, and consistent with the established feminist equality framework, NOW and ACLU depicted pregnancy as a unique condition that is nonetheless comparable to other conditions affecting workers—conditions that invariably involve special needs which society ought to accommodate. Disability due to pregnancy should not, they argued, be privileged over temporary inability to work caused by other conditions. All four briefs thus constructed women as both equal to and different from men. But where Equal Rights Advocates and CREW located sexual difference in women's unique childbearing capacity, NOW and ACLU dispersed the gender specificity of pregnancy among the unique but comparable needs of women and men as individuals.

The Justices Speak

The state of California defended its pregnancy disability statute in a brief written by Deputy Attorney General Marian M. Johnston.[35] Implicitly, the brief relied on the episodic analysis of reproductive conduct made by Equal Rights Advocates. The central issue in the case, it observed, is discrimination on the basis of pregnancy, for "if an employer's leave policy is inadequate, female employees who become mothers but not male employees who become fathers, risk losing their jobs because of childbirth." The brief defended the state pregnancy disability statute as designed to enhance equal employment opportunity by eliminating the disparate impact of inadequate leave policies on pregnant employees.[36]

The California brief hinted also at CREW's position on procreative choice. It suggested, for example, that the existence of California's pregnancy disability statute means that "women, like men, are guaranteed the opportunity to decide whether or not to have children without being vulnerable to loss of employment because of the choice to bear children." In oral argument before the Supreme Court, Johnston used this approach more extensively. A man has no problem keeping his job if "he's decided to have a child"; similarly, women shouldn't have to "risk losing their jobs if they decide to have families."[37]

While focusing on the validity of the pregnancy disability statute, California's brief acknowledged that California Federal Savings could comply with both the state and federal statutes by extending benefits to all temporarily disabled workers. The question of extension was also posed during oral argument, when Justice Lewis Powell asked Johnston whether California regards as "perfectly fair" its practice of denying benefits to nonpregnant disabled workers. "No," she replied, "I don't think it's perfectly fair. I think that it's not unlawful. . . . California has no problem if the Court chooses to interpret Title VII to say that other employees shall get that same benefit." For the state of California, where the issue of mandating that employers provide job-protected leave to all temporarily disabled workers had already been considered in the legislature, extension was a tenable option, although one that had not yet been exercised.[38]

On January 13, 1987, the United States Supreme Court delivered its decision in the case of *California Federal Savings and Loan Association v. Guerra*. The majority opinion, written by Justice Thurgood Marshall, endorsed California's arguments and rejected the bank's claim that the Pregnancy Discrimination Act preempts the state pregnancy disability statute. Although the California law mandates special treatment of pregnant workers, Marshall concluded that it is not inconsistent with the intent of Congress in enacting the Pregnancy Discrimination Act. The PDA's legislative history suggests that Congress's main concern was to overrule the Supreme Court decision in *Gilbert* in order to provide equal employment opportunity to pregnant workers. Where California Federal Savings claimed that Congress meant to prohibit special treatment of the pregnant worker, Marshall found the legislative record mute—"devoid of any discussion of preferential treatment of pregnancy." Congress was aware of the existence of statutes similar to California's, he observed, but no opposition to the PDA was voiced by those endorsing preferential treatment of pregnancy. Congress intended the PDA to be "a floor beneath which pregnancy disability benefits may not drop—not a ceiling above which they may not rise."[39]

In upholding California's special pregnancy law, Marshall

emphasized that the California statute is "narrowly drawn to cover only the period of *actual physical disability* on account of pregnancy, childbirth, or related medical conditions." That is, it can be distinguished from traditional protective legislation and "does not reflect archaic or stereotypical notions about pregnancy and the abilities of pregnant workers." Pregnancy legislation must be narrowly drawn to be valid, Marshall noted; for example, "a State could not mandate special treatment of pregnant workers based on stereotypes or generalizations about their needs and abilities." In these comments, the Court seemed to be warning legislators against a return to traditional maternity legislation.[40]

Marshall also considered the question of extending pregnancy disability benefits to all temporarily disabled workers, noting that the state law "does not compel California employers to treat pregnant workers *better* than other disabled employees; it merely establishes benefits that employers must, at a minimum, provide to pregnant workers." Against California Federal Savings's argument that the state and federal statutes are in absolute contradiction, Marshall observed that extension of the benefits could have been imposed. "Extension is a remedial option to be exercised by a court once a statute is found to be invalid."[41] Through these remarks, the Court indicated a certain level of interest and even approval of this route to bringing the two statutes into harmony.

Marshall echoed the episodic analysis implicit in the California brief when he commented that the state law "ensures that [women] will not lose their jobs on account of pregnancy disability." As for procreative freedom, the opinion offered only the barest suggestion: "By 'taking pregnancy into account,' California's pregnancy disability leave statute allows women, as well as men, to have families without losing their jobs."[42] The theme of women's right to "choose to have families" was nonetheless prominently featured in media coverage of the decision.[43] That is, where the Court emphasized the argument from episodic physiological difference, the media constructed the case in terms of women's and men's family commitments.

The majority opinion in *California Federal* recalls *Geduldig* and *Gilbert* insofar as it concluded that different treatment of

pregnant workers is not always and inevitably unequal treatment. Here, however, the reasoning focuses not on the sui
generis character of pregnancy but on equal employment opportunity. And the decision has the practical consequences of providing rather than denying benefits on the basis of pregnancy.

Three Justices—Rehnquist, Powell, and Byron White—dis-
sented from the majority opinion. In an opinion authored by
White, they agreed with California Federal Savings that the
plain language of the Pregnancy Discrimination Act "leaves no
room for preferential treatment of pregnant workers." The legislative history likewise shows, they claimed, that Congress intended to foster identical rather than "preferential" treatment
of pregnancy. The dissenters vigorously rejected, furthermore,
the majority's interest in extension of benefits to all temporarily
disabled workers as "strange" and "untenable." Meanwhile,
Justice Antonin Scalia concurred with the majority on narrow
grounds, but was grimly agnostic on the question of, as he put
it, "whether or not the PDA prohibits discriminatorily favorable
disability treatment for pregnant women." Although the official
tally was six Justices in favor and three against, one senses only
a five to four majority on the question of providing special
benefits to enhance the equal employment opportunity of
women. For Scalia and the three dissenters, man remained at
center stage as the standard against which the treatment of
pregnant women must be measured. From this point of view,
pregnancy disability benefits are construed as treatment that is
unfairly preferential—a form of reverse discrimination.[44]

Once the Supreme Court decided the California case, the
disagreements among feminist attorneys abated to some extent. Practically speaking, however, the decision did not settle
the debate over pregnancy policy. States are free to follow California's lead, that is, to enact narrowly tailored laws providing
special treatment for pregnant workers. But they may also opt
to extend benefits to all workers equally. The Supreme Court
has left the strategic question open.

6

Questioning Equality

Knots and Entanglements

The preceding chapters have traced the evolution of policies concerning motherhood and employment in the United States. Reformers and feminists seeking to improve the situation of women have sometimes supported and other times opposed female-specific measures. Public policy has more consistently endorsed female specificity, at least for white women, only recently shifting to a framework centered on equality. The discourse that has accompanied these policy views has also been dichotomized, moving around the equality/difference divide. For much of the twentieth century, only one polar position could be held at a time. Where the woman movement had earlier managed to construct women as both different from and equal to men, after the 1920s activists on behalf of women generally had to choose. The rift between National Women's Party feminists and the reform movement required that woman be constituted as either globally different or absolutely equal. Not until the 1960s and 1970s did the opposition begin to ease.

When the Supreme Court ruled in 1987 that Lillian Garland was entitled to her pregnancy disability leave, it offered a jurisprudential theory that seemed to bridge the equality/difference opposition. In *California Federal v. Guerra*, the Court established the legal viability of narrowly drawn female-specific pregnancy disability statutes within the framework of antidiscrimination law. The decision means that the U.S. legal system makes two options available to address women's special needs as childbearers. Policies can be designed on a female-specific basis, as in pregnancy disability legislation, or they can be framed in gender-neutral terms, as in the 1972 EEOC Guidelines and the Pregnancy Discrimination Act (PDA). Although the California case is settled, feminist legal activists continue to be divided on the question of advocating sex-specific policies to meet the needs of women. Likewise, legislators are often uncertain, even confused, about the relative merits of female-specific and gender-neutral approaches to the treatment of maternity in the workplace.

Concerns about the advisability of female-specific measures intersect a broader contemporary questioning of equality by scholars and activists. Within the legal community, the sometimes ambiguous results of implementing equality strategies in the areas of race and sex startled many in the 1970s and 1980s; in place of an earlier confidence in the equality framework came criticism of its failure to encompass real difference. Feminist challenges to equality jurisprudence now span many areas, including family law and the criminal justice system as well as employment practices.[1] Difference and the dilemma of equality are likewise central to the work of contemporary feminist philosophers and political theorists.[2] Feminist historians have also extensively discussed the meaning of equality and the construction of sexual difference.[3] Feminist labor and reform activists contrast Lillian Garland's situation to that of women in Europe and suggest that equality thinking fails to address the needs of mothers.[4] Similarly, feminists who identify with the left or socialist-feminist tendency within the modern women's movement often interpret the Lillian Garland case as confirming their suspicions about the limits of liberalism when confronted with class difference. Equality, they claim, is an inherently bourgeois illusion.[5]

Feminist legal discussion of equality concerns remained at the level of the equal-treatment/special-treatment debate for some time. Polarized by the need to take a stand on the pregnancy disability litigation, participants often stereotyped the two positions. Activists and commentators outside the legal profession also conceptualized the pregnancy policy controversy in terms of a fairly simplistic opposition. By the late 1980s, however, the dichotomous formulation began to be questioned. Feminist lawyers Nadine Taub and Wendy Williams asked, for example, "Are we . . . doomed forever to oscillate between dualities—group versus individual equality, assimilation versus accommodation, 'formal' equality versus 'real' equality? Or is there a way to move legal doctrine beyond these dualities to some richer synthesis?"[6] Efforts to transcend the oppositions haunting the equality/ difference debate have generally been articulated in quite abstract terms, however, often leaving the strategic consequences unspecified or vague. At the practical level, the fault lines reappear, for only two options seem available: special or equal treatment. That is, policy is still understood in terms of a bipolar choice between symmetrical and asymmetrical models of how pregnant workers are actually to be treated.

Attempts to go beyond the established terms of the pregnancy policy debates have been hindered by disagreement and confusion. At least four kinds of issues should be distinguished. First, conflicts about the meaning of pregnancy have constituted a powerful riptide in the controversy, undermining efforts to pose questions clearly. Second, critics and supporters of equality thinking have divergent evaluations of current gender-neutral policies. In particular, they disagree about the extent to which the Pregnancy Discrimination Act has helped women workers, and they vary in their enthusiasm for new equality-based initiatives, for example, family and medical leave legislation. Third, little attention has been paid to the problem of the larger strategic setting; the debate about the viability of female-specific statutes needs to be placed in the context of the general problem of developing and evaluating strategy for women. Fourth, the theoretical implications of the various positions in the debates have been insufficiently explored. In the next section I consider the first of these topics. Strategic and theoretical concerns are addressed in the chapters that make up the rest of this book.

At the end of the twentieth century, the equality-versus-difference dichotomy appears to be dissipating, and the desire to embrace its poles simultaneously has returned. In the pages that follow, I look at the processes by which pregnancy policy is being reconstructed in terms of revised understandings of the equality/ difference opposition. What emerges from my examination is a case, for the 1990s, in favor of a version of the equality approach as the best way to move beyond the dilemma.

Is Pregnancy So Different?

Tension between supporters and critics of female-specific policies has been exacerbated by the diversity of meanings assigned to pregnancy. For many feminists, ideological rather than strategic issues are at the core of their passionately held views on pregnancy litigation. At stake is their conception of how gender difference is to be represented. Supporters of equal treatment are committed to incorporating sexual difference in general, and pregnancy in particular, within a unitary framework that represents the diverse needs of all persons in a similar manner. Proponents of female-specific treatment are repelled by this project, for they believe it obliterates the distinctive character of women's lives. In their view, gender differences are best recognized through policies that explicitly reflect the asymmetry of women's and men's experience.

Advocates of female-specific policies particularly reject the portrayal of pregnancy as a disability, which they understand to be integral to the equal-treatment approach. For example, they vilify the Pregnancy Discrimination Act for its supposed identification of pregnancy with disability and the consequent stigmatization of childbearing as a pathological departure from a neutral standard that is implicitly male. Pregnancy is a condition that is both normal and unique, the critics note, and should not be distorted to fit male norms and the medical model. In physician Wendy Chavkin's words, "Pregnancy . . . is not an illness. Rather, it is a unique condition, that may be accompanied by special needs, and sometimes by illness."[7] Moreover, the need for prenatal care cannot be incorporated within the disability analogy, nor can the requirement for time to nurse and care for infants. In sum, special-treatment advocates view the PDA, and the equality framework on which it is based, as irreparably tainted by an assimilationist linkage of pregnancy to disability.

Equal-treatment advocates have made little reply to the critics' charges, concentrating their efforts instead on litigational and legislative strategy. Their general silence lets stand the assumption that advocacy of an equality-based strategy is necessarily associated with the identification of pregnancy with disability, assimilationist views of feminist goals, and disregard for the special nature of woman. But, as I discuss in later chapters, the equality framework entails a relationship between strategy, politics, and theory that is more complicated. Here I examine the essentially ideological undertow of disagreement and confusion that has muddied discussions of pregnancy policy.

Strictly speaking, the critics of equal treatment were inaccurate in their reading of the Pregnancy Discrimination Act. The PDA does not describe pregnancy as a disability, nor does it even use the word. It simply specifies that "women affected by pregnancy, childbirth, or related medical conditions shall be treated the same for all employment-related purposes . . . as other persons not so affected but similar in their ability or inability to work." Yet the perception that the PDA equates pregnancy with disability has been widespread. Many think, indeed, that the statute's name is the Pregnancy Disability Act.[8]

Why has the notion that the PDA defines pregnancy as a disability been so durable? The answer to this question lies in part in the history of feminist strategic thinking, which sought in the 1960s and 1970s to reject the common practice of citing the normalcy of pregnancy as reason to deny women benefits. Feminist policy analysts deliberately linked pregnancy to disability, campaigning, for instance, to have benefit plans treat pregnancy and childbirth as temporary disabilities. When the 1972 EEOC Guidelines declared that pregnancy-related disabilities "are, for all job-related purposes, temporary disabilities," feminist activists felt they had achieved an important victory. Likewise, disability benefits were the main concern of PDA supporters and the central theme in the legislative hearings.[9]

The enactment of the PDA in 1978 seems at first glance to have been yet another step in the effort to establish pregnancy as a temporary disability. The actual language of the statute eschews, however, any direct connection between pregnancy and disability. That is, the framers of the PDA explicitly abandoned the linkage and installed instead a standard of comparability across difference. Where the earlier formulations made an analogy or equation between pregnancy and disability, the PDA shifts to an analogy between human beings—pregnant and nonpregnant workers. Wendy Williams, one of the feminist lawyers involved in drafting the PDA, describes the change as a move from identity of conditions to comparability of persons. "The litigators sought incorporation [of pregnancy] not by insisting that pregnancy was 'the same' as other physical events but that the position of pregnant workers was analogous to the position of other workers." Older notions nonetheless persisted, surfacing, for example, in the amicus brief presented by the American Civil Liberties Union to the Supreme Court in *California Federal*. The brief defended the PDA's standard of comparability—the ability or inability of employees to work—but it sometimes drifted into language that reflects earlier definitions of pregnancy as a disability. "Is pregnancy so different a disability," it asks, for instance, "as to negate the Congressionally-mandated right to legal equality between the sexes in the workplace?" Such a question not only assumes pregnancy to be a disability, it also seems to reflect a purely formalistic view of sexual difference.[10]

Strangely overlooked in the controversy was the fact that the pregnancy statutes favored by special-treatment advocates generally designate benefits as disability-dependent. That is, they provide benefits only insofar as a woman worker is temporarily disabled by pregnancy or childbirth. In effect, the pregnancy disability legislation associates pregnancy with disability far more explicitly than does the PDA. The issue, then, is not really the PDA's supposed emphasis on pregnancy as disability. Rather, what concerns supporters of female-specific policies is the manner in which the PDA addresses the difference that pregnancy makes. From their perspective, a gender-neutral standard of comparability attempts inappropriately to assimilate women's experience to that of men, and thereby devalues pregnancy's special biological and social nature.

Proponents of special-treatment policies seem to prefer an image of pregnancy that responds to their sense of sexual difference as anchored in woman's uniqueness. In various ways, they find that being a woman constitutes a profound and definitional difference. Whether the difference is thought located in physical phenomena associated with childbearing or in social traits such as interconnectedness and caring, it marks all women, providing a strength and source of unity but also creating specific needs. In this view, policies that positively acknowledge the uniqueness of childbearing and motherhood, such as those in many European countries, need not be measured in terms of equality.

Special-treatment representations of pregnancy and sexual differences are in many ways compelling. They emphasize the inadequacy of traditional liberal views that deny sexual difference and seek individualistic assimilation to a single standard, implicitly male. They offer a vision of women and their special needs as not only unique but also profoundly important. They present themselves as the best defense of those women who are most needy, and as the foundation for the far more adequate support for pregnancy and mothering found in other countries. And they resonate with feminist aspirations to go beyond conventional formulations toward more radical solutions. For many, both within and without the legal community, these characteristics have proven irresistible.

Contributing to the spontaneous support many feel for the special-treatment approach are four additional factors, ordinarily left unarticulated in formal discussions of the pregnancy leave controversy. The first is the power of personal experience. Numerous women and men have told me, for instance, how deeply drawn on a personal level they are to the emphasis on pregnancy as special, often punctuating their stories with examples taken from their own family lives or from incidents at work. The second is a confusion about what constitutes special, or female-specific, benefits. Most people interpret any benefits associated with maternity and child rearing as special treatment, even when in fact they derive from gender-neutral plans or policies. Teachers in New York City, for example, often think they have access to maternity leave in the traditional female-specific sense, but their leaves are actually a combination of disability and parental leave, both available on a gender-neutral basis since 1975.

The third unrecognized factor is a feeling on the part of many that any analogy made between the needs of pregnant workers and those of workers who have, for example, an ulcer or a broken leg debases the societal importance of nurturing. From this perspective, public policy needs to acknowledge the uniqueness of the connection between women workers and the children they bear by making special provision for maternity. Some would appeal more broadly to collective ideals, arguing that society has an obligation to specially honor the important work of mothering the next generation.[11]

Lastly, a great deal of bewilderment surrounds discussion of the concept of equality. Contrary to popular understanding, equality does not mean sameness in the sense of identity. Philosophers, political theorists, and legal scholars have long concurred that equality can only be envisioned in the presence of difference. That is, in order to be equal, two things must differ in some respect; if they are the same in every way they are in fact not equal but identical—indeed, the same thing. For example, if we say two servings of beef stew are equal, what we probably mean is that about the same amount of stew is in each bowl, not that the bowls are the same color or that the same chef made the stew they contain. If by chance the two servings are the same in every respect (amount, bowl, chef, etc.), then they are, strictly speaking, identical. Applied to persons in their social environment, equality locutions entail more complicated amalgams of identity and dissimilarity. In general, however, to say two persons are equal is to indicate that, although certainly not the same in all respects, they are or should be the same in one or more relevant respects.

The conceptual network of equality is dauntingly difficult to unravel. Especially perplexing is the slippage between descriptive and prescriptive (or normative) usages of equality terms. Take equal treatment, for instance. On the one hand, equal treatment may be understood as same treatment; a person who is treated equally is treated the same in some respect as others are treated. On the other hand, equal treatment can mean just or fair treatment; a person who is treated equally is treated in the way she or he should be, that is, justly or fairly. What leads to confusion is the fact that same treatment does not always produce a fair outcome. For example, if we give those equal servings of beef stew to a starving person and a satiated person, we are treating them the same but are we treating them fairly?

What if both are starving, and one is a Hindu? In short, the conceptual network of equality is entangled with that of justice. Amid these various interconnections and entanglements, it is nonetheless obvious that the bottom line is to distinguish equality from sameness or identity. As philosopher Hugo Bedau puts it, "equality . . . not only does not imply identity, it implies nonidentity." Equality requires difference.[12]

Taken together, these four factors—compelling emotional associations, assumptions about the female-specific nature of all child-related benefits, desire to honor nurturing and motherhood, and popular linking of equality to sameness—becloud efforts to understand and evaluate the debate over pregnancy policy. In particular, they further muddle what is already a difficult set of issues by supporting common misperceptions of the debate's practical implications. On the one hand, any policy that addresses the special needs of women as mothers is assumed to derive from the special-treatment framework. On the other, the equal-treatment approach is believed to advocate identical treatment of women and men and therefore no benefits for pregnancy and child-rearing—a policy position most feminists would rightly abhor. Viewed through the lens of this interpretation of the controversy, equality indeed seems an ineffectual strategy. But, as I have argued, the lens is faulty and the images it offers distorted.

7

The Equality Framework Extended

The Pregnancy Discrimination Act and Women Workers

The equal-treatment/special-treatment debate centered on the question of which type of legislation would be best for pregnant workers: gender-neutral laws like the Pregnancy Discrimination Act (PDA) or female-specific pregnancy disability statutes like that upheld in *California Federal v. Guerra*. By the time of the debate, the PDA had been in place for several years, and an evaluation of its impact seemed likely to shed light on the controversy. Participants in the debate disagreed about how the act had affected women workers.

Equal-treatment proponents believed the Pregnancy Discrimination Act offered protections of critical importance to working women. In their view, the PDA is a step in the several-decade process of extending the equality framework to encompass pregnant workers' special needs. Pursuing the policy approach initiated by the 1972 EEOC Guidelines, the statute affirms the right of pregnant women to be treated the same as other workers insofar as they are comparably able or not able to work. Employers are thus prohibited from forcing a pregnant worker onto leave or even out of her job altogether, and they cannot treat a worker disabled by pregnancy less favorably than other temporarily disabled employees. In these ways the PDA addresses common discriminatory practices that disadvantaged women well into the 1970s. Its effect, according to its advocates, is to establish a minimum standard for the treatment of pregnant workers.

Feminists favoring female-specific legislation acknowledged the good intentions incorporated in the Pregnancy Discrimination Act but painted a gloomy picture of how it has actually affected women. In this view, the statute's immediate practical impact has been mixed at best, benefiting some women but harming many others in the name of a purely formal equality. The PDA's mandate of comparability is said to require employers and workers to unnaturally constrict the experience of childbearing and mothering to conform to the medical model of disability. Pregnant workers scramble to maximize a chaotic combination of sick leave, disability, vacation, unpaid leave, and unemployment insurance. Employers maneuver to treat this "illness" like any other. They may refuse to grant extended unpaid personal leaves for maternity, require repeated medical certifications of disability, and insist that "sick" employees return to work as soon as possible. Litigation over the PDA in Montana and California has had, furthermore, an inhibiting effect on employers and unions who wish to find ways to accommodate the special needs of pregnant workers.[1]

Focusing mainly on employee benefit plans, special-treatment advocates implied that on balance the PDA has not been good for women. It fails to meet the needs of the women it covers, they claimed, and it bypasses the many poor and working-class women employed by firms so small they are exempt. In the critics' view, equal-treatment legislation mainly benefits upper-middle-class professional women who can conform to male career norms.[2] The facts in *California Federal* seemed to epitomize this critique, for here was an employer trying to use the PDA to deny pregnancy benefits to Lillian Garland, a black single mother caught in the low-wage ghetto of routine clerical work.

Evidence for the feminist critique of the Pregnancy Discrimination Act has been largely anecdotal. An adequate evaluation of the statute's impact requires more extensive data, weighing gains and losses on several dimensions over time and on a national scale. Although comprehensive studies have not yet been done, some data exist. In particular, researchers have looked at the effect of the PDA on medical coverage of pregnancy and on leave policies.

Before the passage of the PDA in 1978, health plans usually treated pregnancy differently from other conditions requiring medical attention. The act mandated that employers revise their plans to cover pregnancy-related care in a way comparable to coverage of other conditions. In most cases, the changes produced substantially improved benefits. For example, a study of twenty-one medium-sized companies in Iowa, Missouri, and Indiana finds that before 1978, medical benefits for pregnancy in the firms were inferior to benefits for other conditions; four offered no coverage whatsoever for either normal or caesarean delivery. After implementation of the PDA, all the firms covered pregnancy and pregnancy-related conditions on the same basis as other conditions.[3] Surveys conducted by the Health Insurance Association of America (HIAA) show expanded coverage of the medical costs of childbearing. Eighty-nine percent of employees with private health insurance under new policies written in 1982 had some kind of maternity benefits compared with only 57 percent in 1977; new policies written in 1984 covered maternity care for 97 percent of workers in groups with more than twenty-five members.[4] Provisions for the medical care of preexisting conditions and for the extension of benefits after termination have also been brought into line with those pertaining to other conditions. Generally speaking, the changes in benefits for preexisting conditions have represented a gain, but the limitations on extended benefits have been a loss.[5]

A 1987 study of the medical costs of maternity care by the Alan Guttmacher Institute (AGI) found compliance with the PDA to be generally good. Coverage of maternity care in medium- and large-sized firms is now "virtually universal." Small firms are exempt from the PDA and more likely to treat maternity differently from other conditions. Data from HIAA show that perhaps 15 percent of employees in small firms that have health insurance policies either have no maternity coverage or have maternity benefits inferior to benefits provided for other medical conditions. A 1986 study by the Small Business Administration found that the health plans of 18 percent of employers with fewer than twenty-five workers did not cover maternity, compared to 4 percent of those with more than a hundred employees. Although the many women who work in small firms continue to have no or inferior medical coverage for maternity, the AGI views the Pregnancy Discrimination Act as having had a "dramatic [effect] in increasing access to full health insurance coverage for maternity care expenses for large numbers of American women."[6]

In the past decade and a half, employers have generally revised their health plans to cover maternity on a basis comparable to other covered conditions. Within a few years of the enactment of the Pregnancy Discrimination Act, many more women have access to health coverage for pregnancy and childbirth. The act's impact on maternity leave policies and benefits is harder to evaluate, but the evidence points in the same direction.

Paid maternity leave in the United States generally takes the form of short-term disability leave, often provided through insurance plans intended to protect employees against temporary loss of income due to illness or accident. Most women workers do not have access to paid maternity leave, and those who do usually have fewer than six weeks. A study of the impact of the PDA by the Institute for Women's Policy Research (IWPR) estimates that only about 41 percent of women workers of childbearing age are covered by short-term disability insurance. Scant though this level of benefits is, it marks a sharp improvement. One study shows, for example, that the percentage of women workers giving birth to their first child who had some form of paid maternity leave rose from 23 percent in 1971–1975 to 34 percent in 1976–1980 to 47 percent in 1981–1985.[7]

Business opposition to enactment of the PDA in part reflected fears that short-term disability costs for maternity leave would be prohibitively expensive and that women malingerers would abuse benefits. Several studies using information from the insurance industry, which provides employers with policies to cover employee benefits, indeed find generally higher short-term disability costs due to payment of benefits required by the PDA.[8] Their conclusions are confirmed in the IWPR study, which estimates added costs to employers of temporary disability insurance mandated by the PDA at 5 percent of their total TDI costs.[9] The five states with compulsory TDI systems also experienced increased costs after passage of the PDA. In Rhode Island, for example, women workers temporarily disabled by pregnancy got a $250 lump sum payment in the 1970s, while the nonpregnant disabled received benefits according to a percentage-of-wage formula for up to twenty-six weeks. That is, the state-mandated temporary disability insurance program provided benefits for pregnancy that were substantially inferior to those available for other conditions. Once the PDA was implemented, maternity benefits as a percentage of total disability benefits doubled, rising from 5.1 percent in 1977 to 10.2 percent in 1982. Similarly, maternity benefits in New Jersey rose from 12.5 percent of total disability benefits in 1977 to 18.1 percent in 1981.[10] In sum, employers have experienced increased costs due to the PDA, but the amounts have been quite small. According to the authors of the IWPR study, "the costs to business of the PDA do not appear to be catastrophic and they are offset by savings . . . in reduced unemployment insurance benefits and premiums, plus uncounted additional savings in hiring, training, and recruitment costs, because women with disability benefits return to work more and sooner."[11]

Increased expenditures for pregnancy disability suggest that the Pregnancy Discrimination Act has improved access to paid maternity leave for many women. No one knows, however, just who these women are. The rise in monetary outlay could mean that the PDA has benefited working-class women, generally more in need of cash and less able to sustain the unpaid leaves that professional women can sometimes afford.[12] At the same time, the PDA has probably done little to alter the lack of paid maternity leave for women at the very bottom of the employment hierarchy.

Whether temporary leave is paid or unpaid, the PDA requires that it be made available to all employees on the same basis. Company leave policies can no longer treat pregnancy in a less favorable manner than other conditions, as was common practice through the 1970s. A firm that gives time off to a worker who has a heart attack must provide the same job-protected leave to a pregnant employee. Such revised policies represent an important improvement in benefits for women workers. Critics of the PDA often focus on instances where same treatment appears to harm women. An employer who formerly permitted lengthy unpaid maternity leaves, for example, may now expect new mothers to return to work after childbirth sooner than before. Such instances are relatively rare and could be amended by the implementation of a parental leave policy.

With the passage of the Pregnancy Discrimination Act, companies increasingly monitor pregnancy disability leaves in the same way they monitor other leaves taken for reasons of temporary disability, for example, by requiring periodic physician certification. Invasive and demeaning though these policies seem, they are not only associated with the PDA; employers use the same methods to oversee pregnancy disability leaves mandated by female-specific legislation. Such business practices should not be blamed on faulty strategizing by PDA proponents. Like the frustrating struggle to round up benefits from various sources in order to maximize time off for motherhood, they are a reflection of the historic meanness of social welfare provision in the United States.

More studies are necessary, but available evidence on the PDA's immediate impact suggests that it has resulted in improved medical and temporary disability benefits for large numbers of working women who become mothers. Although a few pregnant employees may find themselves with less coverage than they would have received before the PDA, and most continue to lack truly adequate maternity benefits, such data must be set in a larger context. As late as 1970, most women workers in the United States had little or no maternity coverage, or had maternity benefits that were inferior to benefits for other conditions. The policies initiated in the early 1970s—then threatened by the Supreme Court in *Geduldig* and *Gilbert* but reconfirmed through the Pregnancy Discrimination Act—have enabled many women to enjoy maternity benefits for the first time and have raised other women's maternity benefits to the level of comparable conditions.

Any overall evaluation of the PDA's impact must also go beyond the focus on maternity benefits to consider the question of women's access to and tenure in employment. The existence of the PDA means that women workers now have more security than before that being pregnant will not cause them to lose their job or force them to take an unwanted, unpaid maternity leave. Without the Pregnancy Discrimination Act, pregnant women's rights to be hired, to enter training programs, and to continue working while pregnant would be vulnerable. In an economy in which women increasingly participate in the labor force, the issues of access to and tenure in work are at least as important to poor and working-class women as they are to women in less onerous circumstances. In terms of practical results, then, the Pregnancy Discrimination Act cannot be evaluated as negatively as the feminist critics who support female-specific measures would claim.

Family and Medical Leave Legislation

In the late 1980s, a new type of legislation was proposed to address women workers' needs as childbearers and child rearers. Designed by feminist advocates of the equality framework, family and medical leave legislation provides maternity benefits within a gender-neutral package. Thus it offers a way to meld respect for difference and commitment to equality without departing from the use of gender-neutral legal rules. Where pregnancy disability legislation singles out pregnant women as deserving special treatment for appropriately delimited periods, family and medical leave legislation posits all persons as at times needing special treatment for special needs. Both approaches address female-specific needs, but they diverge in their understandings of how to incorporate difference within a policy framework that also endorses equality.

Family and medical leave legislation has been forcefully promoted in the U.S. Congress by Representative Patricia Schroeder of Colorado. The proposed legislation would make benefits available for a variety of individual and family situations that require employees temporarily to stop working. At its core is the provision of a minimum level of job security to workers who must attend to compelling medical or family needs. "The legislation is terribly important," testified Schroeder in 1989, "because it says that the United States is now going to make it okay for you to be a good employee and a good family member. For so long, we have said you could not be both. We have to find a way to be both, because in our economy, almost everybody is in that dual role."[13] Family and medical leave legislation constitutes the worker as both an individual with certain needs and rights and a family member enmeshed in a variety of caretaking obligations.

Introduced in Congress since 1985, the various versions of the Family and Medical Leave Act (FMLA) provide two kinds of leave: medical leave to an employee unable to work because of her or his own serious health condition; and family leave to an employee who needs to stop working in order to care for another family member.[14] Both kinds of leave are available on a gender-neutral basis. Medical leave includes but is not limited to pregnancy disability leave; family leave includes but is not limited to parental leave. Maternity leave in the traditional sense is covered as medical leave insofar as pregnancy and childbirth render a woman temporarily unable to work for medical reasons, and as family leave insofar as the newborn needs the special attention of a parent. In this way, the sex-specific biological phenomenon of pregnancy and the woman-associated social role of child rearing are incorporated within the equality framework.

Schroeder's bill has gone through several incarnations, evolving from a narrow to a more inclusive definition of family benefits. The first version, titled the Parental and Disability Leave Act of 1985, proposed that job-guaranteed unpaid leaves, with health insurance preserved, be available to covered employees who are unable to work because of their own serious health condition or because they must care for a newborn, newly adopted, or seriously ill child. In 1986 the bill was introduced in both the House and Senate as the Parental and Medical Leave Act; the House version proposed a commission to study ways of providing income replacement for employees on leave. The 1987 House bill, renamed the Family and Medical Leave Act (FMLA), extended coverage to include care for a parent or handicapped child over age eighteen with a serious health condition; both House and Senate versions now proposed a study to explore the feasibility of providing some income replacement. More recent versions of the FMLA broadened family leave to cover care of spouses with serious health conditions and to preserve seniority as well as health insurance for employees on medical leave.[15] On the horizon although not yet under active consideration is the extension of family leave to cover the care of close family members other than children, spouses, and parents, for example, siblings, grandchildren, or life partners. Despite determined opposition from business and the Reagan and Bush administrations, the FMLA gathered increasing support in Congress. In spring 1990 it was at last approved by both House and Senate majorities, only to be vetoed by President George Bush.

According to its feminist proponents, the FMLA would establish an important new minimum labor standard: an employee who stops working to take care of her or his own medical or family needs has the right to an unpaid job-protected leave with some benefits preserved. The bill is modest in comparison to existing provisions in other countries, yet it represents a major step forward in the American setting—"historic legislation," in the words of former Equal Employment Opportunity Commission chair Eleanor Holmes Norton. Supporters emphasize that the bill confronts the bottom-line need of workers for job security in the presence of severe medical or family problems. They insist that this need is as pressing for employees at the lower end of the occupational ladder as for those in the middle and upper layers. As Karen Nussbaum of Service Employees International Union told lawmakers, the legislation will benefit workers across the economic spectrum, despite its lack of income replacement: "Though it is hard for a low-wage worker to take an unpaid leave, it is harder to lose your job entirely and start looking for a new one after the birth or illness of a child."[16]

The Family and Medical Leave Act reflects years of feminist efforts to extend the equality framework to incorporate the female-specific needs of motherhood. By disassembling maternity leave into component parts, the bill places the needs of working mothers within the larger context of the needs of families, on the one hand, and of workers, male and female, on the other. In this way it challenges the boundary between work and family life, addresses some of the tensions in each, yet eschews the risks of singling out women or mothers as a separate class.

Feminist critics of the equality framework are often wary of family and medical leave legislation. In their view, the bill provides too little and mainly benefits the privileged. Political theorist Zillah Eisenstein, for example, doubts the FMLA will be of use to poor and working-class women, arguing that it actually bolsters class inequality. "In the name of sex neutrality, economic class privilege is simply institutionalized along sexual lines." Legal scholar Martha Minow observes that nonnuclear and gay families are not included, and she believes that these and other "problems of exclusion hobble the bill and expose it to charges of cultural, racial, and class myopia."[17] Other than general support for comprehensive European-style social welfare programs, on the one hand, and specific endorsements of pregnancy disability statutes, on the other, the critics offer no alternative strategies.

Some supporters believe family and medical leave legislation to be the logical sequel to pregnancy disability legislation. Like the Supreme Court in *California Federal*, they see no contradiction between pregnancy disability legislation and the principle of equality. Gender-neutral family and medical leave legislation simply goes further than female-specific pregnancy legislation, these proponents believe, extending its benefits to more workers. Thus six weeks after the decision in *California Federal*, U.S. Representative Howard Berman of California suggested to a congressional committee holding hearings on the Family and Medical Leave Act that the California statute was part of a long-term campaign to achieve equal employment opportunity for women:

> We are going through an evolutionary process in terms of these fundamental issues. Given the small number of states that have adopted [pregnancy disability] legislation and the fact that all workers, not simply women disabled by virtue of pregnancy, but all workers face the prospect of needing to take time off due to disability or serious family responsibilities, I want to join your battle to extend to all workers that concept which is afforded to some workers under California law.

Referring obliquely to the controversy over his state's pregnancy disability statute, of which he had been chief sponsor, Berman commented that it was "never my intention that the California pregnancy leave law be viewed as the enemy of the necessary solution to the problems posed by family responsibilities and medical disability."[18]

Many proponents of the FMLA, especially feminist lawyers and policy analysts who took the equal-treatment position in the debate over special treatment of pregnancy, see the FMLA as the logical sequel not to pregnancy disability legislation but to the Pregnancy Discrimination Act. In this view, pregnancy statutes represent a well-intentioned diversion from the effort to extend equality to women. These legal activists continue to draw a distinction between the gender neutrality of the PDA and FMLA, on the one hand, and what they believe to be the dangerous sex-specificity of pregnancy disability legislation, on the other. In testimony on the FMLA, for example, Eleanor Holmes Norton described how pregnancy disability laws may offer a pretext for discrimination against women and worried that the California statute might become model state legislation; she urged Congress to approve "a more comprehensive and effective model," the Family and Medical Leave Act.[19]

The FMLA discussed in Congress since 1985 constitutes a major example of the equality approach to designing family policy. At the state and municipal levels, lawmakers have introduced legislation ranging from narrowly female-specific pregnancy disability statutes to comprehensive gender-neutral laws modeled on the FMLA. In effect, the Supreme Court in *California Federal* returned the debate over special treatment of pregnancy in the workplace to local legislatures. The flurry of legislative activity following the *California Federal* decision in early 1987 shows, however, that state and municipal lawmakers seeking to address workers' needs for family and medical leave are befuddled. Faced with the option of adopting either a female-specific or a gender-neutral approach to substantively addressing women's needs, even those with the best of intentions often do not know which way to go. And, of course, the multifaceted coverage promised by family and medical leave legislation appears to be more costly than the narrower benefits offered by pregnancy disability statues.[20]

As of early 1990, twenty-six states had laws mandating some sort of job-protected leave for workers who must temporarily stop work for medical reasons or to care for family members; others are currently considering such measures. The state statutes take several forms.[21] About half provide pregnancy disability leave only, emulating the narrowly female-specific California legislation upheld by the Supreme Court in *California Federal*. Only three—Connecticut, Maine, and Wisconsin—echo the approach of the FMLA by mandating both medical and family leave. Some states provide family leave without any accompanying provisions for either pregnancy or general disability. Of these, most limit the coverage to parental leave to care for a newborn or newly adopted child. Some states' provisions seem quite idiosyncratic. Florida and Vermont, for example, offer pregnancy disability leave together with a parental leave available only to women after birth; biological fathers are ignored.[22] The logic here appears to be an attempt to encase traditional maternity leave within new statutory forms. In sum, the response at the state level to the decision in *California Federal* has been a cacophony of legislative initiatives, including many that provide the most limited kind of female-specific support and some that threaten to revive old stereotypes.

The business community has vigorously fought family and medical leave legislation. Republican lawmakers flaunt their party's rejection of feminist aspirations and argue that the family and medical leave bills go too far. Among the alternatives often suggested is the narrower option of covering only pregnancy by means of female-specific disability leave laws similar to that in California. Claiming that workers with special family and medical needs might be subject to employment discrimination, for example, Representative Harris Fawell of Illinois worried during the 1987 FMLA hearings that "this bill [is] much more than the California bill. . . . Perhaps we ought to center on a pregnancy bill at this point and not unthinkingly do more harm than good." And then Senator Dan Quayle of Indiana energetically opposed the FMLA in 1988, offering a substitute that would make it an unfair employment practice under Title VII of the 1964 Civil Rights Act for an employer to refuse to grant reasonable pregnancy disability leave. Quayle justified his proposal as an appropriately limited first step:

> Of all these leaves, the one with legislative precedent is maternity leave. Congress has already proscribed discrimination on the basis of pregnancy. To expand the Pregnancy Discrimination Act is eminently sensible and fair. Disability leave is for the disabled; disability is objective. It is measurable. . . . Disability due to pregnancy and childbirth is a reasonable place to start.[23]

With these somewhat incoherent remarks, Quayle linked pregnancy to physical disability, on the one hand, and to traditional maternity legislation, on the other. And he joined Fawell and other conservative lawmakers in their effort to forestall passage of more comprehensive family and medical leave legislation by appearing to support a female-specific pregnancy disability statute.

This was not the first time conservatives attempted to transform a broadly conceived proposal concerning pregnancy into a more limited disability statute. In the hearings that preceded the enactment of the Pregnancy Discrimination Act of 1978, opponents similarly questioned the inclusive scope of the proposed legislation and suggested instead a narrow focus on pregnancy disability. Representatives of the insurance and manufacturing industries testified that the sole issue in the *Gilbert* case had been disability policy and that Congress should therefore legislate only limited disability leave benefits and perhaps medical coverage for pregnancy. Senator Orrin Hatch of Utah repeatedly attacked the proposed antidiscrimination bill as overly broad and inappropriately formulated in terms of the equality provisions of Title VII. Pregnancy is a unique but normal condition, he argued, entailing "physical, psychological, and emotional factors not present in other disabilities." Motherhood is special, in short, and best addressed through a pregnancy disability leave statute capped at six weeks.[24]

Conservative efforts to thwart Congress's support for the Pregnancy Discrimination Act came to naught, but an analogous strategy is being revived for family and medical leave legislation more than a decade later. In a period of greater economic distress and political reaction, family and medical leave bills have a good chance of being converted into pregnancy disability legislation, if not rejected outright. Such female-specific statutes seem cheaper, and they are ideologically less threatening. Like it or not, feminist proponents of narrowly focused special-treatment laws have allies in the conservative camp. Where feminist advocates might justify pregnancy disability legislation on the basis of notions of women's equal opportunity to develop themselves, conservative support is clearly framed in other terms. Traditional stereotypes of women's primary functions as mothers and family members lurk in the conservative formulations that promote pregnancy disability statutes over family and medical leave legislation. Feminist supporters of pregnancy disability legislation therefore face a difficult strategic context in which to back such statutes. Indeed, as the next chapter suggests, issues of strategy constitute some of the strongest arguments in favor of continued feminist reliance on the equality framework in shaping pregnancy policy.

8

Difference as Strategy

So Great a Change

The debate sparked by the Montana and California pregnancy disability cases took place in a charged strategic context. Lawyers, activists, and policymakers involved in the issues had to take a practical position on the litigation. For feminists, only two possibilities appeared available. One either supported pregnancy disability statutes as an appropriate acknowledgment of female specificity or opposed them on the basis of some version of the equality approach. In the heated atmosphere of the developing litigation, too little attention was paid to evaluating the competing positions as strategies proposed for a given time and place—strategies that were perhaps equally fraught with dangers and contradictions.

Initially, the strategic questions posed by pregnancy disability laws seemed similar to those associated with early twentieth-century protective labor legislation. Participants on both sides of the pregnancy policy debate accordingly framed their arguments in terms of the history of protectionism. From this perspective, the problem became the similarity of modern pregnancy statutes to traditional protectionist laws. If essentially identical to the older statutes, modern pregnancy disability legislation threatened to reinforce occupational sex-segregation and the disadvantageous treatment of women workers. If the narrowly delimited character of the modern laws distinguished them from protectionism, however, they might escape such implications. Advocates in the debate variously contrasted or likened contemporary pregnancy statutes to the turn-of-the-century legislation, but they shared a simplified and an a-contextual evaluation of protection's negative effects on women workers and of the motivations that drove its enactment. A more considered examination of the historical record is therefore necessary. In particular, the comparability of strategic contexts nearly a century apart should be assessed. Two questions are of special concern. How does the situation of women workers today differ from that of eighty to a hundred years ago? What shifts have taken place in the policy framework within which reforms are sought?

At the turn of the twentieth century, many women worked, but wage work was not the norm for women. Women workers were generally young, and most worked only up to the time they married. The notable exception was African-American women. Still concentrated in the South, most black women were employed their entire lives, usually as domestic servants or farm laborers. Nine decades later, participation in the labor force has become the norm for women, regardless of age, marital status, motherhood, or race. Fifty-eight percent of adult women are now in the labor force, three-quarters of whom work full time. Of wives living with their husbands—presumably the least likely to work—58 percent are in the labor force, up from 44 percent in 1975, 31 percent in 1960, and 24 percent in 1950. Working mothers account for the largest recent increases in labor-force participation. In 1952, 35 percent of mothers of school-age children worked; in 1960, the percentage had risen to 43 percent, in 1980 to 64 percent, and in 1988 to 73 percent. Mothers of preschool children are also working, and at alarmingly high rates given the limited availability of child care. Looking just at mothers of preschoolers, married and living with their husbands, 57 percent hold jobs, compared with 12 percent in 1950, 19 percent in 1960, and 37 percent in 1975. Of married, husband-present mothers of children under three, 55 percent work, up from 38 percent only a decade earlier. More than half of married mothers of infants under one are in the labor force, compared to 31 percent in 1977. Black women continue to participate in the labor force at higher rates than white women, but the gap has closed significantly. In sum, since the

1950s, and especially since the economic hard times that began in the early 1970s, women have become increasingly permanent members of the labor force.[1]

The labor market that women encounter is still sex-segregated, with women concentrated in poorly paid, dead-end jobs. Wages for women remain low, on average hovering around two-thirds the pay men receive. Because of the midcentury rise in the standard of living, however, women's wages provide them with more independence than earlier. Hard though it often is, women who need or want their own households are establishing them in increasing numbers. Women are still less likely than men to hold unionized jobs, but female union membership has been rising since the 1950s. In 1990, 13 percent of employed women were union members. African-American women are more likely than white women to belong to unions: 18 percent of black women workers compared to 12 percent of white women workers. Women's increasing union participation is especially significant because it has taken place in opposition to the long-term steady decline in the proportion of the labor force that is organized. By 1990, women made up 37 percent of the total membership of unions, compared to 30 percent in 1980 and 17 percent in 1954.

The overall situation of women workers today is evidently quite distinct from that at the turn of the twentieth century. Although still in a disadvantaged position within a stratified labor market, women have moved toward more equal involvement in terms of labor-force participation, commitment to the workforce, and union membership. And if the relative level of women's wages has hardly improved, their ability to be self-supporting on the pay they receive has.

The policy setting has changed as well. Eighty to a hundred years ago, neither the state nor organized labor was interested in placing a floor under the hours, pay, or working conditions of all workers. In such decisions as *Lochner v. New York*, the state endorsed the individual worker's right to contract freely with his or her employer. The labor movement attempted to assert the right of workers to bargain collectively with their employers, but insisted on doing so free of state involvement. Given these positions, reformers seeking to better the situation of women workers had few strategic options. They campaigned for female-specific labor legislation, and they made the legal argument that women constitute a distinct group not subject to the principle of freedom of contract. Protective labor legislation depended on the legal rationale that woman constitutes "a class by herself."[2]

In the 1930s, the environment for policy and regulation shifted. On labor legislation, the Supreme Court reversed itself, concluding now that "freedom of contract is a qualified and not an absolute right."[3] Where appropriate, the state could therefore regulate hours, working conditions, and wages. The new approach was consolidated when the Court upheld the 1938 Fair Labor Standards Act. Meanwhile, trade unions dropped their opposition to state involvement in collective bargaining. Alternatives to the reformers' strategic focus on female-specific legislation thus became more feasible. In these years the strategy was becoming increasingly problematic, moreover, and complaints grew that protective legislation harmed more than helped women workers. Some old-time reformers acknowledged the new circumstances and changed their position on female-specific legislation. Writing to a critic in 1953, Alice Hamilton explained her new views: "I have seen so great a change in the position of women workers in the last fifteen years or so that it seemed to me there was no longer any need to oppose the formal granting of equality."[4]

In sum, activists today operate within a policy framework that differs sharply from that of the early twentieth century. The state is more involved in the regulation of the working conditions of all workers; for better or worse, it oversees collective bargaining as well. Under state protection, organized labor has increased its representation, although it remains weak relative to the labor movements in other industrial nations. With respect to women's employment, two decades of social and legislative activism have advanced the principle that women and men are in essential respects more alike than different. At the same time, the Supreme Court's pregnancy decisions of the mid-1970s and the litigation and debates over pregnancy disability statutes demonstrate that the principle is not definitively established.

Given that the strategic context at the end of the twentieth century is very different from the one in which protective legislation originally functioned, the question of female specificity in public policy should be evaluated anew. The effort to enact protectionist labor legislation was a problematic strategic choice constrained by difficult circumstances. At the time, the campaign to emphasize difference in order to obtain substantive benefits for women workers made a great deal of sense, for alternatives did not really exist. By contrast, a range of strategic options is now open.

A hundred years ago the issues activists are today discussing could not be clearly seen nor the debate over special treatment of pregnancy adequately undertaken. In the current controversy we have a second chance, as it were, to explore the problem of strategizing about difference in the workplace, mindful of both the earlier history and the contemporary setting.

Strategizing for Justice

According to feminist advocates of female-specific policies, equality strategies have been useful in combating overt sex discrimination but cannot confront the structural realities of a society that systematically disadvantages women. Far better, they argue, to develop carefully designed female-specific measures to meet substantively the needs created by the physiology of procreation: pregnancy, childbirth, postpartum recovery, and lactation. Such special benefits will offer women a real rather than illusory equality. Some would broaden the scope of special treatment beyond the strictly physiological phenomena associated with pregnancy, proposing that policy must compensate for the ways cultural and social as well as biological sex differences contribute to women's subordination.

Whether narrowly or broadly framed, the critique of the equality strategy and the search for a more perfect feminist legal formulation have drawn the attention of feminist legal scholars for the past decade. Relatively little energy has been devoted to exploring questions of implementation and evaluation, however. Advocates simply presume that the female-specific legal strategy they design will have the impact they intend. In particular they trust that their proposed statutes will not become pretexts for disadvantageous treatment in the manner of protective labor legislation. The correctness of the formulation itself will serve, they seem to assume, as the guarantor of the strategy's effectiveness. These practitioners act, in sociologist Carol Smart's words, "as if law were merely an instrument to be utilized by feminist lawyers with the legal skills to draw up the statutes." In this way they sidestep treacherous issues of strategy and disregard the difficulties of "transforming any feminist analysis of women's oppression into a legal practice." The puzzle that sex difference creates for equality thinking ought to be placed more realistically in specific strategic context.[5]

Dilemmas concerning equality strategies might usefully be recast as questions about reforms. Given the constraints of the contemporary American setting, how successful has the women's movement's use of the equality framework been for women? What are the prospects for new kinds of measures— some gender-neutral, others female-specific—being proposed by feminists? Such questions have only begun to be addressed by students of social movements, as sociologist Carol McClurg Mueller points out. Mueller argues that the evaluation of reforms has to proceed along several dimensions, including that of consciousness, and with attention to how a particular outcome can become a resource for further mobilization. In more popular terms, feminist theorist and activist Charlotte Bunch likewise emphasizes the complex relationship between reform and long-term strategies for social transformation.[6]

Bunch distinguishes the promotion of a reform—a change that "*re-forms*, or forms anew, the way things are"—from reformism, the assumption that women can be liberated within the existing system. The issue is not whether to work for reforms, but how a particular reform contributes to long-range goals. The usefulness of a feminist reform strategy can be evaluated, Bunch suggests, by looking at the answers to five questions. First, does the reform "materially improve the lives of women and if so, which women, and how many?" For example, reforms that address the problems of daily life, such as child care or employment discrimination, are important to all women; but if they primarily help white, heterosexual, upper-middle-class professionals, they reinforce the existing structure of privilege. Second, does the reform "build an individual women's self-respect, strength, and confidence?" Such self-respect and independence on the part of women is key, argues Bunch, to building the women's movement. Third, does working for the reform "give women a sense of power, strength, and imagination as a group and help build structures for further change?" Women need to win and to see that one victory prepares the way to struggle for the next. Writing in 1977, Bunch cites the example of abortion law reform—a reform achieved through women's own efforts, not one handed them by the government. Fourth, does the effort to achieve the reform "educate women politically, enhancing their ability to criticize and challenge the system in the future?" Whether successful or not, each reform fight should show women something about the nature of politics and the limits of the system. Fifth, does the reform "weaken patriarchal control of society's institutions and help women gain power over them?" For example, women's health clinics empower women and challenge the hegemony of the medical profession. While a given reform struggle may not meet all five criteria, it should not go against any of them.[7]

Lawyer Elizabeth Schneider uses a similar approach in her discussion of recent critiques, emanating from within the legal profession, of the limited nature of rights and equality. In her view, it is possible both to acknowledge the limitations of strategies based on the assertion of rights and to take advantage of their empowering and consciousness-raising aspects. Struggles that use the language of rights and equality dialectically open the way for new liberatory claims and revised reform strategies. They should be evaluated in terms of multiple criteria. "The assertion or 'experience' of rights can express political vision, affirm a group's humanity, contribute to an individual's development as a whole person, and assist in the collective political development of a social or political movement." In the case of the women's movement,

> the use of rights and legal struggle . . . started the "conversation" about women's role in society. Assertion of equal rights, reproductive rights, rights to be free from sexual harassment and

battering assisted political organizing and education at least early in the women's movement. Rights discourse encouraged the articulation of feminist vision and furthered the process of political assertion. . . . But once a right is articulated, or even won, the issues change.

In particular, contradictions may arise that reveal new questions needing to be addressed or that shift the discussion into a new framework. Instead of dismissing rights claims as irredeemably limited by their liberal origins, feminist litigators can both recognize the limits of equality and use it to move the struggle forward. "The radical impulse behind the notion of women's equality and reproductive control . . . is powerful. By concretizing an abstract idea and situating it within women's experience, these rights claims did not simply 'occupy' an existing right, but rather modified and transformed the nature of the right."[8]

Legal scholar Patricia J. Williams also defends the utility of rights claims. Recent efforts to reject or replace rights strategies have been misguided, she believes, with damaging practical as well as ideological consequences. Focusing on the lives of African-Americans, Williams argues compellingly that the assertion of rights has a significance to subordinate groups that is different from what that assertion means to, for example, white male legal academics.

> For the historically disempowered, the conferring of rights is symbolic of all the denied aspects of humanity: rights imply a respect which places one within the referential range of self and others, which elevates one's status from human body to social being. For blacks, then, the attainment of rights signifies the due, the respectful behavior, the collective responsibility properly owed by a society to one of its own.

Lack of rights has been a crushing constituent of the experience of being African-American. Williams underscores its injuries to psyche and identity and the redemptive possibilities of redress. Rights discourse can be "deliciously empowering," even while it is clear that its pledges are rarely paid. "To say that blacks never fully believed in rights is true; yet it is also true that blacks believed in them so much and so hard that we gave them life where there was none before. . . . This was not the dry process of reification [but] the resurrection of life from 400-year-old ashes."[9]

Female-Specific Policy and Twentieth-Century Politics

The question of the transformative potential of rights claims has been central to the evolution of the contemporary women's movement. Advocates and critics often disagree about the ways in which a particular reform effort—for example, the campaign for equal treatment in the workplace—can contribute to fundamental change, on the one hand, and succumb to co-optive legitimation processes, on the other. Such disagreements pervaded the pregnancy policy debates.

Viewed as alternative reform strategies, gender-neutral and female-specific policy responses to the pregnancy dilemma need to be carefully evaluated from a number of points of view. I have already argued that the gender-neutral Pregnancy Discrimination Act (PDA) provides tangible help to large numbers of working mothers, and perhaps especially to those in the middle and lower layers of the job hierarchy. As Bunch might put it, the PDA materially improves the lives of women. In subsequent chapters I consider the basis in feminist theory for alternative approaches to pregnancy policy. Unlikely though it may sound, I suggest that a version of the gender-neutral approach can be on the cutting edge of feminist thinking. Here I want to consider the problem of the strategic vulnerability of feminist reform efforts.

Activists in social movements may initiate a reform, but in the course of promoting it they generally must cede control, at least in part. At various stages, alliances are made with other forces, and eventually legislators, judges, policymakers, bureaucrats, and the media become involved. Willy-nilly, issues are redefined and practical details altered. Reformers cannot always anticipate the ramifications of the positions they support. In the case of measures designed to provide maternity benefits, a particular concern is the extent to which feminist-backed proposals may be vulnerable to antiwoman revision in the courts and legislatures. For a number of reasons, I find arguments that question the viability of special-treatment strategies persuasive. The issue is less the similarity of modern female-specific statutes to protective legislation or the adequacy of the benefits provided than the uncertain nature of the contemporary strategic context.

As promoted by feminist legal advocates, the so-called special-treatment strategy actually entails a combination of female-specific and gender-neutral policies. In the presence of certain "real" differences, female-specific measures are to be adopted. In all other areas of work and life, gender-neutral rules are to remain in force. Female-specific pregnancy disability legislation is of course insufficient to meet the needs of workers who are mothers, and special-treatment proponents back a comprehensive package of support for the ongoing work of mothering, in addition to supporting pregnancy disability statutes. In the area of parenting they, like their critics, generally prefer the model of gender neutrality currently being developed in Swedish social policy.

Key to the special-treatment legal strategy is its proponents' confidence that female-specific statutes can be narrowly framed to avoid the stereotypes and disadvantageous understandings of sexual difference that accompanied protective legislation. In this view, it is possible to restrict the scope of gender-specific legislation to match only "real" characteristics, however defined. The benefits of equality policies are in this way preserved alongside those of special treatment. Pregnancy disability leave statutes, for example, attempt just this. Feminist advocates of such measures hope to challenge conventional oppositions of private to public spheres, transcend the work/family boundary, and promote a more advanced conceptualization of difference as compatible with equal opportunity. In this sense, the approach rests on assumptions that are truly distinct from the constructions of motherhood, family, and employment that were dominant in the early twentieth century.

The fact that it may be possible to design narrowly framed female-specific statutes that can be meshed with a gender-neutral legal framework does not, however, make it strategically advisable. What appears to be promising in the abstract will not necessarily accomplish its intended purpose in the actual context of contemporary American society. Given the nature and makeup of state and federal legislative bodies, attempts to enact modern female-specific legislation can trigger a process with uncertain results for women. As in the past, efforts to incorporate feminist perspectives into public policy face the hostility of conservatives, on the one hand, and the well-meaning incomprehension of many liberals, on the other.

Ambiguity and confused motivation seem to have characterized, for example, the legislative history of the Montana pregnancy disability statute, the Montana Maternity Leave Act (MMLA). The MMLA was enacted in 1975 as part of an effort to bring Montana law into compliance with the state's 1972 Equal Rights Amendment, which prohibited sex discrimination. Although the Montana ERA was paradigmatically gender-neutral, the legislators chose to utilize a female-specific approach to address the need for maternity leave. A hint of their thinking processes can be glimpsed in a legislative subcommittee's report, which spoke of the legislature's desire to promote "real sexual equality while encouraging stable and workable family and societal relationships." Responding to "the doubts and fears of many citizens," the subcommittee drafted its legislation with the intention of protecting "the rights of individuals who wish to assume traditional roles in the family and society."[10] Rather than a feminist special-treatment approach, these statements appear to reflect both traditional protectionist views and conservative profamily pressures.

The history of the California pregnancy disability statute offers another example of a muddled legislative process. Introduced in 1977, it was designed to override the Supreme Court's decision in *General Electric v. Gilbert*. From the start, the measure took the form of an inconsistent collection of female-specific and gender-neutral provisions. As the bill moved through the legislative process, it came under intense criticism from conservative legislators and cost-conscious business interests. In the ensuing compromises, the bill's gender neutrality was further toned down and the preferential aspects of its female-specific provisions substantially reduced. Of the nine provisions in the enacted legislation, two provide benefits but seven are more ambiguous, permitting female-specific practices that can be harmful. For example, employers are required to provide pregnant workers with the unpaid job-protected pregnancy disability leave that was at the center of *California Federal*, but they are also allowed to exclude pregnancy from medical plans.[11]

The permission the California statute gave to employers to deny medical benefits for pregnancy is, of course, precisely the kind of disadvantageous practice the Pregnancy Discrimination Act was meant to prohibit. Because the PDA covers workplaces with more than fifteen employees, the California legislation's mixed bag of benefits and exclusions is only in effect for California firms with six to fourteen workers.[12] If Lillian Garland had not worked for a big bank, she might have found herself with unpaid disability leave but without medical coverage for her difficult and expensive pregnancy. All women workers need both medical benefits and adequate leave provisions, but it would seem that for working-class women the financial support provided by medical coverage is especially important. In California, then, the rigors of the legislative process resulted in a compromised special-treatment statute that treated pregnancy in contradictory and sometimes unfavorable ways.

Efforts to enact laws that treat motherhood in the workplace in accordance with the feminist special-treatment model confront, as these examples indicate, very stubborn obstacles. While a few supporters might grasp the policy subtleties involved in targeting "real" differences in order to achieve "real" equality, the older legacy of protectionist good will toward motherhood would probably dominate the thinking of most as they defended the bill against conservative budgetary and ideological assaults. Practically speaking, any legislation that must survive such a process cannot be assured of conforming to the most advanced precepts of contemporary feminist thinking about difference.[13]

Once enacted, legislation still has to be implemented, and disputes over its proper interpretation must be adjudicated in the courts. Here again, it is questionable whether today's increasingly conservative civil and court bureaucracies will be able to grasp the subtle views of difference projected in the feminist special-treatment strategies. Like the legislators who enacted the California and Montana pregnancy disability statutes, most civil servants and judges are not particularly sophisticated when it comes to questions of gender difference. With the best of intentions they will likely miss the fragile distinction between modern female-specific treatment and old-fashioned protectionism.

In effect, proponents of special treatment agree with the Supreme Court that pregnancy creates for women an extra burden not suffered by men. Where the Court in *Geduldig* and *Gilbert* absolved employers of the responsibility of helping support the weight of that burden, advocates of female-specific policies demand that society shoulder it by requiring employers to provide favorable treatment. But they have no sure way of preventing a return to more damaging and exclusionary understandings of gender difference, particularly in the context of a conservative legislative and judicial drift.

Hovering in the background of the feminist defense of special treatment is a strategically perilous argument of another sort. This is the formulation that justifies female-specific measures by appealing to the importance of motherhood. For example, the theory that the state has an obligation to protect working women's procreative rights challenges the work/family boundary, but it also shifts the focus onto motherhood.[14] Despite its feminist origins, the argument can be heard in quite conventional ways and could contribute to a redefinition of women as primarily childbearers, or even as vessels for incubating unborn children—all presumably within the context of the heterosexual two-parent family. Feminists quite rightly assert the importance of motherhood, but doing so outside a securely prowoman context can have unanticipated consequences. In the larger society, to privilege maternity in discussing women ordinarily evokes patriarchal, not feminist, ideology.

Those who make a motherhood argument in support of female-specific policies approach, in short, the domain of protectionism in a particularly risky way. In the early twentieth century, celebration of motherhood was part of a package that also included patriarchal assumptions concerning sexuality and the family. Similar assumptions are held by modern conservatives, with their revival of so-called traditional family values. Emphasis on motherhood thus has the ominous potential to intersect both protectionism and contemporary profamily, pronatalist, and heterosexist insistence on woman's vocation as wife and mother. Policy alternatives need to be devised that support motherhood without implicating these conventions.

In the controversy over pregnancy disability legislation, benefits of immediate usefulness to women are at stake, as is the categorization of women as a class within the U.S. legal framework. Questions of immediate impact and short-term strategy thus converge with problems of long-term feminist vision. Feminist critics of the equality framework emphasize the strategic dilemma it encounters when confronted with the phenomenon of childbearing. To resolve the dilemma and deal with women's special needs, many turn logically but all too trustingly to female-specific measures. A more cautious approach is necessary, however. Female-specific legislation is better evaluated as one of several policy options available today, all of which require careful scrutiny. On the issue of maternity and employment, these include gender-neutral proposals such as family and medical leave, universal temporary disability benefits, and parenting leave as well as female-specific initiatives such as pregnancy disability leave and programs to support the special needs of mothers. In considering this spectrum of possibilities, advocates for women must recognize that any feminist strategy—whether difference- or equality-based—is vulnerable to misogynist distortion.

9

Beyond Equality
versus Difference

A Radical Edge

The previous chapters of this book suggest that the strategy of enacting carefully focused female-specific statutes to address the special needs of women workers is problematic. Although both attractive and to some extent feasible, it is liable in the 1990s to founder on the shoals of legislative, judicial, and ideological processes. While some such laws could be rationally differentiated from traditional protective legislation, the strategic context in which to do so is probably not in place. Classifications based on difference have always had, in the U.S. context, a sinister capacity to be used to disadvantage groups so categorized. Nothing has occurred during the Reagan and Bush years that might suggest a reduced vulnerability to such disadvantageous interpretations, nor is there much basis to predict a major shift in the near future. Moreover, workplace equality strategies—flawed and incomplete though they are—have in fact served American women of diverse class and race backgrounds relatively well.[1] Equality is a diffuse and limited notion, but those who on that basis reject all equality strategies spin a risky discourse and practice. From the perspective of subordinate groups, denial of equality is a burden too heavy to bear, while the assertion of rights can be practically useful and politically empowering. On the specific issue of providing benefits to pregnant workers, finally, a gender-neutral approach—as developed, for example, in family and medical leave legislation—begins to incorporate women workers' special needs within the general framework of inclusivity that has characterized progressive approaches to employment legislation for half a century. It thereby participates in a well-established tradition of efforts to use the equality framework to meet workers' needs across different sectors in the workforce.

Given the current strategic context, in short, the equality framework remains a viable basis for developing pregnancy policy. In this chapter I consider the theoretical implications of such a position. Although my discussion focuses on the feminist legal literature, I address questions that resonate well beyond the legal community. These questions center on difference and how it has been constructed in tension with equality.

Feminist legal analysis operates in several arenas. In the mainstream feminist policy community, the equal-treatment perspective still dominates. Activists work to extend the equality framework to encompass all aspects of women's experience, even their special needs as childbearers and child rearers. Among legal academics, by contrast, the special-treatment approach commands the most interest. Critics condemn the equality framework for its indifference to women's special nature and support the adoption of carefully delimited female-specific measures. Little theoretical inquiry has been undertaken by equal-treatment advocates, who tend to justify gender-neutral policies on the basis of practical imperatives. Supporters of special treatment have paid more attention to theoretical questions. They seek a new feminist paradigm on which to base their female-specific policy suggestions.

Equal-treatment and special-treatment feminists often lose sight of what they have in common. As Wendy Williams puts it, they share "a perception of a world constructed on a male model, a perception which is poorly or not at all grasped by nonfeminists. [They] both see the need, as the central focus for feminist legal theory, to restructure, revise, and reinvent the legal world to undo the maleness of that world and to project femaleness into it."[2] Williams's assessment notwithstanding, it is the special-treatment advocates, concentrated in the academy, who have put the most effort into establishing the foundations for a feminist restructuring of legal thinking.

Supporters of special treatment argue that their adversaries make theoretical errors with political consequences. Equal-treatment proponents are said to endorse a formal equality that ignores real inequality, denies difference, and requires women to conform to male norms. They constitute women, like men, as abstract individuals, thus overlooking the ways women are embodied, encumbered by family responsibilities, enmeshed in social relations, embedded in contexts, and the like. Advocates of equal treatment are also said to disregard the possibility that men are encumbered and embedded. The heart of the equal-treatment strategy is revealed, in this account, to be a form of assimilationist individualism.

This analysis caricatures the equality approach and overlooks important distinctions among those who endorse equal-treatment strategies. While some no doubt hold assimilationist views, the major participants in the pregnancy policy debate have generally espoused a far more transformational feminist vision. The equality framework is not, in other words, an inflexible structure. Rooted in nineteenth-century liberalism, equality thinking has changed in the course of the past century, and the current critiques point to further evolution. At any point, the concept of equality is contested, as diverse groups construct and reconstruct its meaning. Like liberalism itself, moreover, gender equality can sometimes present a radical edge.[3] In order to map this promising perimeter in more detail, theoretical issues that pertain to equality need to be examined.

In the pages that follow I explore the theoretical terrain on which the debate over pregnancy policy developed, looking in particular at the presumed poles of the equality-versus-difference debate. I begin with a survey of the various perspectives that advocates of equal treatment and special treatment have used to justify the strategies they support. I then pose some questions in light of recent critiques of dualism and the current interest in diversity and the politics of difference.

The Critique of Equality

After years of debating pregnancy policy in terms of equality versus difference, many feminist scholars now reject the choice.

They argue instead that the dichotomized opposition of equality to difference must be transcended. Just what is meant by this much-repeated exhortation remains obscure, however. The critique is often made at an extremely general level and requires substantive content. Problems are revealed most clearly when feminists attempt to negotiate the gap between their allegiance to transcendence in the abstract and the need to take specific stands on policy issues. Notwithstanding their refusals of the equality/difference dichotomy, participants in the debate often fall easily to one side or the other of the policy opposition.

Dismantling the equality/difference dichotomy turns out to be a difficult task. Efforts to address the theoretical aspects of the project have been hindered by the persistent assumption that only two positions are involved. That is, the construction of the problem of pregnancy policy as an equality/difference dilemma has made it difficult to attend to variations among the views that have been advanced. A careful reading shows, however, that a spectrum of theoretical positions accompanies the equal-treatment and special-treatment approaches to pregnancy strategy. This section examines these positions more closely in order to render visible their range and diversity.[4]

Before beginning the survey it will be helpful to shift away from the equal treatment/special treatment terminology that has dominated the debate. Christine Littleton suggests the opposition could be better conceptualized as one between symmetrical and asymmetrical approaches to gender difference. The suggestion has many strengths. It disrupts the assumption, implicit in the equal/different formulations, that men are the norm in comparison to whom women are either different or the same. It decenters the debate's focus on women; as Littleton points out, "the more fundamental question [is] whether and how the existence of two sexes should shape law and society."[5] And it reduces the opportunities for certain kinds of rhetorical confusion inherent in the positive connotations of the term equality. Use of a symmetry/asymmetry terminology can challenge, in sum, the tendency for the critique of the equality/difference dichotomy to itself reproduce the problems feminists wish to overcome.

Littleton's language of symmetry and asymmetry is especially appropriate for describing the strategies advocated by participants in the pregnancy policy debate. The categorization is less apt as a means to differentiate their theoretical positions, at least partly because it still connotes the dualism of its predecessors. In the following overview of the positions in the pregnancy policy debate, I adopt a modified version of Littleton's use of the terms asymmetry and symmetry. In my usage, schematically represented in figure 9.1, symmetry and asymmetry designate strategic positions only. Asymmetrists are those who support carefully designed female-specific policies; symmetrists are those who oppose such policies, arguing instead for a continuation of the equality-based strategic orientation of the 1970s.

I start with the equal-treatment position—the symmetrists. The symmetrist approach to gender difference has played a central role in second-wave feminism. The theoretical implications of the strategy have received relatively little attention, however. Symmetrists have justified gender-neutral policies mainly on practical rather than theoretical grounds, focusing on institutional constraints and strategic dangers. Within their arguments, at least two relatively distinct theoretical orientations can be discerned: assimilation and androgyny.

Assimilationism is the traditional liberal approach to social recognition of categorical differences, and it is the one the courts most easily understand. In this view, race and gender, like eye color, are characteristics that should not be allowed to matter. Individuals who are similarly situated with respect to a particular purpose should be treated alike, regardless of group differences—real or imagined, biologically or culturally constituted. Applied to women, assimilationism assumes that women really are, or given the opportunity could be, just like men in all important respects. Gender specificities of course exist, but they should not be permitted to make a difference.

Because assimilationism constructs women as fundamentally the same as men, it has difficulty incorporating the physical differences associated with procreation. Traditionally, it set sex-based physiological differences aside, as in the nineteenth-century liberal feminist focus on equal rights and opportunities in the public sphere. More recently, assimilationism addresses physical sex differences by making a close analogy or equation of female-specific traits to general characteristics—converting

THEORETICAL POSITION	STRATEGIC ORIENTATION
Assimilation	Equal-treatment (symmetrist)
Androgyny	
Special rights	Special-treatment (asymmetrist)
Dominance	
Accommodation	
Acceptance	

Fig. 9.1

pregnancy, for example, into a temporary disability. In this way, women's needs are validated as exactly like those of men. Whether physiological sex difference is ignored for the particular purposes at hand or converted to supposedly universal terms, assimilationism takes the experience of men to be the norm. The role of social policy, for assimilationists, is to eliminate the obstacles that block women's ability to participate in society's institutions on the same basis as men. No structural changes to those institutions are necessary.

An assimilationist model was implicit in the efforts of many feminist activists in the 1960s and 1970s. Campaigns to overturn the policy legacy of early twentieth-century protectionism, for example, usually reflected on assimilationist view. Female-specific measures seemed based on unwarranted assumptions of women's absolute and global difference, and feminists fought for women to have the same rights and access as men in all areas of social life. At a time when employers could fire women who became pregnant, reached a certain age, or married, and when women were treated unfavorably with respect to education, training, promotion, and basic citizenship rights, the equation of equality with same treatment appeared to make sense.

Assimilationism is not the only theoretical model associated with the symmetrist approach to gender difference. The view has in fact rarely been voiced by participants in the recent debate over pregnancy policy.[6] Symmetrist commentators on the sameness/difference dilemma most frequently embrace an equality vision they call androgyny. Like assimilationists, these legal androgynists—for example, Wendy Williams and Nadine Taub—use analogy to deal with the stubborn specificity of sex-unique traits, but they shift its object from physiological characteristics to persons. That is, they invoke analogies not in order to convert sex-specific physical conditions to a universal basis, but to draw out the commonalities in the lives of differently sexed persons. In the case of pregnancy, for example, the two approaches produce different analyses and have different practical implications. Where the assimilationist likening of pregnancy to disability seems to obliterate the specificity of women's needs, androgyny constructs women and men as different but with analogously special needs when temporarily disabled. Meeting those needs may require social institutions to change. More generally, androgyny requires "a redefinition of what a typical employee is that encompasses both sexes." The work environment will therefore have to be restructured. It is not enough to drop the obvious barriers to women becoming pilots, firefighters, and professors; airplane cockpits, firefighting equipment, and lecture podiums must be redesigned to accommodate women. In this way, the androgynist use of the equality framework can "overcome the definition of the prototypical worker as male and . . . promote an integrated—and androgynous—prototype."[7]

The 1978 Pregnancy Discrimination Act is conceptualized in legal androgynist terms. Rather than define pregnancy as a disability, the act requires employers to make analogies among their employees. If able to work, pregnant and nonpregnant employees must be treated the same; likewise, workers temporarily disabled by reason of pregnancy or for other reasons can expect same treatment. To promote the substantive change envisioned by the androgyny perspective, Taub and Williams suggest that feminist legal activists make more use of disparate impact theory. In the pregnancy context, this could mean that an employer whose inadequate disability leave policy has a disparate impact on pregnant employees would be required to redesign benefits to provide not just pregnancy leave but more adequate disability leave for all workers. In this way, the employer is forced "to modify the male-defined workplace so as to encompass the experience of both sexes. Disparate effects doctrine thus encourages an androgynous rather than male model in the workplace."[8]

The concept of androgyny, which posits the intermingling of the various characteristics of women and men, was popular among feminists in the 1970s. Unlike assimilationism, androgyny seems to affirm and respect female specificity. For some, androgyny connotes a melding of the best of women's and men's natures. Others conceptualize it as a kind of sex-trait pluralism, offering an assortment of possibilities from among which individuals can choose. Symmetrist advocates of androgyny have focused on practical politics and have not really spelled out what they mean by the term. But where symmetrists have left the issues vague, feminist philosophers and political theorists have not. Their investigations of the notion of androgyny suggest that it offers a powerful but illusory vision. Seeming to aim at a human wholeness that encompasses difference, the androgynous ideal ultimately dismantles gender difference in favor of a universalized personhood. Thus the integrated approach to androgyny abolishes sex distinctions, and the pluralist version dissolves them in an abundance of individual choice. Both types of androgyny ignore the workings of power and hierarchy. A strategy built on a commitment to androgyny has, in short, shaky or at least insufficiently specified foundations.[9]

Assimilation and androgyny, the two theoretical positions most frequently used to justify symmetrist strategies, are generally rejected by feminist legal academics, who support female-specific policies on a limited basis. These asymmetrists, who dominate legal scholarship, tend to dismiss all equal-treatment positions as irredeemably simplistic applications of formal equality. In Lucinda Finley's formulation, equality doctrine "inherently assumes that the goal is assimilation to an existing standard without questioning the desirability of that standard and thus it limits the debate to what policies will best achieve the assimilation."[10] Asymmetrists' theoretical efforts focus on developing analyses of how gender makes a difference and what to do about it. Four versions of a theoretical model justifying female-specific policies can be distinguished: special rights, dominance, accommodation, and acceptance.

The special-rights perspective was articulated in 1980 by philosopher Elizabeth Wolgast. Linking a critique of equality thinking to a rejection of liberal individualism, Wolgast argues against the allure of the notion of androgyny. For her, human beings are in essence a divided species and "justice requires men and women to be treated differently." Real differences between women and men can be documented, she claims, in their behavior, psychology, and moral reasoning as well as physiology. As mothers, women have special needs that require the installation of a system of special rights alongside equal rights. "The two kinds of rights, equal and differential (or special), work very differently. With regard to an equal right, taking a person's individual qualities into account may constitute discrimination. But with special rights, they *must* be taken into account, for these rights are based on human differences." Just as ramps enable persons in wheelchairs to have equal access to buildings and public spaces, the provision of special measures to address women's needs promotes a real sexual equality. Only on this basis can women "make their own distinctive contribution to the culture and society."[11]

Wolgast developed the argument for special rights through analysis of the Supreme Court decisions of the 1970s concerning gender, and her scrutiny of equality thinking was extremely influential in the feminist legal community. Her expansive characterization of special rights comes dangerously close to traditional protectionism, however, as many immediately observed. Because would-be advocates of the special-rights model have "their feet precariously planted on the slippery slope of judicial stereotyping," few participants in the equal-treatment/special-treatment debate actually espouse Wolgast's argument. Rather, like assimilationism, the special-rights position has mainly functioned in the controversy as a point of departure.[12]

The dominance perspective is at the opposite end from the special-rights model on the spectrum of positions held by asymmetrists. Its central premise is an absolute rejection of the notion of difference. In this view, pioneered by Catharine MacKinnon, difference is as chimerical a basis for the analysis of gender asymmetry as equality, for both are defined by male power. "The question of equality . . . is at root a question of hierarchy, which—as power succeeds in constructing social perception and social reality—derivatively becomes a categorical distinction, a difference." Feminists mired in the special-treatment/equal-treatment debate fail to see that the two positions are "two different versions of the male standard. If you see gender as a hierarchy . . . you realize that the options of either being the same as men or being different from men are just two ways of having men as your standard." By contrast, the dominance perspective situates the issue of concern as not women's difference but their domination by men. Likewise, the goal is not to achieve equality but to address hierarchy directly in order to end women's subordination. The dominance perspective suggests that policies and practices be evaluated according to whether they reinforce or reduce the domination of women by men.[13]

Dominance analysis has launched a radical challenge to the conventions of legal thinking and has been pivotal in the development of feminist legal theory. Proponents of the perspective have not, however, been able to force the legal system to respond to their challenge. While feminist dominance theorists refine and perfect their analyses, the law continues to look at women in terms of sameness and difference. In Deborah Rhode's evaluation, "the sources of this theory's strengths are also the sources of its limitations. . . . As a foundation for an alternative legal framework, dominance paradigms are too often theoretically reductive and strategically counterproductive." Essentialist and deterministic as theory, dominance has also proven unreliable as a guide to the formulation of policy.[14]

The asymmetrist approaches most commonly endorsed in feminist legal scholarship are accommodation and acceptance. Like the dominance perspective, these orientations shift the emphasis "from gender difference to gender disadvantage," that is, to the adverse consequences of gender difference in women's lives.[15] Unlike dominance, these perspectives permit feminist policy proposals to be formulated within more conventional legal terms. Both the accommodation and the acceptance approaches justify sex-specific measures in appropriately bounded circumstances on the basis of certain differences in the experience of women and men. They diverge, however, in their delineation of the boundaries of relevant gender difference.

The accommodation perspective posits a dualism in the treatment of women that is strictly limited. It endorses gender neutrality as the standard in most situations, but proposes that narrowly defined female-specific measures be used to accommodate physiological sex differences. Such an approach was first described by Ann Scales in her 1980–1981 discussion of "incorporationism." Rejecting Wolgast's notion of special rights as too broad, Scales suggests that "women should be recognized to have rights different from men only insofar as pregnancy and breastfeeding, the only aspects of childbearing and childrearing completely unique to women, are directly concerned." Sylvia Law likewise proposes that measures pertaining to pregnancy and breastfeeding be evaluated using MacKinnon's dominance standard; all other differences are to be addressed by gender-neutral means. Herma Hill Kay suggests that conventional equality analysis cannot be applied in the presence of real physiological differences. Her "episodic" approach would acknowledge biological difference by validating some sex-specific treatment of pregnant, nursing, or menstruating women, as well as of men who rape.[16]

The accommodationist model—the notion that special treatment is valid when used to accommodate "real," that is, physiologically based, difference—has occasionally been acknowledged in public policy. The federal government's WIC program, which provides nutritional supplements to pregnant and nursing mothers, infants, and young children, is one established example; special treatment to address the needs of the physically disabled is another. In *California Federal,* the United States Supreme Court used accommodationist reasoning to affirm pregnancy disability legislation that is "narrowly drawn to cover only the period of *actual physical disability* on account of pregnancy, childbirth, or related medical conditions."[17]

The acceptance perspective has been advanced by Christine Littleton. Where accommodation validates female-specific measures on an extremely limited basis, acceptance throws the difference net more broadly, encompassing both biological and cultural sex differences. The goal is to achieve "equal acceptance" for male and female activities and attributes as they are currently constructed. The acceptance model targets the unjust consequences of difference regardless of its source. "Whether the gender 'difference' is seen as biological or social, it must be rendered costless in order to achieve true equality." Like the special-rights perspective, acceptance proposes that women and men be treated differently where the asymmetry of their lives requires it. Unlike special rights, acceptance recognizes the need for a systematic procedure to determine the appropriateness and limits of sex-specific measures. Littleton's method is to identify complementary ways women and men "stand in asymmetrical positions to a particular social institution." Where society encodes difference in such "gender complements," an equalizing analysis is to be applied. In the employment context, for example, socially "male" and "female" skills should be equally valued and compensated. With respect to pregnancy, women who become mothers and men who become fathers constitute gender complements and ought to be able to choose to combine parenthood and employment to the same extent. More generally, Littleton suggests that society constructs warriors and mothers as gender complements: "Both occupations involve a lot of unpleasant work, along with a real sense of commitment to a cause beyond oneself that is culturally gussied up and glamorized culturally to cover up the unpleasantness involved. Both involve danger and possible death." Perhaps, she speculates, society ought to compensate mothers as soldiers, or make motherhood an unofficial qualification for running for political office.[18]

The theory of equality as acceptance is attractive, for it promises to go beyond the limits of the accommodation model without re-creating the difficulties of Wolgast's special-rights approach. CREW, the coalition that submitted an amicus brief in *California Federal*, used an acceptance argument to defend Lillian Garland's right to her job. A number of feminist legal scholars produce work that can be placed within the acceptance framework, even if they do not adopt Littleton's methodology for evaluating sex-specific measures. Finley, for example, suggests "responsibility analysis" should supplement equality analysis "where women appear to be truly different from men—in their capacity to become pregnant and their traditional relegation to the sphere of childrearing." She is thus able to recommend an array of female-specific policies to address the cultural as well as physiological specificity of women.[19]

Asymmetrist positions are vulnerable to criticism based on strategic considerations. As equal-treatment proponents often point out, female-specific measures can easily be converted into pretexts for the disadvantageous treatment of women. Affirmations of cultural and biological sex difference have risky ideological and theoretical implications as well. Littleton herself comments that "matching gendered complements in order to equalize across cultural differences may sound like marching directly into the valley of the stereotypes."[20]

The pregnancy policy controversy has appeared to construct equality and difference as polar opposites, offering only two options. Either one supports equality theory and a same-treatment strategy, or one explores various ways to affirm woman's difference in order to endorse female-specific treatment on some limited basis. The foregoing survey shows that most positions in the debate actually attempt to theorize an equality that acknowledges difference. Even assimilationism, the staunchest in its commitment to a notion of women as essentially the same as men, does not deny difference. Rather, it views gender distinctions as characteristics that are present but for virtually all purposes should not matter. Three of the asymmetrist perspectives—special rights, accommodation, and acceptance—as well as androgyny in the symmetrist category incorporate female specificity more wholeheartedly. That is, they construct concepts of gender equality that depend, at bottom, on an affirmation of female difference. In this way they seek to shape policies that can better serve women by retaining elements of gender specificity alongside or within the equality framework established in the 1960s and 1970s.

Toward a Politics of Diversity

Feminist legal scholars have made important contributions. In particular, through their consideration of the limits of equality thinking, they have developed a range of theoretical perspectives. Too frequently, however, the new perspectives reproduce in new forms the theoretical dilemmas from which their creators had hoped to escape. Several difficulties, all pertaining to the representation of difference, stand out in particular: use of dualist and essentialist notions of difference; insufficient recognition of the pervasiveness of difference; and concepts of difference and diversity that focus on individuals and occlude social structure.

The concept of difference has been at the center of recent feminist theorizing.[21] Within the legal community, asymmetrists reject equality in favor of an exploration of difference. "Equality analysis cannot give us the tools" to confront gender subordination, they insist. To move forward, the equality/difference opposition must be discarded, for "implicit in the whole process of feminist scholarship . . . is a rejection of dualism, a rejection of polarized thinking at all points along the consciousness-theory-strategy continuum." Some would renounce the notion of equality altogether, for "the word has come to equate difference with stigma, and to exalt similarity as the ideal."[22]

Asymmetrist critics of equality often claim a series of postmodern theoretical accomplishments. They forswear such staples of conventional scholarship as dualism, essentialism, objectivity, neutrality, and universality. In place of fixed oppositions and totalizing scholarly practices, the critics embrace ambiguity, subjectivity, particularity, the validity of multiple voices, and the partiality of situated knowledge. These new allegiances notwithstanding, the various theoretical models proposed by legal asymmetrists too frequently reintroduce the rejected characteristics.

Their reappearance is particularly striking in accommodation-ism, the most widely accepted special-treatment theory.

Accommodationism, as described in the previous section, justifies narrowly focused female-specific policies on the basis that special treatment is valid in the presence of physiological sex differences. Those who support the model—for example, Herma Hill Kay, Sylvia Law, and the Supreme Court in *California Federal*—argue in diverse ways for a two-track system. Gender neutrality is to be the general rule, but sex-specific measures can be used to accommodate real physiological characteristics. The two tracks implicate two standards. On the one hand, conventional equality norms are to govern in most situations; on the other, special sex-specific norms can be invoked on a limited basis. As a theoretical model, accommodationism posits an opposition between normal persons, to whom equality rules apply, and (temporarily) abnormal persons, for whom special measures are necessary.

Paradoxically, accommodationism's two-track approach resurrects formulations proposed by feminists two decades earlier. The 1971 *Yale Law Journal* article on the Equal Rights Amendment, for example, allowed that gender-specific legislation concerning sex-unique physical traits is permissible so long as it is "closely, directly and narrowly confined to the unique physical characteristic." Of course, as Sylvia Law observes, the authors of the article underestimated the centrality of the issue of female-specific treatment and proposed no independent principle to justify special measures. But their argument that female-specific policies can be consistent with the equality framework actually reflects a dualism that is well-established in U.S. law. Traditional jurisprudence quite comfortably endorses broadly neutral rules applying to all alongside a carefully delimited set of exceptions.[23] The invocation of basically the same theoretical model by advocates of both difference- and equality-based policies suggests, moreover, that the pregnancy policy debate has indeed laid a false trail.

Many feminist legal scholars deploy a dualistic notion of difference in another way when they focus their concerns solely on gender. Whether theorized in terms of assimilation, androgyny, special rights, dominance, accommodation, or acceptance, difference is repeatedly constructed as exclusively grounded in gender. For example, actors are depicted as male or female but somehow lacking other defining characteristics. Where race and class are mentioned, little effort is made to incorporate them theoretically. Such accounts articulate an unmodulated opposition of female to male and disregard other kinds of categorical difference. Strenuously condemning the dichotomous formulations haunting the pregnancy policy debate, participants do not see the ways in which their own work reproduces a dualistic focus on gender.

Feminist legal scholarship only rarely acknowledges what has elsewhere become a commonplace observation: the pervasiveness of difference throughout social life. In their inattention to the full range of human heterogeneity, feminist legal scholars are oddly out of step with a great deal of recent work. Over the past decade, scholars in a number of fields have become increasingly sensitive to the diversity of social experience. In the best of their accounts, such characteristics as race, ethnicity, class, gender, age, ability, and affectional preference are recognized as always present and active. For example, if other distinctive characteristics go unmentioned in a study of gender difference, it is understood that they only appear to be effaced. The omission actually signals an underlying assumption that the women and men of concern are white, middle-class, English-speaking, able-bodied, heterosexual, and so forth. Silence on these aspects of identity does not obliterate them as dimensions of difference. To the contrary: silence eloquently privileges what is already hegemonic and thereby reinforces hierarchy.[24]

Recent research not only recognizes diversity, it also attempts to address it theoretically. Feminist theorists in particular have sought an integrated theoretical framework that could respond to the specificity of all differences. Some suggest that such a diversity-inclusive framework may require a radical decentering of sexual difference. Here again, feminist legal scholarship has fallen short, focusing mainly on gender and drawing on a remarkably limited range of theory. Carol Gilligan's *In a Different Voice* has been the main theoretical influence. Circumscribing their discussion of theoretical issues within Gilligan's consideration of two voices, feminist legal scholars produce an account in which the ethic of care wins easily over the logic of justice—and dualism is once again in place.[25] The only other theoretical option feminist legal scholars acknowledge is Catharine MacKinnon's radical rejection of difference; while this position also has a following, it is harder to translate into legal practice.

The task of theorizing gender with attention to diversity is, of course, extremely difficult. Significant progress has been made, most especially by feminists of color, and particularly in the last decade. Living at the structural intersection of the most salient categorical oppressions—those based on race and gender as well as, often, class—women of color are well placed to produce a knowledge that encompasses diversity. Since the late 1960s they have sought to theorize the position of women of color in a way that is inclusive of a broad range of differences.

One of the earliest contributions to the development of what may be called black feminist thought was made by Frances Beale, at the time a coordinator of SNCC's Black Women's Liberation Committee. In "Double Jeopardy: To Be Black and Female," first published in 1969, Beale argued that black women are oppressed as both women and blacks in a context dominated by capitalist exploitation.[26] The article, much discussed and widely reprinted, constituted a starting point from which feminist thinkers have gradually developed more complex understandings of the ways categorical oppressions intersect. In particular, Beale's formulation in terms of double jeopardy was quickly reworked into a notion of triple oppression based on race, class, and sex. Whether envisioned as a double or triple jeopardy, the underlying model being proposed was insufficiently specified. It conceptualized the oppressions as comparable or parallel phenomena of more or less equal weight, but it did not address the dynamics of how they related to one another. Simultaneously distinct and inextricably intertwined, sex, race, and class factors were assumed simply to accumulate in an additive manner.

By the late 1970s, some feminists were expressing discomfort with the inadequacies of a theoretical model that paralleled race, class, and sex. What, they wondered, did it mean to analyze oppressions as "inextricably intertwined?" How were the interrelationships to be theorized? In contrast to the dominant trends in the mostly white radical women's movement of the period, which were emphasizing sisterhood and the common experience of women, feminists of color continued to insist on the special character of women's lives as members of particular groups. At the same time, they launched a search for a more adequate theorization.[27]

The 1980s saw a variety of efforts to modify the additive model while preserving its respect for the diverse experience of women. Sociologist Deborah King, for example, proposed a more interactive theorization in terms of multiple, rather than double, jeopardy. In her view, "the relative significance of race, sex, or class in determining the conditions of black women's lives is neither fixed nor absolute but, rather, is dependent on the socio-historical context and the social phenomenon under consideration." Psychologist Aida Hurtado argued that the issue was less the interrelationship of sex, race, and class than the relative positioning of particular oppressed groups with respect to white men. Thus, "the definition of *woman* is constructed differently for white women and for women of Color, though gender is the marking mechanism through which the subordination of each is maintained." Anthropologist Karen Brodkin Sacks suggested a reconceptualization of class that would encompass race and gender diversity within notions of membership in a community. "Not only is class experienced in historically specific ways, but it is also experienced in racially specific, gender-specific, and kinship-specific ways." Sociologist Patricia Hill Collins explored how an Afrocentric feminist epistemology might reveal a many-leveled matrix of domination. In her account, "Black feminist thought fosters a fundamental paradigmatic shift that rejects additive approaches to oppression." These and other contributions indicate that recent efforts to theorize race, class, and gender in a nonadditive manner are significant and promising.[28]

The work just outlined took the relationship of race and gender as its central concern. An analogous yet largely independent project attempted to theorize women's oppression in terms of an integrated system of class and sex stratification. Originating in the late 1960s in the socialist-feminist wing of the women's liberation movement, this work sought to radically transform socialist theory to encompass women's oppression. Socialist-feminist theorists began by proposing various sorts of dual-systems theories, arguing, for example, that women's oppression can be explained in terms of parallel mechanisms of capitalism and patriarchy. By the late 1970s, the mechanistic and additive character of dual-systems theory was being subjected to severe criticism. As with the feminist theorists interested in race, a search began for a more unified theorization of the relationship among group oppressions.[29]

Early efforts to theorize categorical difference were rooted, as this brief survey shows, in the oppositional social movements of the 1960s and 1970s. In the past decade, interest in difference and diversity has expanded well beyond communities of radical activists and scholars. This important and very welcome development, coming in the mid-1980s for a variety of reasons, entails a struggle over terms and meaning that is political as well as theoretical. Multiple discourses can center on difference and diversity, not all of them compatible with what feminists and people of color might intend. Disparate notions of diversity, for example, are implicated in the many-layered controversies surrounding multiculturalism. In some quarters, the term diversity functions as code for the resuscitation of an official pluralism that ultimately denies the specificities and hierarchies associated with group differences. That is, the way diversity is often promulgated and understood can serve to disguise the specific character of collective subordination. Where formerly we were all expected to dissolve our specificity in the melting pot, now we are said to retain some hard core of cultural identity as a tessera in the gorgeous mosaic. Either way—whether considered one ingredient among others in the social soup, or one flinty chip among others in the social mosaic—the distinctiveness of historically constituted subordinate positions within various social hierarchies appears lost.

The meaning of diversity is, in other words, contested. The point has been made with respect to difference, and I am here emphasizing that the notion of diversity also requires scrutiny. Some facets are already under examination. For example, hard though it has turned out to be to transcend dualistic accounts of diversity by means of a nonadditive analysis, the importance of doing so is now widely acknowledged. Two other issues are less frequently identified as problems: the representation of difference in relation to social hierarchy and the conceptualization of diversity.

As suggested above, discussion of difference and diversity is often accompanied by a lack of attention to structural relations of power. This occurs when, for instance, diversity is celebrated as a rich reflection of human individuality and social variation, but little mention is made of any associated penalties or oppression. By simultaneously acknowledging cultural heterogeneity and remaining silent about the ways different social groups are positioned within a hierarchical order, such celebrations mask domination. A few commentators have pointed to this problem. Historian Linda Gordon, for example, argues that "the concept of 'difference' . . . implies a pluralist multiplicity of stories that benignly coexist or interact; it may obscure relations of inequality, domination, and even exploitation among women." Likewise, literary critic Hazel Carby suggests that the language of difference and diversity is currently being used to marginalize analysis of structures of dominance.[30]

More rarely recognized as a problematic issue is the question of the meaning of diversity as a concept. Commentators ordinarily do not make a distinction between difference as a characteristic of individuals and as a group phenomenon, often using difference or diversity to refer to both.[31] In most accounts, difference at the level of groups—which could be distinguished by such terms as categorical diversity or group diversity—is represented as a simple extension of the specificity attached to individuals: sex, race, age, affectional preference, and so forth. Diversity is thus understood to refer simultaneously to the existence of differences between individuals and among collections of individuals sharing particular characteristics—for example, women, men, African-Americans, whites, children, adults, lesbians and gays, heterosexuals, and so forth. Group diversity is conceptualized, in other words, as a series of aggregated individual specificities, and individuals appear to be constituted, improbably, as members of many such groups. What is missing from this picture is an adequate account of social structure, on the one hand, and of identity, on the other.

In sum, categorical diversity is often thought of as individual difference crystallized, writ large, and innocent of power. This elision of levels and specificities has the political correlates flagged by Carby and Gordon. That is, once diversity is stripped of its special character as a power-laden and irreducibly heterogeneous group phenomenon, it becomes possible to put difference in the service of an unoffending pluralism.

Legal scholar Martha Minow's recent effort to theorize difference provides a good example of the consequences of disregarding diversity's variegated and structural character.[32] Minow wishes to produce a complex nonmechanical portrayal that respects the broad range of diversity, but her account is undermined by its inadequate construction of the concept. Despite her intentions, she tends to reduce human heterogeneity to a single, supposedly characteristic opposition—embodied in her repeated positing of children and the physically and mentally disabled as oppression's paradigmatic victims. For Minow, the injuries of difference are located in processes of interpersonal labeling and stigmatization. Difference becomes an issue of relations between competent adults and incompetent, voiceless, dependent individuals who do not belong to historically constituted communities. Diversity is represented not only as invariant in form but also as an individualistic phenomenon that is largely independent of culture and history—indeed, a product of the irrational human tendency to stigmatize individual others as different.

Minow's policy suggestions envision transforming the perspective of the individuals involved in stigmatizing processes. Once they understand difference as a function of the stigmatizing relationship between normals and abnormals, connection can be established and disadvantageous treatment halted. For example, hearing children can learn sign language, thereby transforming the classroom into a little commonwealth of sensitive communicators. Not surprisingly, examples of race or sex stigmatization are virtually absent from Minow's text, for these phenomena pose disruptive questions concerning social power and categorical subordination. With the discussion centered on differences of age and ability, structural hierarchy and group specificity vanish in a cornucopia of liberal good will.

It isn't easy to see how a more adequate theorization of diversity can be developed. Certain steps could be taken to clarify the issues. In the first place, diversity should be conceptually distinguished from difference as a term associated with groups; assumptions that map individual specificities into group diversity can thus be problematized. Second, diversity must be located within a structural understanding of power, domination, and hierarchy—at least insofar as diversity is characteristic of today's complex societies. Third, diversity should be recognized as relentlessly heterogeneous; for example, sex, race, and class cannot simply be paralleled to one another as if they were fully comparable phenomena. Fourth, the construction of identity needs to be understood as an ongoing, inherently contested process of negotiation across many divides. In short, the conceptualization of diversity must acknowledge the existence in modern societies of hierarchically interrelated groups with specific and irreducibly various characteristics. As a provisional definition, diversity might usefully be taken to refer to the phenomenon that all individuals are multiply positioned as members of groups within a diversely hierarchical social structure.

Feminist legal scholarship has only begun to confront the theoretical complexity of the concepts implicated in the construction of the opposition of difference to equality. This chapter has examined the complexity in the briefest of terms, looking in particular at its bearing on what might be called a politics of diversity. My purpose here has been to indicate how difficult and tangled these questions are, and how critical to a more satisfactory feminist response to the equality-versus-difference dilemma.

───10───

Different but Not Unequal

Motherhood and Policy

When I began research for this book, I had both policy concerns and theoretical questions. My policy concerns centered on women and their families. How, I wondered, ought U.S. social policy address the needs of mothers? Should the special burdens created by maternity, child rearing, and family life be addressed with female-specific measures, on the model of the European social welfare tradition? Is the choice between treating women the same as or different from men the only option available to policymakers? My theoretical questions focused on the concepts of equality and difference in feminist thought. Does equality require the denial of difference, as some feminists seemed to argue? Is equality merely a liberal notion that at the end of the twentieth century has reached the limit of its usefulness? Must the category "woman" be constituted on the basis of an opposition between difference and equality?

As a path into this cluster of questions, I chose to look at one of the key components of family policy, the treatment of pregnancy in the workplace. The results of my investigations have been presented in the previous chapters of *Mothers on the Job*, structured in the form of a double account. On the one hand, I have tracked the strategic issues and debates surrounding pregnancy policy as they have unfolded. On the other, I have examined how the problem of pregnancy policy has been constructed in terms of notions of difference and equality. In this chapter I bring the book to a conclusion by returning to the questions that motivated it.

One impediment to thinking about these questions is the perplexing contrast between U.S. and European-style family policies. Feminists are often frustrated by the absence in the United States of a social welfare system committed to comprehensive support for the needs of women and families. Examination of U.S. maternity policies demonstrates that this peculiarity is well rooted in American traditions. Steeped in ideologies of individualism and liberty conceived of as freedom from state interference, on the one hand, and in assumptions of racism and the inherent unfreedom of certain groups, on the other, U.S. social welfare policy has developed in a manner quite different from the experience in Europe. Policy deliberations have rejected universalistic conceptualizations that posit a linkage between citizens' needs, state responsibility, and the collective social good. Instead, the reproduction of gender and race hierarchies has been central to policy evolution in the United States. Thus women have been constructed as not only different from or equal to men but also differentiated by race and ethnicity; gendered identity is always also racial, particularly in the American setting. Contemporary efforts to design programs in support of mothers' needs must acknowledge this history. However much advocates for women may envy the comprehensive social entitlement programs common elsewhere, U.S. social policy is not likely to emulate them.

We can learn a good deal about the potential in the United States for policy advocacy on behalf of women by looking at the past. Within a deeply racialized context, the equality/difference dichotomy has provided the framework. Activists and reformers seeking to better the condition of women have contended with the framework in complex ways. They have chosen sides, often with passion and commitment, and they have tried as well to bridge the opposition by understanding woman to be both different and equal. That is, even as advocates for women have participated in the reproduction of the dichotomy, they have sought to resist or transcend it. The nineteenth-century woman movement was, for example, notable for its ability to construct woman in terms of a female specificity that to some extent also entailed equality. Usually unacknowledged but present in this construction was a presumption that she was white.

After World War I, American feminists and reformers divided over protective labor legislation and the Equal Rights Amendment (ERA). The equality/difference dichotomy hardened into a sharp antagonism, producing a chasm that lasted nearly half a century. When the weight of opinion and activism shifted from difference to equality in the 1960s, the polarization survived. But where before woman had been constituted as essentially different, now she was seen as fundamentally equal.

Feminist understandings of the relationship between equality and difference started to become more elastic in the 1980s. Pressed by developing contradictions in policy and in women's lives, the dichotomy gradually lost its hold. Once again feminists could construct woman as simultaneously different and equal. To some extent, moreover, the construction now stretched across racial and ethnic divides. Good evidence for this new pliability is provided by the range of positions in the pregnancy policy debate, most of which show a paradoxical double-sidedness. Participants retain the opposition of difference to equality, and they simultaneously attempt to transcend or reconstruct it. Amid the fervor, acrimony, and polarization of their discussions, they combine commitment to woman's equality with assertion of her difference.

Advocates for women have not been the only architects of the opposition of difference to equality. The construction of "woman" is always contested, with consequences for social policy. One such contest occurred at the start of this century, when reformers yoked a particular version of the equality/difference relationship to their support for female-specific labor legislation. As projected in the Brandeis/Goldmark brief for *Muller v. Oregon,* woman's difference was above all physiologically based and had a limited bearing on her status. But the reformers could not ensure that their framing of the issues would be incorporated into public policy. When the United States Supreme Court decided the case, it backed the female-specific strategy but insisted on a different construction of the dichotomy. For the Justices, woman's difference was global in scope, linked eternally to her role as mother. Rather than equal citizen with special physiological needs, woman was to be constituted as dependent on man and primarily mother and homemaker.

Early twentieth-century reformers did not challenge the Supreme Court's construction of woman and motherhood in *Muller*. They were delighted by the decision's validation of protective labor legislation. Moreover, many among them shared the Court's views on motherhood and family. The Court's version became hegemonic—the ideological counterpart to a maternity policy projected as universal but actually directed primarily at white women. What is striking about this story is not that the reformers' formulation lost out, but that they seem not to have noticed the distance between their and the Court's construction. As the years passed, and their opposition to the ERA intensified, reformers moved farther and farther away from a conceptualization of woman as both different and equal. To many, woman's difference now seemed self-evidently determinant of her place in society.

The positioning of woman on the cusp between difference and equality is again being contested today. Discussion of the relationship between equality and difference is diverse and still in development. It includes not only the feminist debate but also a spectrum of views that claim feminism from a conservative viewpoint. Arising in the 1980s, this new trend within women's politics celebrates woman's difference as the foundation for a gender equality said to be truer than that promised by the feminism of the 1960s and 1970s.[1] Farther to the right, antifeminist conservatives more boldly assert woman's difference and what they call traditional family values, but even they do not entirely reject equality norms. From a variety of political directions, then, the conventional polarization of difference and equality is being reevaluated. The softening of the opposition of difference to equality is not the exclusive achievement of feminists with a radical perspective.

Given the range of efforts to constitute woman as both different and equal, I am wary when the Supreme Court renders decisions—for example, *California Federal v. Guerra*—that seem to converge with feminist thinking. Can the Justices' affirmation of woman's simultaneous difference and equality be the same as that of feminists? The Court's enthusiasm for acknowledging female specificity alongside women's equality could in the long run have quite damaging consequences. The dilemma of difference is, after all, that both special treatment and same treatment have the potential to be disadvantageous. Thus female-specific characteristics can be the basis not only for providing benefits to women but also for denying them—as the Court decided in *Geduldig* and *Gilbert*. The more positive practical outcome of its approval of difference in *California Federal* should not, I think, tempt us to lower our guard. Although the legal reasoning that won Lillian Garland her job back sought to justify only favorable special treatment, endorsement of women's difference is always vulnerable to disadvantageous reinterpretation.

Equality-versus-difference questions are probably never settled, even for the moment, as the twists and turns of policy development suggest. Difference and equality can each cut several ways, and advocates for women usually lack the power to enforce their reading of the issues. Pregnancy policy, which has evolved in the context of the changing and contested interpretation of the equality/difference dilemma, is a case in point.

Pregnancy has traditionally been the quintessential marker of woman's difference. Viewed as both normal and unique, the phenomenon of pregnancy justified a special treatment of women in the twentieth-century American workplace that was often unfavorable. Motherhood was assumed to be incompatible with the labor-force participation of white women in particular. In the 1960s and 1970s the meaning of pregnancy in the employment context began to change. By the late 1970s, a new legal basis, framed in terms of equality, had been established for the treatment of pregnant workers. As codified in the 1978 Pregnancy Discrimination Act (PDA), an employer cannot discriminate on the basis of pregnancy. If pregnancy impairs a woman's capacity to work, her employer now has to treat it comparably to other disabling conditions; the employer is required to ignore a worker's pregnant condition if it does not affect her performance. In this way, a standard of comparability links the pregnant employee to her co-workers. Despite conservative opposition, this approach remains dominant in U.S. pregnancy policy today. Pregnancy no longer signifies a woman worker's utter uniqueness; rather, it stands for the ways she should be seen as different but not unequal.

I take the recent changes in pregnancy policy as emblematic of a more general transformation in U.S. family policy. Expansion of the scope of equality thinking has not been limited to pregnancy. Wherever one looks, there is evidence of an extension of the equality framework into areas traditionally shaped by assertions of gender and race specificity. Policies concerning marriage and divorce have been in the lead. More recently, employment-based proposals have sought to reinterpret the relationship of family and work in terms of equality principles. Examples include efforts to enact parental leave statutes or to embed them within more comprehensive family and medical leave bills. These and other initiatives suggest that a new, equality-oriented family policy is being consolidated in the United States.

The practical consequences of the shift in family policy are not yet clear, and feminists are quite properly on the alert. Examination of the implementation of equality policies in the areas of divorce and child custody suggests that the alarm is justified. Given the disparities of power, resources, and commitments among family members, gender-neutral rules have not produced equitable outcomes. The debate over the treatment of pregnancy in the workplace reveals the presence of analogous contradictions. Studies could be undertaken for other policies affecting women and family life, but I think there is already enough information to draw a conclusion. Family policy based on the equality framework is potentially as burdened with danger to women's interests as that produced through the discourse of difference.

Some might conclude that the equality framework must be abandoned.[2] I do not. Female-specific treatment had devastating consequences on women's employment position, lasting into the 1970s. Insofar as all women were constructed as potential mothers, pregnancy came to be the pretext for much of the unfavorable treatment of women in the workplace. In my view, the alternative to basing pregnancy policy on woman's difference is some sort of equality-based strategy, but not the stingy motherhood-denying version sought in *California Federal* by Lillian Garland's employer. Parenting leave is one option. Family and medical leave legislation, designed by feminist policy analysts in response to the controversy over pregnancy disability leave statutes, is a better one.

On the issue of the treatment of pregnancy in the workplace, then, we have a range of policy choices, both female-specific and gender-neutral. Pregnancy disability statutes provide leave, usually unpaid but job-protected, to employees temporarily disabled by pregnancy. Such laws address the pressing female-specific issue of combining childbearing with employment, and they are relatively easy to implement. They are, however, strategically risky, as are mother-only parenting leave statutes. Gender-neutral parenting leave legislation, which offers leave for child rearing to both mothers and fathers, is also popular and seems ideologically attractive from a feminist point of view. But parenting leave does nothing for the worker temporarily unable to work because of pregnancy-related disability. Forcefully promoting the image of gender equality, parenting leave proposals ignore female-specific physiological needs. Practically and ideologically, they ask for too little, even in the meager context of U.S. maternity policy. In addition, parenting leave statutes usually do not support caretaking responsibilities toward other family members—for example, spouses, elderly parents, siblings, and grandchildren.

Family and medical leave legislation is the most comprehensive of the approaches currently under consideration to address the needs of mothers. Although complicated and seemingly costly, it is popular and has been enacted in several states and municipalities. Employers are required to provide job-protected leaves for a worker's own illness or to take care of sick or dependent family members. Family and medical leave legislation thus addresses the special needs of pregnancy and motherhood within a gender-neutral legal framework that encompasses a spectrum of workers' special needs. It is the policy proposal that to me seems most to deserve feminist support.

Differential Consideration

Support for family and medical leave legislation does not necessarily entail endorsing gender-neutral rules across the board.

Here I would agree with sociologist Carol Smart that no general approach to formulating policy for women is possible.[3] Policy is best analyzed as a set of separable questions, and different issues may call for different approaches. The fact that policy interpretation and implementation are not likely to be in the hands of feminists also suggests the need for differentiated and practice-based analysis. For each specific policy issue, an approach must be developed that has a reasonable chance of being implemented, is not too haunted by strategic danger, and moves well beyond existing ideological and structural configurations—an approach that ventures, in short, onto the radical edge of the possible.

Rather than debate the choice between equal treatment and special treatment, feminists should recognize the spectrum of possibilities available within each camp. For example, female-specific approaches vary in the ways they incorporate difference alongside equality. The limited, physiologically based female specificity of pregnancy disability statutes offers one model, endorsed by the Supreme Court in *California Federal*. Proposals to provide caretaking leave only to mothers imply another. Gender-neutral policies also differ in their approach to the opposition of difference to equality, with some more able to blur or challenge it than others. In the area of child custody, for instance, the rigidity of gender neutrality in mandatory joint custody policies denies the possibility that mothers and fathers play different roles in child rearing. Fathers' rights rhetoric takes advantage of that rigidity to launch a covert attack on sex equality. In contrast, gender-neutral custody policies framed around primary caretaking allow for a differentiated consideration of particular cases.

Policies that encase female specificity within a larger gender-neutral context effectively transcend the equality/difference dichotomy in practice. This is what distinguishes family and medical leave legislation not only from the employer's miserly interpretation of equality in *California Federal* but also from parental leave proposals. Similarly, gender-neutral child custody guidelines that use primary caretaking as the standard can acknowledge the tendency of parenting responsibilities to be met by mothers. And comparable worth policies likewise adhere to the equality framework while simultaneously defying it through an acceptance of job specificity. Such strategies aggressively resist the opposition of difference to equality. Taking an inclusive approach to the particularity of experience, they seek to differentially consider needs without giving up equality norms. They are so far removed from their gender-neutral or female-specific origins that it makes sense to call them by another name. I suggest the term differential consideration.[4]

The differential consideration policy that has the longest track record is comparable worth. Comparable worth (or pay equity) emerged as a strategy for confronting the economic impact of occupational segregation on women. Given that women and men do not, in general, do the same work, comparable worth analysis proposes that their jobs can be evaluated as comparable and the pay appropriately readjusted. Alongside affirmative action policies, which tend to push individuals in disadvantaged groups into different job slots, comparable worth plans provide a way to improve the situation of those who remain in jobs they already have. They leave the sex segregation of the occupational structure in place while simultaneously establishing standards of comparability across it. Developed to address gender stratification, comparable worth analysis was soon extended also to problems of racial stratification in the workplace.

Comparable worth policies have mainly been implemented in state and local public employment, with the intention of benefiting women and minorities in clerical work and in client-oriented service occupations. The results have been mixed and some feminists are pessimistic, arguing that comparable worth is a partial and somewhat risky reform strategy in a world that needs radical restructuring. Proponents do not entirely disagree with the various criticisms of comparable worth campaigns, but they have a more complex approach to the problem of evaluation. As sociologist Roslyn Feldberg speculated in one of the earliest discussions of the radical possibilities of the strategy, comparable worth "has the potential to redress some of the inequalities among women and to initiate an open discussion of the wage system. Its theoretical and political impact will reach far beyond the liberal framework in which it was conceived and force a rethinking of assumptions underlying gender hierarchy and the dominance of the market." Analysts note the challenge that comparable worth presents to race and class as well as gender hierarchies.[5]

Family and medical leave legislation is a differential consideration policy that, like comparable worth, has been the subject of feminist skepticism. Critics claim family and medical leave proposals offer too little to women and represent merely a liberal reform that does not go far enough. In the American context, however, family and medical leave legislation provides more than has ever been available before and constitutes an important challenge to existing social arrangements—in particular to gender oppositions, work/family boundaries, and notions of family definition. In terms of benefits for working mothers, family and medical leave legislation delineates, in other words, the frontier of what is currently possible.

Family and medical leave legislation is gender-neutral in form, as is its predecessor, the 1978 Pregnancy Discrimination Act. Its gender neutrality moves beyond the PDA's defensive and pregnancy-focused stance, however, for it has substantive content. Where the PDA prohibits discrimination, family and medical leave legislation provides benefits. Moreover, gender is not the only group specificity acknowledged. Combining a number of different medical and caring needs into a single package, the legislation provides leaves regardless of sex, parenthood, family status, and stage in the life cycle. In this way the approach recognizes that all workers have their own medical needs, that women workers who become mothers have particular needs, that fathers as well as mothers can parent infants and sick children, that adults must care for elderly parents, and that caretaking obligations extend outside immediate family boundaries.[6] These various concerns, many new to U.S. policy discussion, push forcefully at the limits of American social policy conventions. This is the approach that can come closest in the American context to the comprehensive benefit plans of European welfare states.

Differential consideration policies like comparable worth and family and medical leave set a new kind of policy standard. They are symmetrist in their strategic orientation, for they derive from the feminist equality analysis of the 1960s and 1970s and rely on gender-neutral legal rules. In terms of practical politics, they can therefore take advantage of the strategic safety net provided by the equality framework. But differential consideration policies depart from earlier types of symmetrist policies in key ways. Insofar as they energetically incorporate difference—that is, specificity—alongside equality, they challenge the limitations of the equality framework even as they rely upon it. They perforce provide mechanisms enabling policy to be tailored to particular situations and individuals. And although initiated by activists seeking to address the needs of women, they are quickly seen to be applicable to other groups. Thus comparable worth turns out to be as pertinent to racial stratification in the workplace as it is to gender stratification, and family and medical leave legislation offers benefits of importance to family members other than women.

Still to be articulated is the theoretical position that supports differential consideration policies. It cannot be assimilationism or androgyny, for both these frameworks assume a quite straightforward gender dualism and an unproblematized notion of equality. There must be, then, additional theoretical positions within the symmetrist camp discussed in the previous chapter. These positions have not yet been explicitly delineated, but they are implicit in the intentions of a number of scholars, particularly those attempting to understand difference, diversity, and multiculturalism as phenomena constructed through power. The goal of such theoretical inquiry is not simply to deconstruct or transcend the equality/difference dichotomy. Rather, the aim is to cast a theoretical net that can capture the unstable and messy ambiguities of a human heterogeneity constituted in contradiction.

Differential consideration analysis thus goes beyond the kinds of arguments put forth in the pregnancy policy debate. Refusing to be constrained by the equality/difference dichotomy, it aims to include all persons in their motley specificity, not separate out those who are not "the same." Among the specificities can be relations with and responsibilities toward others. That is, differential consideration thinking has the potential for constituting persons not just as simultaneously different and equal but also as enmeshed in social relations and encumbered by commitments. Difference, diversity, and en-cumberedness become, in principle, unexceptional rather than phenomena to be suppressed or accommodated. Differential consideration analysis envisions, in sum, a just equality of a new sort.

I think of differential consideration as the policy direction that best responds to the desire of feminist theorists to tran-scend the opposition of difference to equality. Campaigns for differential consideration open a space for concepts of equality that do not require the denial of specificity. They can challenge assumptions about the market, the family, and gender, class, and race hierarchy. Likewise, they may problematize notions of individualism and the separation of family from work. In the difficult and contradictory climate of the 1990s, proposals for differential consideration policies have a chance, I also think, to win some ground for women. On the terrains that count most—those of practical politics and moral vision—differential consideration has already staked a claim.

Notes

1. The Dilemma of Pregnancy Policy

1. Patricia Schroeder, "Parental Leave: The Need for a Federal Policy," in *The Parental Leave Crisis: Toward a National Policy*, ed. Edward F. Zigler and Meryl Frank (New Haven: Yale University Press, 1988), 326; Edward F. Zigler, Meryl Frank, and Barbara Emmel, "Introduction," in *Parental Leave Crisis*, xxiii. The term maternity policy conventionally encompasses policies that address both childbearing and child rearing; I therefore use the term pregnancy policy to refer more specifically to policies that concern pregnancy and childbirth.
2. The definition and boundaries of the concept of family policy are contested. See, for example, Phyllis Moen and Alvin L. Schorr, "Families and Social Policy," in *Handbook of Marriage and the Family*, ed. Marvin B. Sussman and Suzanne K. Steinmetz (New York: Plenum, 1987), 795; Martin Rein, *Notes for the Study of Tacit Family Policy*, Family Policy Note 1 (Cambridge: Joint Center for Urban Studies of the M.I.T. and Harvard University, 1977); Gilbert Y. Steiner, *The Futility of Family Policy* (Washington, D.C.: Brookings Institute, 1981); Sheila Kamerman and Alfred Kahn, *Family Policy* (New York: Columbia University Press, 1978); Ruth Sidel, *Women and Children Last: The Plight of Poor Women in Affluent America* (New York: Penguin Books, 1986).
3. Amy Wilentz, "Garland's Bouquet: A Landmark Supreme Court Ruling Supports Pregnancy Leave," *Time*, 26 January 1987, 15.
4. The opposition that is the subject of the debate is variously named equality versus difference and sameness versus difference. Embedded in this terminological instability are difficult theoretical issues, in particular the conflation of sameness with equality, and the relationship of equality to notions of fairness and justice. The sameness-versus-difference formulation is more precise, but feminists use it in ways that tend to bracket these issues. I therefore generally adopt the equality-versus-difference formulation despite—or perhaps because of—its ambiguities.
5. Feminists studying the impact of divorce, for example, questioned

whether the conventional equality framework could produce equitable outcomes, given the realities of gender difference. Martha L. Fineman, "Implementing Equality: Ideology, Contradiction, and Social Change: A Study of Rhetoric and Results in the Regulation of the Consequences of Divorce," *Wisconsin Law Review* (1983): 789–886; Lenore J. Weitzman, *The Divorce Revolution: The Unexpected Social and Economic Consequences for Women and Children in America* (New York: Free Press, 1985). Feminist understandings of difference and equality were also at issue in the controversial case brought by the Equal Employment Opportunity Commission against Sears, Roebuck and Company. Ruth Milkman, "Women's History and the Sears Case," *Feminist Studies* 12(1986): 375–400.

6. For a sampling of the 1980s literature on difference, see Michele Barrett, "The Concept of 'Difference,' " *Feminist Review* 26(1987): 28–41; Jana Sawicki and Iris Young, "Issues of Difference in Feminist Philosophy," *Newsletter on Feminism and Philosophy* (American Philosophical Association), April 1988, 13–17; Alice Kessler-Harris, "The Debate over Equality for Women in the Work Place: Recognizing Differences," *Women and Work: An Annual Review* 1(1985): 141–161; Joan C. Tronto, "Beyond Gender Difference to a Theory of Care," *Signs* 12(1986–1987): 644–663.

7. Lucinda M. Finley, "Transcending Equality Theory: A Way Out of the Maternity and the Workplace Debate," *Columbia Law Review* 86(1986): 1118–1182; Joan W. Scott, "Deconstructing Equality-versus-Difference: Or, the Uses of Post-structuralist Theory for Feminism," *Feminist Studies* 14(Spring 1988): 33–50; Martha Minow, "Learning to Live with the Dilemma of Difference: Bilingual and Special Education," *Law and Contemporary Problems* 48(Spring 1985): 157–211. For an accessible overview of equality-versus-difference issues in feminist legal theory, see Martha Minow, "Adjudicating Differences: Conflicts among Feminist Lawyers," in *Conflicts in Feminism*, ed. Marianne Hirsch and Evelyn Fox Keller (New York: Routledge, 1990), 149–163.

8. Scott, "Deconstructing Equality-versus-Difference," 42, 43. Ann Snitow, "A Gender Diary," in *Conflicts in Feminism*, 9–43, esp. 9.

9. Snitow, "A Gender Diary," 19.

10. See, for example, Wendy Kaminer, *A Fearful Freedom: Women's Flight from Equality* (Reading, Mass.: Addison-Wesley, 1990); and Carol Lee Bacchi, *Same Difference: Feminism and Sexual Difference* (Sydney, Australia: Allen and Unwin, 1990). I thank Hester Eisenstein for making *Same Difference* available to me.

11. The terms white and women of color are problematic from a number of points of view. The notion that white people are a unified group is relatively recent; the European immigrants who dominated the industrial labor force in the late nineteenth and early twentieth centuries were themselves regarded as distinct races. The term women of color is likewise questionable insofar as it amalgamates different groups or implies that European-Americans lack color, i.e., race; see Hazel V. Carby, "The Politics of Difference," *Ms. Magazine*, September/October 1990, 84–85.

Pending better ways to describe the racial/ethnic hierarchy, I nevertheless use the terms white and of color.

2. Woman's Place

1. The classic discussions of the ideology of separate spheres are Barbara Welter, "The Cult of True Womanhood, 1820–1860," *American Quarterly* 18(1966): 151–174; Carroll Smith-Rosenberg, "The Female World of Love and Ritual: Relations between Women in Nineteenth-Century America," *Signs* 1(1975–1976): 1–29; and Nancy F. Cott, *The Bonds of Womanhood: "Woman's Sphere" in New England, 1780–1835* (New Haven: Yale University Press, 1977). Recent reevaluations include Nancy A. Hewitt, "Beyond the Search for Sisterhood: American Women's History in the 1980s," *Social History* 10(1985): 299–322; and Linda K. Kerber, "Separate Spheres, Female Worlds, Woman's Place: The Rhetoric of Women's History," *Journal of American History* 75(1988): 9–39.
2. Norma Basch, "Invisible Women: The Legal Fiction of Marital Unity in Nineteenth-Century America," *Feminist Studies* 5(1979): 346–366; Marylynn Salmon, "Equality or Submersion? Feme Covert Status in Early Pennsylvania," in *Women of America: A History*, ed. Carol Berkin and Mary Beth Norton (Boston: Houghton Mifflin, 1979), 92–111; Joan R. Gundersen, "Independence, Citizenship, and the American Revolution," *Signs* 13 (1987–1988), 59–77; and, for an overview of the literature, Norma Basch, "The Emerging Legal History of Women in the United States: Property, Divorce, and the Constitution," *Signs* 12(1986–1987): 97–117, esp. 99–106.
3. Hewitt, "Beyond the Search for Sisterhood," 315.
4. *Notable American Women, 1607–1950*, ed. Edward T. James, Janet Wilson James, and Paul S. Boyer (Cambridge: Harvard University Press, 1971), 1: 223–225; Robert M. Spector, "Woman against the Law: Myra Bradwell's Struggle for Admission to the Illinois Bar," *Illinois State Historical Society Journal* 68(1975): 228–242; Steven M. Buechler, *The Transformation of the Woman Suffrage Movement: The Case of Illinois, 1850–1920* (New Brunswick, N.J.: Rutgers University Press, 1986), 62–65; Frances Olsen, "From False Paternalism to False Equality: Judicial Assaults on Feminist Community, Illinois, 1869–1895," *Michigan Law Review* 84(1986): 1518–1541. Contemporary description of Bradwell cited in Spector, "Woman against the Law," 229.
5. Bradwell v. Illinois, 83 U.S. (16 Wall.) 130 (1873), cited in Barbara Allen Babcock, Ann E. Freedman, Eleanor Holmes Norton, and Susan C. Ross, *Sex Discrimination and the Law: Causes and Remedies* (Boston: Little Brown, 1975), 6.
6. Aileen S. Kraditor, ed., *Up from the Pedestal: Selected Writings in the History of American Feminism* (Chicago: Quadrangle Books, 1968), 187.

7. I use the term woman movement to refer to the various organized efforts on behalf of women that occurred before the second decade of the twentieth century. As Nancy Cott documents, the word feminism was not current earlier; *The Grounding of Modern Feminism* (New Haven: Yale University Press, 1987).

8. For good overviews of the situation of women workers at the turn of the century, see Mary Ryan, *Womanhood in America* (New York: Franklin Watts, 1979), chap. 4; Alice Kessler-Harris, *Out to Work: A History of Wage-Earning Women in the United States* (New York: Oxford University Press, 1982), chaps. 5–6.

9. For a brief overview of European legislation and social policy affecting women workers, see Meryl Frank and Robyn Lipner, "History of Maternity Leave in Europe and the United States," in *The Parental Leave Crisis: Toward a National Policy,* ed. Edward F. Zigler and Meryl Frank (New Haven: Yale University Press, 1988), 3–22.

10. Elizabeth Faulkner Baker, *Protective Labor Legislation, with Special Reference to Women in the State of New York* (New York: Columbia University Press, 1925); Kessler-Harris, *Out to Work,* chap. 7; Susan Lehrer, *Origins of Protective Labor Legislation for Women, 1905–1925* (Albany: State University of New York Press, 1987).

11. For consideration of the fate of protective legislation in the courts, see Judith A. Baer, *The Chains of Protection: The Judicial Response to Women's Labor Legislation* (Westport, Conn.: Greenwood Press, 1978), chap. 2; and Ann Corinne Hill, "Protection of Women Workers and the Courts: A Legal Case History," *Feminist Studies* 5(1979): 247–273. See also Baker, *Protective Labor Legislation,* 18–102.

12. *People v. Williams,* 189 N.Y. 131 (1907), cited in Babcock et al., *Sex Discrimination,* 28.

13. *Wenham v. State,* 65 Neb. 394 (1902), cited in Baer, *Chains of Protection,* 54.

14. *Commonwealth v. Beatty,* 15 Pa. super. 5 (1900), cited in Baker, *Protective Labor Legislation,* 61.

15. *State v. Buchanan,* 29 Wash. 602 (1902), cited ibid., 63.

16. For Muller v. Oregon, 208 U.S. 412 (1908), see Kessler-Harris, *Out to Work,* 186–187; Baer, *Chains of Protection,* 56–67; Nancy S. Erickson, "Historical Background of 'Protective' Labor Legislation: *Muller v. Oregon,*" in *Women and the Law: A Social Historical Perspective,* ed. D. Kelly Weisberg (Cambridge, Mass.: Schenkman Publishing, 1982), 2: 155–186; Ronald K. L. Collins and Jennifer Friesen, "Looking Back on *Muller v. Oregon,*" *American Bar Association Journal* 69(March 1983): 294–298; Ava Baron, "Protective Legislation and the Cult of Domesticity," *Journal of Family Issues* 2(1981): 25–38.

17. Lochner v. New York, 198 U.S. 45 (1905), cited in Babcock et al., *Sex Discrimination,* 20, 22.

18. For the strategy of the so-called Brandeis brief, see the citations in note 16, above. Deborah L. Rhode argues that reformers could have challenged *Lochner* directly; *Justice and Gender: Sex Discrimination and the Law*

(Cambridge: Harvard University Press, 1989), 40. Both the brief (hereafter cited as the Brandeis/Goldmark brief) and the Supreme Court decision are available in Louis D. Brandeis and Josephine Goldmark, *Women in Industry* (New York: Arno Press, 1969; first published 1908).

19. Brandeis/Goldmark brief, 10.
20. Ibid., 10, 16.
21. Baer provides an overview and methodological critique of the "facts" in the Brandeis/Goldmark brief; *Chains of Protection*, 58–61.
22. Brandeis/Goldmark brief, 18. Citations not otherwise identified are to the prefatory comments, written by Brandeis and Goldmark, that appear before each group of citations.
23. Ibid., 28.
24. Ibid., 36 (London, 1892), 29 (Massachusetts, 1872), and 30 (Maine, 1888).
25. Ibid., 38, citing an 1875 Massachusetts report.
26. Safety is considered ibid., 42–44, and morals ibid., 44–46.
27. Ibid., 47.
28. Ibid., 109 (1902).
29. Ibid., 113.
30. Ibid., 33, citing factory inspectors' reports, Berlin, 1905.
31. Ibid., 21, citing Dr. Theodore Weyl, Jena, 1894.
32. Ibid., 58, citing factory inspectors' reports, Berlin, 1905.
33. Ibid., 49, citing factory inspectors' reports, Berlin, 1905.
34. Ibid., citing Dr. Theodore Weyl, Jena, 1904. For the larger context in which motherhood became central to dominant definitions of women, see the sources cited in note 50.
35. Ibid., 18.
36. Ibid., 21, citing Dr. Theodore Weyl, Jena, 1894.
37. Ibid., 50, citing Dr. Alice Salomon, London, 1907.
38. For example, Kessler-Harris, *Out to Work*, 186–187; Erickson, "Historical Background," 159–160; Baron, "Protective Labor Legislation," 32–33; Susan Moller Okin, *Women in Western Political Thought* (Princeton: Princeton University Press, 1979), 256–257; Ronnie Steinberg, *Wages and Hours: Labor and Reform in Twentieth-Century America* (New Brunswick, N.J.: Rutgers University Press, 1982), 80–81. Feminist lawyers are particularly prone to assume the identity of the arguments in the Brandeis/Goldmark brief and the *Muller* opinion; for example, Babcock et al., *Sex Discrimination*, 29–32, or Rhode, *Justice and Gender*, 40–43. Baer, *Chains of Protection*, is somewhat more careful, but still leaves the implication that the Brandeis/Goldmark brief made essentially the same points as the Supreme Court opinion.
39. *Muller v. Oregon* (1908), in Brandeis and Goldmark, *Women in Industry*, 6–7; the text of *Muller* is placed at the back of *Women in Industry*, where it is repaginated as pp. 1–8.
40. *Muller*, ibid., 3.
41. Ibid., 4, 5.
42. Ibid., 4.
43. Ibid., 6–7.

44. Jules Simon, speaking in the French Senate in 1891; cited in the Brandeis/ Goldmark brief, 48.

45. *Muller*, in *Women in Industry*, 6.

46. Ibid.

47. Ibid., 7.

48. Ibid., 6.

49. The citations in this paragraph are, respectively, from Bradley's opinion in *Bradwell* and the Court's unanimous opinion in *Muller*.

50. Anna Davin, "Imperialism and Motherhood," *History Workshop Journal* 5(1978): 9–65, esp. 12–13. See also Jane Lewis, *The Politics of Motherhood: Child and Maternal Welfare in England, 1900–1939* (London: Croom Helm, 1980); and Deborah Dwork, *War Is Good for Babies and Other Young Children: A History of the Infant and Child Welfare Movement in England, 1898–1918* (London: Tavistock Publications, 1987). Scholars are just beginning to explore the ways the politics of motherhood took specific shape in the United States; see, for example, Gwendolyn Mink, "The Lady and the Tramp: Gender, Race and the Origins of the American Welfare State," in *Women, the State, and Welfare*, ed. Linda Gordon (Madison: University of Wisconsin Press, 1990), 92–122.

51. Sophonisba Breckinridge, "Legislative Control of Women's Work," *Journal of Political Economy* 14(1906): 107–108. Portions of Breckinridge's article are cited in the Brandeis/Goldmark brief, 49–50.

52. *Woman's Journal*, 21 March 1908, cited in Erickson, "Historical Background," 171–172; see also the citations in Olson, "From False Paternalism," 1538 n.99. It seems likely that these women were aware of comparable critiques long current in England; see chapter 3, note 13.

53. Florence Kelley in 1908, cited in Erickson, "Historical Background," 174.

54. *Ritchie v. Wayman*, 244 Ill. 509 (1910), cited in Baer, *Chains of Protection*, 78.

55. Baer, *Chains of Protection*, 107–108; Baker, *Protective Labor Legislation*, 74; Babcock et al., *Sex Discrimination*, 43. *United States ex rel. Robinson v. York*, 281 F. Supp. 8 (D. Conn. 1968), cited in Leo Kanowitz, *Women and the Law: The Unfinished Revolution* (Albuquerque: University of New Mexico Press, 1969), 171. In 1970, another court recalled *Muller* in a more restricted fashion as taking "account of differences in physical structure, strength and endurance of women"; *Seidenberg v. McSorley's Old Ale House, Inc.*, 317 F. Supp. 593 (S.D.N.Y. 1970), cited in Babcock et al., *Sex Discrimination*, 1045.

56. Mary Van Kleek in 1919, cited in Kessler-Harris, *Out to Work*, 207.

57. Baer, *Chains of Protection*, 75–91; Kessler-Harris, *Out to Work*, 187–188.

58. Baker, *Protective Labor Legislation*, 145, 253–257.

59. Kessler-Harris, *Out to Work*, 181. The illusion that there are two mutually exclusive types of protective labor legislation is widespread; see, for example, Zillah R. Eisenstein, *The Female Body and the Law* (Berkeley: University of California Press, 1989), 201 (citing Kessler-Harris as authority).

60. Kessler-Harris, *Out to Work*, 191–195. For a contemporary discussion of

the coverage, enforcement, and impact of protective legislation, see Baker, *Protective Labor Legislation*, 278–428.

61. "Report on Investigation of 164 Night Workers in Connecticut," cited in Kessler-Harris, *Out to Work*, 192–193.

62. Maurine Weiner Greenwald, *Women, War, and Work: The Impact of World War I on Women Workers in the United States* (Westport, Conn.: Greenwood Press, 1980), 139.

63. Baker, *Protective Labor Legislation*, 427–428.

64. For judicious discussion of the effects of protective labor legislation, see the work of Alice Kessler-Harris; for example, *Out to Work*, chap. 7, and idem, *A Woman's Wage: Historical Meanings and Social Consequences* (Lexington: University Press of Kentucky, 1990). See also Cott, *Grounding of Modern Feminism*, 129–142; and idem, "Historical Perspectives: The Equal Rights Amendment Conflict in the 1920s," in *Conflicts in Feminism*, ed. Marianne Hirsch and Evelyn Fox Keller (New York: Routledge, 1990), 44–59.

3. Mothers at Work

1. Sheila B. Kamerman, Alfred J. Kahn, and Paul Kingston, *Maternity Policies and Working Women* (New York: Columbia University Press, 1983); the authors of this useful summary of current practices emphasize that recent studies have exaggerated the adequacy of current maternity benefits. An expanded view of a minimally adequate maternity policy is sketched in "Accommodating Pregnancy in the Workplace" (November 1987), a report from the research project on Mothers in the Workplace, conducted by the Center for the Child, National Council of Jewish Women, New York, N.Y.; the center notes that, in addition to health insurance, job-protected pregnancy disability leave, and income replacement, pregnant workers need parenting leave, assistance in finding child care, time for medical appointments, flexible scheduling, and an understanding, individualized response from supervisors when unanticipated difficulties arise.

2. *The Financing of Maternity Care in the United States* (New York: Alan Guttmacher Institute, 1987), presented in summary form in the pamphlet *Blessed Events and the Bottom Line: Financing Maternity Care in the United States* (New York: Alan Guttmacher Institute, 1987).

3. *Blessed Events*, 18–19; see also Rachel Benson Gold and Asta M. Kenney, "Paying for Maternity Care," *Family Planning Perspectives* 17(1985): 103–111. I thank Susheela Singh of the Guttmacher Institute for taking the time to introduce me to these data.

4. *Blessed Events*, 21–23.

5. Ibid., 20; Susheela Singh, "Health Insurance of Women of Childbearing Age: United States, 1985," *Metropolitan Life Insurance Company, Statistical*

Bulletin 69, no. 4 (October–December 1988): 16–23. Most of the 83 percent of women aged fifteen through forty-four who have medical coverage are covered through private group plans associated with their own, their husband's, or their parents' employment (67 percent); 6 percent buy private health insurance as individuals, and 10 percent are insured through Medicaid or other government programs. One in six Americans under sixty-five has no health insurance, and the number without coverage is rising; Employee Benefits Research Institute, "A Profile of the Nonelderly Population without Health Insurance," *Issue Brief*, no. 66, May 1987; *Blessed Events*, 1.

6. The figure of 26 percent includes 17 percent without health insurance, plus 9 percent whose private health plans exclude maternity; *Blessed Events*, 43–45. Singh, "Health Insurance of Women," 18–20. For the size of firms, *Financing of Maternity Care*, 273.

7. *Blessed Events*, 24–25.

8. For the 1981 study, see Kamerman et al., *Maternity Policies*, 161–169. For the discussion in this and the following paragraph, ibid., 50–74, and "Medical and Family Leave: Benefits Available to Female Workers in the United States" (March 1987) and "Accommodating Pregnancy in the Workplace" (November 1987), reporting data from the Mothers in the Workplace Study conducted by the Center for the Child, National Council of Jewish Women, New York, N.Y. See also Ellen A. Farber, Marguerite Alejandro-Wright, and Susan Muenchow, "Managing Work and Family: Hopes and Realities," in *The Parental Leave Crisis: Toward a National Policy*, ed. Edward F. Zigler and Meryl Frank (New Haven: Yale University Press, 1988), 161–176.

9. Sylvia Ann Hewlett, *A Lesser Life: The Myth of Women's Liberation in America* (New York: William Morrow, 1986), 374; see also Mary Ann Mason, *The Equality Trap* (New York: Simon and Schuster, 1988). For a fine discussion of *A Lesser Life*, see Deborah Rosenfelt and Judith Stacey, "Second Thoughts on the Second Wave," *Feminist Studies* 13(1987): 341–361.

10. Hewlett, *A Lesser Life*, 195.

11. For Germany see Gaston V. Rimlinger, *Welfare Policy and Industrialization in Europe, America, and Russia* (New York: John Wiley and Sons, 1971), 112–122; for England, Maurice Bruce, *The Coming of the Welfare State* (London: Batsford, 1968), 154–227. For comparative overviews and bibliography, see Rimlinger, *Welfare Policy*; Peter Flora and Arnold J. Heidenheimer, eds., *The Development of Welfare States in Europe and America* (New Brunswick, N.J.: Transaction, 1981); Margaret Weir, Ann Shola Orloff, and Theda Skocpol, eds., *The Politics of Social Policy in the United States* (Princeton: Princeton University Press, 1988), 5–9.

12. For overviews of the history of European welfare policies pertaining to maternity, see Meryl Frank and Robyn Lipner, "History of Maternity Leave in Europe and the United States," in Zigler and Frank, *Parental Leave Crisis*, 3–22; and Susanne A. Stoiber, *Parental Leave and "Woman's Place": The Implications and Impact of Three European Approaches to Family*

Leave Policy (Washington, D.C.: Women's Research and Education Institute, 1989). For England, Margaret Hewitt, *Wives and Mothers In Victorian Industry* (London: Rockliff, 1958). For France, Mary Lynn MacDougall, "Protecting Infants: The French Campaign for Maternity Leaves, 1890s–1913," *French Historical Studies* 13(1983): 79–105. Note that maternity policies can be directed at women as workers or as citizens, a distinction in the basis for entitlement that is not always made clear in the literature.

13. In England, some reformers questioned whether the merits of female-specific protective labor legislation were worth the risk of sex-based disadvantage. Opposition to protection centered in the work of Emma Paterson and the activities of the Women's Protective and Provident League, later the Women's Trade Union League. See Norbert C. Soldon, *Women in British Trade Unions, 1874–1976* (Dublin: Gil and Macmillan, 1978), chaps. 1–2; B. L. Hutchins and A. Harrison, *A History of Factory Legislation* (New York: Burt Franklin, 1903), 173–199; Mary Lyndon Shanley, "Review Essay: Suffrage, Protective Labor Legislation, and Married Women's Property Laws in England," *Signs* 12(1986–1987): 62–77, esp. 67–71; Carol Lee Bacchi, *Same Difference: Feminism and Sexual Difference* (Sydney, Australia: Allen and Unwin, 1990), 36–39.

14. *International Labour Conventions and Recommendations, 1919–1981* (Geneva: International Labour Office, 1982), 691–692 (Convention No. 3). See also S. A. Smirnov, "Maternity Protection: National Law and Practice in Selected European Countries," *International Social Security Review* 32(1979): 420–444.

15. See Anna Davin, "Imperialism and Motherhood," *History Workshop Journal* 5(1978): 9–65; Jane Lewis, *The Politics of Motherhood: Child and Maternal Welfare in England, 1900–1939* (London: Croom Helm, 1980); Deborah Dwork, *War Is Good for Babies and Other Young Children: A History of the Infant and Child Welfare Movement in England, 1898–1918* (London: Tavistock Publications, 1987).

16. Eugenicist physician Caleb W. Saleeby in 1908, cited in Davin, "Imperialism and Motherhood," 28; and Dwork, *War Is Good*, 115.

17. French legislator in 1892, cited in Alisa Klaus, "Maternal and Infant Health Policy in the United States and France, 1890–1920," paper presented at Gender and the Origins of the Welfare State conference, Center for European Studies, Harvard University, 1987–1988.

18. John Burns in 1906, cited in Davin, "Imperialism and Motherhood," 28.

19. British report (1908), cited in Louise A. Tilly and Joan W. Scott, *Women, Work, and Family* (New York: Holt, Rinehart and Winston, 1978), 173. Gwendolyn Mink considers the distinctiveness of American maternalism in "The Lady and the Tramp: Gender, Race and the Origins of the American Welfare State," in *Women, the State, and Welfare*, ed. Linda Gordon (Madison: University of Wisconsin Press, 1990), 92–122.

20. *International Labour Conventions*, 693–696 (Convention No. 103); Smirnov, "Maternity Protection."

21. Kamerman et al., *Maternity Policies*; Sheila B. Kamerman, *Maternity and*

Parental Benefits and Leaves: An International Review (New York: Columbia University Center for the Social Sciences, 1980); Sheila B. Kamerman and Alfred J. Kahn, *Child Care, Family Benefits, and Working Parents: A Study in Comparative Policy* (New York: Columbia University Press, 1981); *Maternity Benefits in the Eighties: A Global Survey* (Geneva: International Labour Office, 1985); Smirnov, "Maternity Protection"; Ruth Sidel, *Women and Children Last: The Plight of Poor Women in Affluent America* (New York: Penguin Books, 1987), chap. 9; Carolyn Teich Adams and Kathryn Teich Winston, *Mothers at Work: Public Policies in the United States, Sweden, and China* (New York: Longman, 1980).

22. In the 1970s some European countries, notably Sweden, began to experiment with an equality approach to family legislation; most remain committed to female-specific practices.

23. For evaluation of the impact of protective labor legislation in this and the following paragraph, see the works cited in chapter 2, note 64.

24. For the workplace maternity practices discussed in this and the following paragraphs, see Women's Bureau, U.S. Department of Labor, *1975 Handbook on Women Workers*, Bulletin 297 (Washington, D.C.: GPO, 1975), chap. 8, "Maternity Standards"; Elizabeth Duncan Koontz, "Childbirth and Child Rearing Leave: Job-Related Benefits," *New York Law Forum* 17(1971): 480–502; and Trudy Hayden, *Punishing Pregnancy: Discrimination in Education, Employment, and Credit* (New York: American Civil Liberties Union, 1973), 21–63. For a sampling of typical pregnancy rules challenged only in the past fifteen years, see Wendy W. Williams, "Equality's Riddle: Pregnancy and the Equal Treatment/Special Treatment Debate," *New York University Review of Law and Social Change* 13(1984–1985): 325–380, esp. nn. 77, 125, 127; or Lucinda M. Finley, "Transcending Equality Theory: A Way Out of the Maternity and the Workplace Debate," *Columbia Law Review* 86(1986): 1118–1182, esp. 1123–1125.

25. Dorothy R. Kittner, "Maternity Benefits Available to Most Health Plan Participants," *Monthly Labor Review* 101, no. 5 (May 1978): 53–56. On coverage of wives, see U.S. Congress, Senate, Subcommittee on Labor of the Committee on Human Resources, *Discrimination on the Basis of Pregnancy, 1977*, 95th Cong., 1st sess., 26, 27, 29 April 1977, 303–304, 369.

26. Domestics, for example, must tend to their employer's family even if it means not seeing their own children. Judith Rollins, *Between Women: Domestics and Their Employers* (Philadelphia: Temple University Press, 1985); Phyllis Palmer, *Domesticity and Dirt: Housewives and Domestic Servants in the United States, 1920–1945* (Philadelphia: Temple University Press, 1989).

27. Further investigation is necessary to specify the evolution of the distinct maternity policies that have been directed at white women and women of color. In the case of African-Americans, the place to start is with the history of practices under slavery. In the case of whites, I hypothesize that the principles underlying maternity policy were not fully in place until after World War I. For other groups, immigration policies played an

important part in setting the initial parameters within which motherhood and employment were combined. For important work on this history, see Mink, "Lady and the Tramp," as well as Linda Gordon, "The New Feminist Scholarship on the Welfare State," in Gordon, *Women, the State, and Welfare*, 9–35. Barbara J. Nelson discusses the history in terms of a gender-based two-channel welfare state in "The Origins of the Two-Channel Welfare State: Workmen's Compensation and Mother's Aid," in Gordon, *Women, the State, and Welfare*, 123–151; in my view, race has been at least as salient as gender in the formation of the American welfare state.

28. Mink, "Lady and the Tramp."
29. For example, many European countries improved maternity benefits and child care provisions in the 1970s. Smirnov, "Maternity Protection"; Kamerman and Kahn, *Child Care, Family Benefits, and Working Parents;* Stoiber, *Parental Leave and "Woman's Place."*

4. Feminism and Equality

1. Nancy F. Cott, "Feminist Theory and Feminist Movements: The Past before Us," in *What Is Feminism: A Re-Examination*, ed. Juliet Mitchell and Ann Oakley (New York: Pantheon Books, 1986), 50. My discussion in this section is indebted to Nancy Cott's work; see also Nancy Cott, "The Crisis in Feminism, 1910–1930," paper presented at the Sixth Berkshire Conference on the History of Women, Smith College, June 1984; idem, *The Grounding of Modern Feminism* (New Haven: Yale University Press, 1987); and idem, "Historical Perspectives: The Equal Rights Amendment Conflict in the 1920s," in *Conflicts in Feminism*, ed. Marianne Hirsch and Evelyn Fox Keller (New York: Routledge, 1990), 44–59. For analogous complexities in the history of other national feminisms, see Karen Offen, "Defining Feminism: A Comparative Historical Approach," *Signs* 14 (1988–1989): 119–157, esp. 134–150; and Carol Lee Bacchi, *Same Difference: Feminism and Sexual Difference* (Sydney, Australia: Allen and Unwin, 1990), chap. 1.
2. Helen Philleo Jenkins in 1899, cited in Aileen S. Kraditor, ed., *Up from the Pedestal: Selected Writings in the History of the American Feminism* (Chicago: Quadrangle Books, 1968), 269–270; Carrie Chapman Catt in 1914, cited ibid., 287; Alice Stone Blackwell in 1914, cited ibid.
3. Rosalyn Terborg-Penn, "Discontented Black Feminists: Prelude and Postscript to the Passage of the Fourteenth Amendment," in *Decades of Discontent: The Women's Movement, 1920–1940*, ed. Lois Scharf and Joan M. Jensen (Westport, Conn.: Greenwood Press, 1983), 261–278; Bettina Aptheker, "Woman Suffrage and the Crusade against Lynching, 1890–1920," in *Woman's Legacy: Essays on Race, Sex, and Class in American History* (Amherst: University of Massachusetts Press, 1982), 53–76.

4. Mollie Schepps in 1912, just after the Triangle Shirtwaist Factory fire; cited in Rosalyn Baxandall, Linda Gordon, and Susan Reverby, eds., *America's Working Women: A Documentary History, 1600 to the Present* (New York: Random House, 1976), 218.

5. Susan Levine, *Labor's True Woman: Carpet Weavers, Industrialization and Labor Reform in the Gilded Age* (Philadelphia: Temple University Press, 1984). See also Alice Kessler-Harris, "Problems of Coalition-Building: Women and Trade Unions in the 1920s," in *Women, Work and Protest: A Century of U.S. Women's Labor History,* ed. Ruth Milkman (Boston: Routledge and Kegan Paul, 1985), 110–138, esp. 115–119.

6. For overviews of the National Woman's Party and the dispute over its equal rights strategy, see Nancy F. Cott, "Feminist Politics in the 1920s: The National Woman's Party," *Journal of American History* 71(1984): 43–68; idem, *Grounding of Modern Feminism,* chaps. 2–4; idem, "Historical Perspectives"; Alice Kessler-Harris, *Out to Work: A History of Wage-Earning Women in the United States* (New York: Oxford University Press), 206–212; Susan D. Becker, *The Origins of the Equal Rights Amendment: American Feminism between the Wars* (Westport, Conn.: Greenwood Press, 1981); Christine A. Lunardini, *From Equal Suffrage to Equal Rights: Alice Paul and the National Woman's Party, 1910–1928* (New York: New York University Press, 1986), 150–170. As Cott documents, the term feminism came into use in the United States during the second decade of the twentieth century to refer to a group of women radicals with diffuse liberatory ideals; by the end of the 1920s, however, the term had been restricted to the proponents of equal rights in the narrow NWP sense. In what follows, I generally use the term women reformers to refer to women activists who opposed equal rights leglislation.

7. Harriot Stanton Blatch in 1918, cited in Cott, *Grounding of Modern Feminism,* 121. Alma Lutz, cited in William H. Chafe, *The American Woman: Her Changing Social, Economic, and Political Roles, 1920–1970* (New York: Oxford University Press, 1972), 124. Elizabeth Faulkner Baker, *Protective Labor Legislation, with Special Reference to Women in the State of New York* (New York: Columbia University Press, 1925), 427–428. Blanche Wiesen Cook, ed., *Crystal Eastman on Women and Revolution* (New York: Oxford University Press, 1978), 171–172, citing a British worker in a 1925 article for *Equal Rights.*

8. Cott, "Feminist Politics in the 1920s," 50.

9. Letter to Edith Houghton Hooker, 1922, in Barbara Sicherman, ed., *Alice Hamilton: A Life in Letters* (Cambridge: Harvard University Press, 1984), 256.

10. Various reformers, cited in Cott, *Grounding of Modern Feminism,* 138.

11. Mrs. William J. Carson, testifying at the 1931 Senate Hearings on the Equal Rights Amendment; cited in Kraditor, *Up from the Pedestal,* 301. It would be interesting to trace the evolution of the idea that female-specific treatment can provide "real equality." Louise Newman of Brown University suggests it may have originated in turn-of-the-century conservative

discourse; private communication, June 1990. Sybil Lipschultz hypothesizes its emergence among reformers in the 1920s; "Social Feminism and Legal Discourse: 1908–1923," in *At the Boundaries of Law*, ed. Martha Albertson Fineman and Nancy Sweet Thomadsen (New York: Routledge, 1991), 209–225. Once established, the notion of difference as real equality endured late into the century. For example, in testimony against the ERA at the 1970 Senate Hearings, Myra Wolfgang of the AFL-CIO explained that "we who want equal opportunities, equal pay for equal work and equal status for women, know that frequently we obtain real equality through a difference in treatment, rather than an identity in treatment"; cited in Barbara Allen Babcock, Ann E. Freedman, Eleanor Holmes Norton, and Susan C. Ross, *Sex Discrimination and the Law: Causes and Remedies* (Boston: Little Brown, 1975), 279.

12. Cott, *Grounding of Modern Feminism*, 138; Gertrude F. Brown, cited ibid., 128–129. For an argument that some women activists retained and extended their commitment to combining equality and difference, see Wendy Sarvasy, "Beyond the Difference versus Equality Policy Debate: Postsuffrage Feminism, Citizenship, and the Quest for a Feminist Welfare State," *Signs* 17(1992–1993): 329–362.

13. Women's Bureau, U.S. Department of Labor, *1975 Handbook on Women Workers*, Bulletin 297 (Washington, D.C.: GPO, 1975), chap. 1; Women's Bureau, U.S. Department of Labor, *Time of Change: 1983 Handbook on Women Workers*, Bulletin 298 (Washington, D.C.: GPO, 1983), chap. 1.

14. Cynthia Harrison provides a very detailed discussion of women's activism in the early 1960s in *On Account of Sex: The Politics of Women's Issues, 1945–1968* (Berkeley: University of California Press, 1988). See also the interpretation of these years in Patricia G. Zelman, *Women, Work, and National Policy: The Kennedy-Johnson Years* (Ann Arbor, Mich.: UMI Research Press, 1982). Thoughtful recent overviews are included in Myra Marx Ferree and Beth B. Hess, *Controversy and Coalition: The New Feminist Movement* (Boston: Twayne Publishers, 1985); and Leila J. Rupp and Verta Taylor, *Survival in the Doldrums: The American Women's Rights Movement, 1945 to the 1960s* (Columbus: Ohio State University Press, 1990). See also Judith Hole and Ellen Levine, *Rebirth of Feminism* (New York: Quadrangle Books, 1971), 17–107.

15. Harrison, *On Account of Sex*, 225.

16. *American Women: The Report of the President's Commission on the Status of Women and Other Publications of the Commission* (New York: Charles Scribner's Sons, 1965), 65–66, 119.

17. Ibid., 66; see also 149–151; Harrison, *On Account of Sex*, 126–130.

18. *American Women*, 65–66, 57–58.

19. Ibid., 171–177; Harrison, *On Account of Sex*, 160–161, 184–187.

20. Betty Friedan, *The Feminine Mystique* (New York: Dell, 1963), 351, 361.

21. Zelman, *Women, Work, and National Policy*, 155–171; Harrison, *On Account of Sex*, 126–130; William H. Chafe, *Women and Equality: Changing Patterns in American Culture* (New York: Oxford University Press, 1977); Sara

Evans, *Personal Politics: The Roots of Women's Liberation in the Civil Rights Movement and the New Left* (New York: Alfred A. Knopf, 1979). For recent discussions of the sex-race analogy, see Myra Marx Ferree, "Equality and Autonomy: Feminist Politics in the United States and West Germany," in *The Women's Movements of the United States and Western Europe: Consciousness, Political Opportunity, and Public Policy,* ed. Mary Fainsod Katzenstein and Carol McClurg Mueller (Philadelphia: Temple University Press, 1987), 172–195; Sylvia Law, "Rethinking Sex and the Constitution," *University of Pennsylvania Law Review* 132(1984): 955–1040, esp. 963–966; and Deborah L. Rhode, *Gender and Justice: Sex Discrimination and the Law* (Cambridge: Harvard University Press, 1989), 86–92.

22. The notion of a liberation that transcends formal equality is characteristic of the women's liberation movements of the late 1960s and the 1970s, but it could also be felt in the supposedly more staid efforts of the midsixties. See, for example, the formulations in the National Organization for Women's 1966 Statement of Purpose, envisioning "a new movement toward true equality for all women . . . as part of the worldwide revolution of human rights"; Kraditor, *Up from the Pedestal,* 363–369. I am grateful to Cynthia Harrison for reminding me of this point.

23. *American Women,* 49. For the actual process by which Congress included the ban on sex discrimination in Title VII, see Zelman, *Women, Work, and National Policy,* 60–71; Harrison, *On Account of Sex,* 176–182; Donald Allen Robinson, "Two Movements in Pursuit of Equal Employment Opportunity," *Signs* 4(1978–1979): 413–433.

24. Pauli Murray and Mary Eastwood, "Jane Crow and the Law: Sex Discrimination and Title VII," *George Washington Law Review* 34(1965): 232–256, esp. 235.

25. Harrison, *On Account of Sex,* 186; Murray and Eastwood, "Jane Crow and the Law," 253, 251.

26. Harrison, *On Account of Sex,* 184; Zelman, *Women, Work, and National Policy,* 100–101; Babcock et al., *Sex Discrimination,* 261. For a summary of changes in state protective legislation after 1966, see Barbara A. Brown, Thomas I. Emerson, Gail Falk, and Ann E. Freedman, "The Equal Rights Amendment: A Constitutional Basis for Equal Rights for Women," *Yale Law Journal* 80(1971): 871–986, esp. 925. For the implementation of Title VII, see Zelman, *Women, Work, and National Policy,* 89–107, and Harrison, *On Account of Sex,* 185–191.

27. Harrison, *On Account of Sex,* 190. For the early years of the EEOC, see ibid., 187–191; Zelman, *Women, Work, and National Policy,* 89–99; and Hole and Levine, *Rebirth of Feminism,* 30–35.

28. Kraditor, *Up from the Pedestal,* 369. For the early years of the National Organization for Women, see Harrison, *On Account of Sex,* 192–209; Zelman, *Women, Work, and National Policy,* 104–123; and Hole and Levine, *Rebirth of Feminism,* 81–87.

29. For the legal framework developed by feminists in the early 1970s, see

Murray and Eastwood, "Jane Crow and the Law"; Brown et al., "Equal Rights Amendment"; Babcock et al., *Sex Discrimination*, 71–189; Wendy W. Williams, "Equality's Riddle: Pregnancy and the Equal Treatment/Special Treatment Debate," *New York University Review of Law and Social Change* 13(1984–1985): 325–380, esp. 329–332.

30. Brown et al., "Equal Rights Amendment," 889.
31. Ibid., 893.
32. On disparate impact analysis, see Brown et al., "Equal Rights Amendment," 898–900; Babcock et al., *Sex Discrimination*, 331–349; and Nancy S. Erickson, "Pregnancy Discrimination: An Analytical Approach," *Women's Rights Law Reporter* 5(1979): 83–105. The literacy test example was adjudicated in Gaston County v. United States, 395 U.S. 285 (1969), and the prison guard example as Dothard v. Rawlinson, 433 U.S. 321 (1977). In Griggs v. Duke Power Co., 401 U.S. 424 (1971), the Supreme Court rendered a unanimous decision placing the burden on employers to show that a neutral rule with discriminatory effect is a business necessity; in 1989 the Court gutted *Griggs's* effectiveness in *Wards Cove Packing Co. v. Atonio*, 490 U.S. 642 (1989).
33. Kraditor, *Up from the Pedestal*, 368; Elizabeth Duncan Koontz, "Childbirth and Child Rearing Leave: Job-Related Benefits," *New York Law Forum* 17(1971): 480–502, esp. 481.
34. Brown et al., "Equal Rights Amendment," 893, 894.
35. Citizens' Advisory Council on the Status of Women, *Women in 1970* (Washington, D.C.: GPO, 1971), 16; see also 14. Brown et al., "Equal Rights Amendment," 894. See also Murray and Eastwood, "Jane Crow and the Law," 240, 248 n.87.
36. Citizens' Advisory Council, *Women in 1970*, 4, 21. See also Brown et al., "Equal Rights Amendment," 929–932. Nancy Erickson notes that the effort to identify pregnancy and childbirth as conditions that ought be covered by temporary disability laws goes back at least to 1952, when women reformers in New York proposed to amend the 1950 state disability benefits law; Erickson, "Pregnancy Discrimination," 83 n.5.
37. Citizens' Advisory Council, *Women in 1970*, 4, 21–22.
38. Geraldine Leshin, *EEO Law: Impact on Fringe Benefits* (Los Angeles: UCLA Institute of Industrial Relations, 1979), 15.
39. Women's Bureau, U.S. Department of Labor, *1969 Handbook On Women Workers*, Bulletin 294 (Washington, D.C.: GPO, 1969), 54.
40. In Reed v. Reed, 404 U.S. 71 (1971), the Supreme Court struck down an Idaho law automatically preferring men to women as estate administrators. For a nontechnical overview of the long and frustrating campaign to bring women within contemporary norms of legal equality, see Susan Moller Okin, *Women in Western Political Thought* (Princeton: Princeton University Press, 1979), chap. 11.
41. "A written or unwritten employment policy or practice which excludes from employment applicants or employees because of pregnancy is in

prima facie violation of Title VII." EEOC Guidelines on Discrimination because of Sex, sec. 1604.10(a), *Federal Register*, vol. 37, no. 66, 6837 (5 April 1972), later codified in *Code of Federal Regulations*, vol. 29.

42. "Disabilities caused or contributed to by pregnancy, miscarriage, abortion, childbirth, and recovery therefrom are, for all job-related purposes, temporary disabilities and should be treated as such under any health or temporary disability insurance or sick leave plan available in connection with employment. Written and unwritten employment policies and practices involving matters such as the availability of extensions, the accrual of seniority and other benefits and privileges, reinstatement, and payment under any health or temporary disability insurance or sick leave plan, formal or informal, shall be applied to disability due to pregnancy or childbirth on the same terms and conditions as they are applied to other temporary disabilities." Ibid., sec. 1604.10(b).

43. "Where the termination of an employee who is temporarily disabled is caused by an employment policy under which insufficient or no leave is available, such a termination violates the act if it has a disparate impact on employees of one sex and is not justified by business necessity." Ibid., sec. 1604.10(c).

44. Sheila B. Kamerman, Alfred J. Kahn, and Paul Kingston, *Maternity Policies and Working Women* (New York: Columbia University Press, 1983); Williams, "Equality's Riddle"; Patricia Huckle, "The Womb Factor: Pregnancy Policies and Employment of Women," in *Women, Power and Policy*, ed. Ellen Boneparth (New York: Pergamon Press, 1982).

45. See also Kamerman et al., *Maternity Policies*, chap. 2, esp. 45–46; Virginia Sapiro, "The Gender Basis of American Social Policy," *Political Science Quarterly* 101, no. 1 (1986): 221–238.

46. Lenore J. Weitzman, *The Divorce Revolution: The Unexpected Social and Economic Consequences for Women and Children in America* (New York: Free Press, 1985), chap. 9 and *passim*; Terry Arendel, *Mothers and Divorce: Legal, Economic and Social Dilemmas* (Berkeley: University of California Press, 1986); Martha Albertson Fineman, *The Illusion of Equality: The Rhetoric and Reality of Divorce Reform* (Chicago: University of Chicago Press, 1991). See also Barbara Ehrenreich, *The Hearts of Men: American Dreams and the Flight from Commitment* (Garden City, N.Y.: Anchor Books, 1982).

5. Difference in Court

1. Justice Stewart authored the majority opinion of Geduldig v. Aiello, 417 U.S. 484 (1974), and Justice Rehnquist that of General Electric Company v. Gilbert, 429 U.S. 125 (1976). The two cases have been extensively discussed in the feminist legal literature; see, for succinct expositions, Wendy W. Williams, "Equality's Riddle: Pregnancy and the Equal Treatment/Special Treatment Debate," *New York University Review of Law and Social Change*

13(1984–1985): 325–380, esp. 335–345; and Herma Hill Kay, "Equality and Difference: The Case of Pregnancy," *Berkeley Women's Law Journal* 1, no. 1 (Fall 1985): 1–38, esp. 2–8.

2. *Gilbert,* cited in Williams, "Equality's Riddle," 345.
3. *Geduldig,* cited in Barbara Allen Babcock, Ann E. Freedman, Eleanor Holmes Norton, and Susan C. Ross, *Sex Discrimination and the Law: Causes and Remedies* (Boston: Little Brown, 1975), 318; *Gilbert,* cited in Ann C. Scales, "Towards a Feminist Jurisprudence," *Indiana Law Review* 56 (1980–1981): 375–444, esp. 400. As Scales notes, "This is not just a disagreement about the scope of Title VII: it is an open conflict of values about women's place, about substantive equality. It is significant to note that where the district court referred to women's 'biologically more burdensome place,' the Supreme Court replaced the term with 'differing roles.' The respective normative implications are unmistakable."
4. Joyce Gelb and Marian Lief Palley, *Women and Public Policies* (Princeton: Princeton University Press, 1982), chap. 7; Patricia Huckle, "The Womb Factor: Pregnancy Policies and Employment of Women," in *Women, Power and Policy,* ed. Ellen Boneparth (New York: Pergamon Press, 1982), 144–161; Peg Simpson, "A Victory for Women," *Civil Rights Digest* 2(Spring 1979): 13–21; Scales, "Towards a Feminist Jurisprudence," 401–410.
5. U.S. Congress, House, Committee on Education and Labor, *Prohibition of Sex Discrimination Based on Pregnancy,* 95th Cong., 2d sess. (1978), H. Rept. 95-948, 3.
6. Public Law 95-555, 92 Stat. 2076, adding subsection (k) to section 701 of Title VII. As part of Title VII, the Pregnancy Discrimination Act covers all public and private employers of fifteen or more persons, as well as public and private employment agencies, labor unions with fifteen or more members, and joint labor-management committees with apprenticeship or other training programs. Indian tribes are exempt as employers. Exceptions are permitted when sex is a bona fide occupational qualification that is reasonably necessary to the normal operation of the business.
7. House, Committee on Education and Labor, H. Rept. 95-948, 4.
8. U.S. Congress, Senate, Committee on Human Resources, *Amending Title VII, Civil Rights Act of 1964,* 95th Cong., 1st sess. (1977), S. Rept. 95-331, 4.
9. Geraldine Leshin, *EEO Law: Impact on Fringe Benefits* (Los Angeles: UCLA Institute of Industrial Relations, 1979), 14–15; EEOC Guidelines on Discrimination because of Sex, sec. 1604.10(b), *Federal Register,* vol. 37, no. 66, 6837 (5 April 1972), later codified in *Code of Federal Regulations,* vol. 29. For discussion of early EEOC policy, see chapter 4, above.
10. For an overview of the new maternity legislation, see Nancy E. Dowd, "Maternity Leave: Taking Sex Differences into Account," *Fordham Law Review* 54(1986): 699–765, esp. 720–735. Puerto Rico has had statutes mandating maternity leave since 1942. Other forms of regulation were also used to encourage employers to grant maternity leave. As of the mid-1980s, five states (Hawaii, Illinois, Kansas, New Hampshire, Washington) used regulatory provisions rather than legislation to provide job- and

benefit-protected pregnancy disability leaves. Seven states (Colorado, Iowa, Maine, Michigan, Ohio, Oklahoma, Rhode Island) did not affirmatively require maternity leaves but viewed failure to provide adequate maternity leave as a violation of state antidiscrimination law if such failure had an adverse impact on women.

11. "Interim Study by the Montana Subcommittee on the Judiciary," cited in Kay, "Equality and Difference," 10.

12. The Massachusetts, Connecticut, and Montana statutes were enacted between 1972 and 1975; those of California and Wisconsin in 1978 and 1981 respectively.

13. For accounts of the litigation over Montana's pregnancy leave law, see Kay, "Equality and Difference," 10–12, 15–19, or Williams, "Equality's Riddle," 327–328.

14. Miller-Wohl Co. v. Comm'r of Labor and Industry, 692 P.2d 1243 (Mont. 1984), cited in Kay, "Equality and Difference," 18. Kay observes that the court's opinion concerning the violation of Title VII is vague; ibid., 17 n.96.

15. The Montana legislature did not follow the court's recommendation.

16. For clear accounts of California Federal Savings and Loan Ass'n v. Guerra, 479 U.S. 272 (1987), see Kay, "Equality and Difference," 12–17, 19–20; and Lisa A. Rodensky, "*California Federal Savings and Loan Association v. Guerra*: Preferential Treatment and the Pregnancy Discrimination Act," *Harvard Women's Law Journal* 10(1987): 225–251, esp. 239–247.

17. The early stages of the debate are briefly described in Linda J. Krieger and Patricia N. Cooney, "The Miller-Wohl Controversy: Equal Treatment, Positive Action and the Meaning of Women's Equality," *Golden Gate University Law Review* 13, no. 3 (Summer 1983): 513–572, esp. 515–516. Although the debate is generally characterized as opposing special treatment to equal treatment, proponents on each side noted the diversity of views within their camp and sometimes rejected the terminology. Equal-treatment advocates were generally more comfortable with their label; for consideration of an alternative formulation, see the discussion in Nadine Taub and Wendy W. Williams, "Will Equality Require More Than Assimilation, Accommodation or Separation from the Existing Social Structure?" *Rutgers Law Review* 37(1985): 825–844. Some, but not all, proponents of so-called special treatment rejected the term as a derisive caricature; see, for example, Ruth Colker, "The Anti-Subordination Principle: Applications," *Wisconsin Women's Law Journal* 3(1987): 62.

I generally retain the special-treatment/equal-treatment terminology in this chapter's exposition of the debate, even though neither position is fully captured by its respective label. Special can convey, it seems to me, the sense of difference, affirmatively understood, that feminists want to endorse. Equal may too often be heard to mean "same" or "identical," however, and the equal-treatment perspective might more appropriately be called gender-neutral, although that term also carries connotations of liberal individualism and the denial of difference. I adopted the term gender-neutral rather than equal in the analytical portions of "Debating Difference: Feminism, Pregnancy, and the Workplace," *Feminist Studies* 16(1990): 9–32. I think now, however, that we must retain equality locutions despite their ambiguities and overlays of meaning.

18. Brief for amici curiae American Civil Liberties Union et al., *California Federal Savings and Loan Association v. Guerra,* No. 85-494, U.S. Supreme Court, pp. A2–A3; see also Tamar Lewin, "Pregnancy-Leave Suit Has Divided Feminists," *New York Times,* 28 June 1986, 52.

19. Two articles opened the debate: Wendy Williams, "The Equality Crisis: Some Reflections on Culture, Courts and Feminism," *Women's Rights Law Reporter* 7, no. 3 (Spring 1982): 175–200; Krieger and Cooney, "Miller-Wohl Controversy." See also Scales, "Towards a Feminist Jurisprudence"; and Elizabeth Wolgast, *Equality and the Rights of Women* (Ithaca, N.Y.: Cornell University Press, 1980). The issues were presciently anticipated in Mary C. Segers, "Equality, Public Policy and Relevant Sex Differences," *Polity* 11(1979): 319–339.

20. Krieger and Cooney, "Miller-Wohl Controversy," 533.

21. Briefs for amici curiae Equal Rights Advocates et al., for amici curiae Coalition for Reproductive Equality in the Workplace et al., for amici curiae American Civil Liberties Union et al., and for amici curiae National Organization for Women et al., *California Federal Savings and Loan Association v. Guerra,* No. 85-494, U.S. Supreme Court. I am grateful to Joan Bertin of the ACLU for giving me access to the briefs submitted to the Supreme Court in *California Federal.*

22. This has been a fairly general impression. See, for example, Sylvia Ann Hewlett, *A Lesser Life: The Myth of Women's Liberation in America* (New York: William Morrow, 1986), 144–146; or Mary Ann Mason, *The Equality Trap* (New York: Simon and Schuster, 1988), 42–43, 179.

23. Brief for ACLU, 33–34.

24. Brief for NOW, 11.

25. Ibid., 17.

26. Brief for Equal Rights Advocates, 5.

27. Kay, "Equality and Difference," 22; Kay participated in the drafting of the brief for Equal Rights Advocates. Episodic analysis uses a narrow notion of "reproductive behavior" in order to exclude workers who become parents through means other than their own procreative activity.

28. Brief for Equal Rights Advocates, 6, 7.

29. Ibid., 22–23. Proponents in the debate have sharply distinct understandings of disparate impact analysis, differences that cannot easily be resolved.

30. Brief for CREW, 21.

31. Ibid., 8–9, citing Carey v. Population Services International, 431 U.S. 678 (1977).

32. Ibid., 44–45. CREW's suggestion that the California statute was intended to enhance procreative choice seems suspect. See, for example, the discussion of the legislative history in brief for Respondents, *California Federal*

Savings and Loan Association v. Guerra, No. 85-494, U.S. Supreme Court; and Susan M. Damplo, *"California Federal Savings and Loan Ass'n v. Guerra* and the Feminist Debate: Sameness/Difference Assumptions about Pregnancy in the Workplace," seminar paper, Georgetown University Law Center, 1987.

33. Brief for CREW, 37.
34. Krieger and Cooney, "Miller-Wohl Controversy," 535. Kay, "Equality and Difference," 23 n.125. Christine A. Littleton, "Equality and Feminist Legal Theory," *University of Pittsburgh Law Review* 48(1987): 1043–1059, esp. 1055. In her 1977 testimony on the Pregnancy Discrimination Act, Wendy Williams also acknowledged the possibility of an argument based on procreative rights; U.S. Congress, Senate, Subcommittee on Labor of the Committee on Human Resources, *Discrimination on the Basis of Pregnancy, 1977,* 95th Cong., 1st sess., 26, 27, 29 April 1977, 115, 137.
35. Brief for Respondents. The oral arguments in the case are recorded in "Proceedings before the Supreme Court of the United States, in California Federal Savings and Loan Association v. Guerra, No. 85-494, October 8, 1986," official transcript, Alderson Reporting Company, Washington, D.C., 1986.
36. Brief for Respondents, 17. From the opposing position, Theodore Olson, representing California Federal Savings before the Supreme Court, also recalled episodic analysis when he noted that the case involved "the right to engage in reproductive activity, and not lose your job"; "Proceedings," 8.
37. "Proceedings," 39–40; see also 42, where Johnston explicitly refers to the right to procreation.
38. Brief for Respondents, 21 n.20; "Proceedings," 37, 47.
39. California Federal, 286, 285. Marshall here quotes the decision by the Ninth Circuit Court of Appeals. The briefs by the parties and the amici varied widely in their intepretation of the House and Senate record on the Pregnancy Discrimination Act. In my view, Marshall is correct that a consistent congressional intent with respect to preferential treatment of pregnancy cannot be read out of the legislative history, which focused on discriminatorily unfavorable treatment. See also the discussion in Rodensky, *"California Federal Savings and Loan Association v. Guerra."*
40. California Federal, 290, 285 n.17.
41. Ibid., 291, 291–292.
42. Ibid., 289.
43. See, for example, Stuart Taylor, Jr., "Job Rights Backed in Pregnancy Case," *New York Times,* 4 January 1987, A1 and B10; editorial, *New York Times,* 18 January 1987; Amy Wilentz, "Garland's Bouquet: A Landmark Supreme Court Ruling Supports Pregnancy Leave," *Time,* 26 January 1987, 14–15; Aric Press, "A New Family Issue," *Newsweek,* 26 January 1987, 22–24.
44. *California Federal,* dissent by Justice White, joined by Justices Rehnquist and Powell, 297, 302. Separate concurring opinion by Justice Scalia, 296;

for Scalia, the case turns solely on the question of preemption, not on any substantive issues. Nancy E. Dodd does not distinguish the dissenters' opinion from Marshall's when she claims "the Supreme Court framed the issue as whether 'preferential treatment' was permissible"; "Work and Family: The Gender Paradox and the Limitations of Discrimination Analysis in Restructuring the Workplace," *Harvard Civil Rights–Civil Liberties Law Review* 24(1989): 79–172, esp. 124 n.154.

6. Questioning Equality

1. Carol Smart, *Feminism and the Power of Law* (London: Routledge, 1989); Deborah L. Rhode, *Justice and Gender: Sex Discrimination and the Law* (Cambridge: Harvard University Press, 1989); Martha Albertson Fineman and Nancy Sweet Thomadsen, eds., *At the Boundaries of Law: Feminism and Legal Theory* (New York: Routledge, 1991); Ava Baron, "Feminist Legal Strategies: The Powers of Difference," in *Analyzing Gender: A Handbook of Social Science Research,* ed. Beth Hess and Myra Marx Ferree (Newbury Park, Calif.: Sage Publications, 1987), 474–503.
2. Jana Sawicki and Iris Young, "Issues of Difference in Feminist Philosophy," *Newsletter on Feminism and Philosophy* (American Philosophical Association) April 1988, 13–17; Zillah R. Eisenstein, "Developing Feminist Theory: Sexually Particular, Equal and Free," chap. 10 in her *Feminism and Sexual Equality: Crisis in Liberal America* (New York: Monthly Review, 1984), 231–256; idem, *The Female Body and the Law* (Berkeley: University of California Press, 1988); Susan Moller Okin, *Justice, Gender, and the Family* (New York: Basic Books, 1990); Mary E. Hawkesworth, *Beyond Oppression: Feminist Theory and Political Strategy* (New York: Continuum, 1990); Iris Marion Young, *Justice and the Politics of Difference* (Princeton: Princeton University Press, 1990).
3. Alice Kessler-Harris, "The Debate over Equality for Women in the Work Place: Recognizing Differences," *Women and Work: An Annual Review* 1(1985): 141–161; idem, *A Woman's Wage: Historical Meanings and Social Consequences* (Louisville: University Press of Kentucky, 1990); Joan Wallach Scott, *Gender and the Politics of History* (New York: Columbia University Press, 1988).
4. Wendy Chavkin, "Walking a Tightrope: Pregnancy, Parenting, and Work," in *Double Exposure: Women's Health Hazards on the Job and at Home,* ed. Wendy Chavkin (New York: Monthly Review Press, 1984), 196–213; Ruth Sidel, *Women and Children Last: The Plight of Poor Women in Affluent America* (New York: Viking Penguin, 1986); Mary Ann Mason, *The Equality Trap* (New York: Simon and Schuster, 1988). For a more circumspect discussion of the relevance of the European experience for U.S. public policy, see Nancy E. Dowd, "Envisioning Work and Family: A Critical Perspective on International Models," *Harvard Journal on Legislation* 26(1989): 311–348.

5. For discussion of the socialist critique of equality as merely bourgeois, see Anne Phillips, "Introduction," in *Feminism and Equality*, ed. Anne Phillips (New York: New York University Press, 1987), 1–23.

6. Nadine Taub and Wendy W. Williams, "Will Equality Require More Than Assimilation, Accommodation or Separation from the Existing Social Structure?" *Rutgers Law Review* 37(1985): 825–844, esp. 835–836.

7. Chavkin, "Walking a Tightrope," 202.

8. Instances of the assumption that the PDA defines pregnancy as a disability, and of the substitution of Disability for Discrimination in its name, are easy to find, even among those who support the equal-treatment strategy: Joyce Gelb and Marian Lief Palley, *Women and Public Policies* (Princeton: Princeton University Press, 1982), chap. 7, *passim* (error corrected in the 2d ed.); Sheila B. Kamerman, Alfred J. Kahn, and Paul Kingston, *Maternity Policies and Working Women* (New York: Columbia University Press, 1983), 41, 46, 142, 144–147, 155; Patricia Schroeder, "Parental Leave: The Need for a Federal Policy," in *The Parental Leave Crisis: Toward a National Policy*, ed. Edward F. Zigler and Meryl Frank (New Haven: Yale University Press, 1988), 326–332; Eisenstein, *Female Body and the Law*, 99–100; Carol Lee Bacchi, *Same Difference: Feminism and Sexual Differences* (Sydney, Australia: Allen and Unwin, 1990), 114.

9. EEOC Guidelines on Discrimination because of Sex, sec. 1604.10(b), *Federal Register*, vol. 37, no. 66 (5 April 1972), later codified in *Code of Federal Regulations*, vol. 29.

10. Wendy W. Williams, "Equality's Riddle: Pregnancy and the Equal Treatment/Special Treatment Debate," *New York University Review of Law and Social Change* 13(1984–1985): 325–380, esp. 363; brief for amici curiae American Civil Liberties Union et al., *California Federal Savings and Loan Association v. Guerra*, No. 85-494, U.S. Supreme Court, 5.

11. I have not found such rhetoric openly advanced by feminists in the debate, but it is sometimes voiced in conversation and lurks in the background of the controversy. As discussed above in chapters 2 and 3, emphasis on the link between motherhood and future generations is an old theme, embraced in varying ways by reformers, socialists, and dominant ideology. Contemporary feminists who would invoke this theme need to pay attention to the context within which the claim is made. For a thoughtful discussion of the politics of motherhood and reproduction, see Rosalind Pollack Petchesky, *Abortion and Woman's Choice: The State, Sexuality, and Reproductive Freedom* (New York: Longman, 1984).

12. Hugo Adam Bedau, "Egalitarianism and the Idea of Equality," in *Equality: Nomos IX*, ed. J. Roland Pennock and John W. Chapman (New York: Atherton Press, 1967), 3–27, esp. 8. For helpful explorations of the nature of equality, see ibid.; Bernard Williams, "The Idea of Equality," in *Philosophy, Politics and Society*, 2d series, ed. Peter Laslett and W. G. Runciman (Oxford: Blackwell, 1962), 110–131; Bette Novit Evans, "Thinking Clearly about Equality: Conceptual Premises and Why They Make a Difference," in *Elusive Equality: Liberalism, Affirmative Action, and Social Change in Amer-*

ica, ed. James C. Foster and Mary C. Segers (Port Washington, N.Y.: Associated Faculty Press, 1983), 101–114. See also Deborah L. Rhode, "Feminist Perspectives on Legal Ideology," in *What Is Feminism?* ed. Juliet Mitchell and Ann Oakley (New York: Pantheon, 1986), 151–160. For an early posing of the questions surrounding equality and equal treatment, see Karl Marx, *Critique of the Gotha Programme*, ed. C. P. Dutt (New York: International Publishers, 1970).

7. The Equality Framework Extended

1. Reva B. Siegel, "Employment Equality under the Pregnancy Discrimination Act of 1978," *Yale Law Journal* 94(1985): 929–956, esp. 933.
2. For the implication that the Pregnancy Discrimination Act harms poor and working-class women, see, for example, Linda J. Krieger and Patricia N. Cooney, "The Miller-Wohl Controversy: Equal Treatment, Positive Action and the Meaning of Women's Equality," *Golden Gate University Law Review* 13(1983): 513–572, esp. 545–546; Ann C. Scales, "Towards a Feminist Jurisprudence," *Indiana Law Journal* 56, no. 3 (1980–1981): 375–444, esp. 427; Siegel, "Employment Equality under the Pregnancy Discrimination Act," 932–933; and Wendy Chavkin, "Walking a Tightrope: Pregnancy, Parenting, and Work," in *Double Exposure: Women's Health Hazards on the Job and at Home*, ed. Wendy Chavkin (New York: Monthly Review Press, 1984), 196–213. For similar charges against the equal-treatment approach in other areas, see Martha Fineman, "Illusive Equality: On Weitzman's *Divorce Revolution*," *American Bar Foundation Research Journal* (1986): 781–790; or Nancy E. Dowd, "Work and Family: The Gender Paradox and the Limitations of Discrimination Analysis in Restructuring the Workplace," *Harvard Civil Rights–Civil Liberties Lew Review* 24(1989): 79–172, esp. 153, 170–171.
3. Janet Witte Burgstahler, "The Impact of the Pregnancy Discrimination Act of 1978 on Employee Health Insurance Benefit Levels," Ph.D. diss., University of Iowa, 1984. For the pre-PDA norms, see Dorothy R. Kittner, "Maternity Benefits Available to Most Health Plan Participants," *Monthly Labor Review* 101(1978): 53–56; despite the article's title, it documents that before the PDA, most workers in plans with maternity benefits "could anticipate less protection for normal delivery pregnancy expenses than for expenses due to other reasons."
4. Rachel Benson Gold and Asta M. Kenney, "Paying for Maternity Care," *Family Planning Perspectives* 17(1985) 103–111, esp. 106; *The Financing of Maternity Care in the United States* (New York: Alan Guttmacher Institute, 1987), 252.
5. For example, the firms of the Midwest study covered pregnancy only if conception occurred while the insured was an employee; after termination, medical benefits for pregnancy-related conditions were extended for

nine months. Thus, a woman worker was not covered for a preexisting pregnancy but could plan on retaining benefits after she stopped work during or at the end of her pregnancy. Once the PDA was in effect, the companies revised their benefit plans to make treatment of pregnancy consistent with that of other covered conditions. Preexisting pregnancy was covered if no treatment for a pregnancy-related condition had occurred in the ninety days prior to becoming insured. After termination, benefits were now extended for only three months. These firms are typical. Kittner, "Maternity Benefits," 54. Burgstahler, "Impact of the PDA," 69–74; similar changes are reported in "The Design of Major Medical Insurance," *EBPR Research Reports* 327.5 (June 1980): 7–8.

6. *The Financing of Maternity Care*, 252–253, 273–274. On coverage in small firms compared to larger ones, see also "Medical and Family Leave: Benefits Available to Female Workers in the United States" (March 1987) and "Accommodating Pregnancy in the Workplace" (November 1987), reporting data from the Mothers in the Workplace Study conducted by the Center for the Child, National Council of Jewish Women, New York, N.Y.

7. Roberta M. Spalter-Roth, Claudia Withers, and Sheila R. Gibbs, *Improving Employment Opportunities for Women Workers: An Assessment of the Ten Year Economic and Legal Impact of the Pregnancy Discrimination Act* (Washington, D.C.: Institute for Women's Policy Research, 1990), 14–15.

8. Carol C. McDonough and Linda H. Kistler, "An Evaluation of the Costs of Pregnancy Disability," *Employee Benefits Journal* 6, no. 4 (December 1981): 7–11f.; Kathryn McIntyre, "Pregnancy Law Hikes Short-Term Disability Costs," *Business Insurance*, 8 February 1982, p. 1, reporting a survey of sixty-eight companies.

9. Spalter-Roth et al., *Improving Employment Opportunities for Women Workers*, 17–18.

10. In Rhode Island, a lawsuit was necessary to force the legislature to amend its paid temporary disability statute to cover pregnancy on a basis of equality. Daniel N. Price, "Cash Benefits for Short-Term Sickness, 1948–81," *Social Security Bulletin* 47, no. 8 (August 1984): 23–38, esp. 37–38; brief for amici curiae National Organization for Women et al., *California Federal Savings and Loan Association v. Guerra*, No. 85-494, U.S. Supreme Court, 25–26; Sheila B. Kamerman, Alfred J. Kahn, and Paul Kingston, *Maternity Policies and Working Women* (New York: Columbia University Press, 1983), 78, 82; Elizabeth Koontz, "Childbirth and Child Rearing Leave: Job-Related Benefits," *New York Law Forum* 17 (1971): 480–502, esp. 484–485. Some of the rise in maternity costs could be due to a relative increase in the numbers of women of childbearing age in the labor force.

11. Spalter-Roth et al., *Improving Employment Opportunities for Women Workers*, 41.

12. Koontz, "Childbirth and Child Rearing Leave," 502; Wendy W. Williams, "Equality's Riddle: Pregnancy and the Equal Treatment/Special Treatment Debate," *New York University Review of Law and Social Change* 13 (1984–1985): 325–380, esp. 350, n. 102.

13. U.S. Congress, House, Subcommittee on Labor-Management Relations of the Committee on Education and Labor, *Hearing on H.R. 770, The Family and Medical Leave Act of 1989*, 101st Cong., 1st sess., 7 February 1989, 5.

14. Early versions of the bill used different terminology: disability leave for medical leave, and parental leave for family leave. For a detailed account of the origins and development of the federal bill, see Anne L. Radigan, *Concept and Compromise: The Evolution of Family Leave Legislation in the U.S. Congress* (Washington, D.C.: Women's Research and Education Institute, 1988). Donna R. Lenhoff and Sylvia M. Becker summarize the bill's trajectory through the House and Senate in "Family and Medical Leave Legislation in the States: Toward a Comprehensive Approach," *Harvard Journal on Legislation* 26(1989): 403–463, esp. 412–415. On the term parenting, see Susan Rae Peterson, "Against 'Parenting,' " in *Mothering: Essays in Feminist Theory*, ed. Joyce Trebilcot (Totowa, N.J.: Rowman and Allanheld, 1984), 62–69, which argues that such gender-neutral locutions disguise the fact that it is still mothers who do most of the work.

15. U.S. Congress, House, "Parental and Disability Leave Act of 1985," H.R. 2020. U.S. Congress, House and Senate, "Parental and Medical Leave Act of 1986," H.R. 4300 and S. 2278. U.S. Congress, House, "Family and Medical Leave Act of 1987," H.R. 925; Senate, "Parental and Medical Leave Act of 1987," S. 249. U.S. Congress, House, "Family and Medical Leave Act of 1988," H.R. 925; Senate, "Parental and Medical Leave Act of 1988," S. 2488. U.S. Congress, House and Senate, "Family and Medical Leave Act of 1989," H.R. 770 and S. 345.

16. U.S. Congress, House, Subcommittee on Civil Service and Subcommittee on Compensation and Employee Benefits of the Committee on Post Office and Civil Service, *Family and Medical Leave Act of 1987*, 100th Cong., 1st sess., 2 April 1987, 31. U.S. Congress, House, Subcommittee on Labor-Management Relations and Subcommittee on Labor Standards of the Committee on Education and Labor, *Family and Medical Leave Act of 1987*, 100th Cong., 1st sess., 25 February and 5 March 1987, 219.

17. Zillah R. Eisenstein, *The Female Body and the Law* (Berkeley: University of California Press, 1988), 216. Martha Minow, "Adjudicating Difference: Conflicts among Feminist Lawyers," in *Conflicts in Feminism*, ed. Marianne Hirsch and Evelyn Fox Keller (New York: Routledge, 1990), 149–163, esp. 155. See also Dowd, "Work and Family," 122–128; and Carol Lee Bacchi, *Same Difference: Feminism and Sexual Difference* (Sydney, Australia: Allen and Unwin, 1990), 119.

18. House, Education and Labor, *Family and Medical Leave Act of 1987*, 25 February and 5 March 1987, 13.

19. House, Post Office and Civil Service, *Family and Medical Leave Act of 1987*, 2 April 1987, 37.

20. Legislators do not usually pay attention to the kinds of costs—to new mothers, to parents of sick children, to family members caring for elderly parents, to workers who miss work because of their own illness,

to taxpayers who must often make up the difference, etc.—documented in Roberta M. Spalter-Roth and Heidi Hartmann, *Unnecessary Losses: Costs to Americans of the Lack of Family and Medical Leave* (Washington, D.C.: Institute for Women's Policy Research, 1988).

21. For information on state family and medical leave legislation, see Lenhoff and Becker, "Family and Medical Leave Legislation in the States." See also the chart "State Laws and Regulations Guaranteeing Employees Their Jobs after Family and Medical Leaves," published in early 1990 by the Women's Legal Defense Fund, Washington, D.C.

22. Florida mandates parental leave to adoptive parents. Female-specific parental leave may be unconstitutional; see Judith L. Lichtman, Donna R. Lenhoff, and Helen Norton, " 'Mothers Only' Leave Laws Are Unconstitutional," manuscript, Women's Legal Defense Fund, March 1990.

23. House, Education and Labor, *Family and Medical Leave Act of 1987*, 25 February and 5 March 1987, 41. U.S. Congress, Senate, Committee on Labor and Human Resources, *Parental and Medical Leave Act of 1988*, 100th Cong., 2d sess. (1988), S. Rept. 100-447, 57, 69.

24. U.S. Congress, Senate, Subcommittee on Labor of the Committee on Human Resources, *Discrimination on the Basis of Pregnancy, 1977*, 95th Cong., 1st sess., 26, 27, 29 April 1977, 39–45, 80–84, 397–419.

8. Difference as Strategy

1. For good overviews of the situation of women workers, see Alice Kessler-Harris, *Out to Work: A History of Wage-Earning Work in the United States* (New York: Oxford University Press, 1982), chaps. 5, 6, and 11; Jacqueline Jones, *Labor of Love, Labor of Sorrow: Black Women, Work, and the Family from Slavery to the Present* (New York: Vintage, 1986), chaps. 3–5; Mary Ryan, *Womanhood in America* (New York: Franklin Watts, 1979), chap. 4. For the contemporary statistics in this and the following paragraph, see Women's Bureau, U.S. Department of Labor, *1969 Handbook on Women Workers*, Bulletin 294 (Washington, D.C.: GPO, 1969); idem, *Time of Change: 1983 Handbook on Women Workers*, Bulletin 298 (Washington, D.C.: GPO, 1983); Bureau of Labor Statistics, U.S. Department of Labor, "Half of Mothers with Children under 3 Now in Labor Force," News Release USDL 86-345, 20 August 1986; idem, "Labor Force Participation Unchanged among Mothers with Young Children," News Release USDL 88-431, 7 September 1988; Women's Bureau, U.S. Department of Labor, "Working Mothers and Their Children," *Facts on Working Women*, No. 89-3, August 1989; Bureau of Labor Statistics, U.S. Department of Labor, "Employment in Perspective: Women in the Labor Force," Report 801, Fourth Quarter 1990; Women's Bureau, U.S. Department of Labor, "Earnings Differences between Women and Men," *Facts on Working Women*, No. 90-3, October 1990; *Employment and Earnings* 38, no. 1 (January 1992): 228.

2. *Muller v. Oregon*, 208 U.S. 412 (1908).
3. *West Coast Hotel Co. v. Parrish*, 300 U.S. 379 (1937), cited in Judith A. Baer, *Chains of Protection: The Judicial Response to Women's Labor Legislation* (Westport, Conn.: Greenwood Press, 1978), 99. For the significance of the Supreme Court's shift on freedom of contract, see ibid., 91–101; Alice Kessler-Harris, "The Debate over Equality for Women in the Work Place: Recognizing Differences," *Women and Work: An Annual Review* 1(1985): 141–161; and idem, *A Woman's Wage: Historical Meanings and Social Consequences* (Lexington: University Press of Kentucky, 1990).
4. Cited in Kessler-Harris, "Debate over Equality," 151. See also Barbara Sicherman, *Alice Hamilton: A Life in Letters* (Cambridge: Harvard University Press, 1984), 384–385. Unlike Hamilton, most labor and reform activists refused to abandon their pro-protection and anti-ERA stance. Some persisted in their opposition to equal rights legislation into the early 1970s.
5. Carol Smart, *Feminism and the Power of Law* (London: Routledge, 1989), 136–137. For an exception to the general disinterest in practical questions of strategy, see Diana Majury, "Strategizing in Equality," *Wisconsin Women's Law Journal* 3(1987): 168–187.
6. Carol McClurg Mueller, "Collective Consciousness, Identity Transformation, and the Rise of Women in Public Office in the United States," in *The Women's Movements of the United States and Western Europe: Consciousness, Political Opportunity, and Public Policy*, ed. Mary Fainsod Katzenstein and Carol McClurg Mueller (Philadelphia: Temple University Press, 1987), 89–108.
7. Charlotte Bunch, "The Reform Tool Kit" (1977), in *Passionate Politics: Feminist Theory in Action* (New York: St. Martin's Press, 1987), 103–117.
8. Elizabeth M. Schneider, "The Dialectic of Rights and Politics: Perspectives from the Women's Movement," *New York University Law Review* 61(1986): 589–652, esp. 590, 650–651, 642. Schneider's arguments are directed toward the movement known as Critical Legal Studies (CLS).
9. Patricia J. Williams, "Alchemical Notes: Reconstructing Ideals from Deconstructed Rights," *Harvard Civil Rights–Civil Liberties Law Review* 22(1987): 401–433, esp. 416, 431, 430. See also Kimberle Williams Crenshaw, "Race, Reform, and Retrenchment: Transformation and Legitimation in Antidiscrimination Law," *Harvard Law Review* 101(1988): 1331–1387; and Judy Scales-Trent, "Black Women and the Constitution: Finding Our Place, Asserting Our Rights," *Harvard Civil Rights–Civil Liberties Law Review* 24(1989): 9–44. Williams, Crenshaw, and Scales-Trent, like Schneider, are responding to the work of CLS scholars.
10. "Interim Study by the Montana Subcommittee on Judiciary," cited in Herma Hill Kay, "Equality and Difference: The Case of Pregnancy," *Berkeley Women's Law Journal* 1(Fall 1985): 1–38, esp. 10.
11. For the text of the California legislation, see Herma Hill Kay, "Equality and Difference," 12 n.69. For its history, see brief for amici curiae National Organization for Women et al., *California Federal Savings and Loan*

Association v. Guerra, No. 85-494, U.S. Supreme Court, 14–17; and Susan M. Damplo, *"California Federal Savings and Loan Ass'n. v. Guerra* and the Feminist Debate: Sameness/Difference Assumptions about Pregnancy in the Workplace," manuscript, Georgetown University Law Center, 1987.

12. The California statute, enacted while the PDA was under consideration in Congress, stipulates that only its pregnancy disability leave provision applies also to the larger employers who are subject to Title VII of the 1964 Civil Rights Act.

13. Recent efforts to enact family and medical leave legislation at the state level have followed just such tortuous paths. The evolution of a parental leave bill introduced in Oregon in 1987 provides an interesting instance of legislative good intentions combined with strategic bewilderment. Conceived as a gender-neutral measure, it was transformed in committee to a gender-specific (and probably unconstitutional) maternity leave bill. Legislators who supported it were pleased they had achieved something for the good of mothers, and few perceived the significance of the alteration. Only strenuous efforts on the part of women's group lobbyists persuaded them to return the measure to gender neutrality. Private correspondance and telephone conversations, Oregon House of Representatives, August 1987.

14. This argument was used, as discussed above in chapter 5, in brief for amici curiae Coalition for Reproductive Equality in the Workplace et al., *California Federal Savings and Loan Association v. Guerra,* No. 85-494, U.S. Supreme Court; see also Christine A. Littleton, "Equality and Feminist Legal Theory," *University of Pittsburgh Law Review* 48(1987): 1043–1059.

9. Beyond Equality versus Difference

1. The skepticism voiced by many feminists concerning the results of equality legislation, seems to me especially on the economic front, too negative. As with any reform, equality legislation can only be evaluated through a complex multileveled analysis, which includes the perspective of subordinate groups; see chapter 8. The particular question of women's economic situation needs to be analyzed in the context of the general economic deterioration of the past two decades; my guess is that without equality legislation, women today would be even worse off than they are.

2. Wendy W. Williams, "Notes from a First Generation," *University of Chicago Legal Forum* (1989): 99–113, esp. 108.

3. Zillah Eisenstein pioneered the discussion of the radical possibilities within liberal feminism; see *The Radical Future of Liberal Feminism* (New York: Longman, 1981); and idem, *Feminism and Sexual Equality: Crisis in Liberal America* (New York: Monthly Review, 1984). See also Juliet Mitchell, "Women and Equality," in *The Rights and Wrongs of Women,* ed. Juliet Mitchell and Ann Oakley (Harmondsworth, England: Penguin, 1976),

379–399. For an overview of feminist critiques of liberalism, see Anne Phillips, "Introduction," in *Feminism and Equality*, ed. Anne Phillips (New York: New York University Press, 1987), 1–23.

4. For early attempts to disentangle various positions within the poles of the debate, see Ann C. Scales, "Towards a Feminist Jurisprudence," *Indiana Law Review* 56(1980–1981): 375–444; Sylvia Law, "Rethinking Sex and the Constitution," *University of Pennsylvania Law Review* 132 (1984): 955–1040; Herma Hill Kay, "Models of Equality," *University of Illinois Law Review* (1985): 39–88. Political philosophers and social scientists likewise discuss a range of positions covered by the notion of equality; early discussions within second-wave feminism include Alice S. Rossi, "Sex Equality: The Beginning of Ideology," *The Humanist* 29(September–October 1969): 3–6f.; Jean Bethke Elshtain, "The Feminist Movement and the Question of Equality," *Polity* 7(1975): 452–477; Mary C. Segers, "Equality, Public Policy and Relevant Sex Differences," *Polity* 11(1979): 319–339.

5. Christine Littleton, "Reconstructing Sexual Equality," *California Law Review* 75(1987): 1279–1337, esp. 1287.

6. Littleton suggests that male legal scholars are sometimes drawn to assimilationist theories, perhaps because "it appears to offer [them] a share in the feminist enterprise"; "Reconstructing Sexual Equality," 1294–1295. See, for example, Richard A. Wasserstrom, "Racism, Sexism, and Preferential Treatment: An Approach to the Topics," *UCLA Law Review* 24(1977): 581–621.

7. Wendy W. Williams, "Equality's Riddle: Pregnancy and the Equal Treatment/Special Treatment Debate," *New York University Review of Law and Social Change* 13(1984–1985): 325–380, esp. 368, 363 (citations in text); see also 367, 369. Nadine Taub and Wendy W. Williams, "Will Equality Require More Than Assimilation, Accommodation or Separation from the Existing Social Structure?" *Rutgers Law Review* 37(1985): 825–844, esp. 836, 838. Littleton uses the example of the adjustable lecture podium to illustrate her claim that restructuring flows only from her ˉequality-as-acceptance approach; "Reconstructing Sexual Equality," 1314.

8. Taub and Williams, "Will Equality Require More," 838.

9. Kathryn Pauly Morgan, "Androgyny: A Conceptual Critique," *Social Theory and Practice* 8(1982): 245–283; Alison M. Jaggar, *Feminist Politics and Human Nature* (Totowa, NJ: Rowan and Allanheld, 1983), 38–39, 85–88; Ellen Carol Dubois, Gail Paradise Kelly, Elizabeth Lapovsky Kennedy, Carolyn W. Korsmeyer, and Lillian S. Robinson, *Feminist Scholarship: Kindling in the Groves of Academe* (Urbana: University of Illinois Press, 1985), 129; Deborah L. Rhode, *Justice and Gender: Sex Discrimination and the Law* (Cambridge: Harvard University Press, 1989), 313–315.

10. Lucinda M. Finley, "Transcending Equality Theory: A Way Out of the Maternity and the Workplace Debate," *Columbia Law Review* 86(1986): 1118–1182, esp. 1143. Some asymmetrists discuss several variants of the equal-treatment perspective, all of which are said to reduce to the same disadvantaging demand that women conform to standards developed for

men. See, for example, Littleton's discussion of the symmetrical models in "Reconstructing Sexual Equality," 1291–1295.

11. Elizabeth Wolgast, *Equality and the Rights of Women* (Ithaca, N.Y.: Cornell University Press, 1980), 14, 42, 129.

12. Scales, "Towards a Feminist Jurisprudence," 433. Scales calls the special-rights position "bivalence," but this is probably a misapplication of Wolgast's use of the term; see Wolgast, *Equality and the Rights of Women*, 16. Andrew Weissman utilizes a special rights model in "Sexual Equality under the Pregnancy Discrimination Act," *Columbia Law Review* 83(1983): 690–726.

13. Catharine A. MacKinnon, *Feminism Unmodified: Discourses on Life and Law* (Cambridge: Harvard University Press, 1987), 40; Isabel Marcus, Paul J. Spiegelman, et al., "Feminist Discourse, Moral Values, and the Law—A Conversation," *Buffalo Law Review* 34(1985), 11–87, esp. 21. Among other dominance analyses, see Kathleen A. Lahey, "Feminist Theories of (In)Equality," *Wisconsin Women's Law Journal* 3(1987): 5–28; and Ruth Colker, "The Anti-Subordination Principle: Applications," *Wisconsin Women's Law Journal* 3(1987): 59–80.

14. Rhode, *Justice and Gender,* 83. See also Carol Smart, *Feminism and the Power of Law* (London: Routledge, 1989), 75–82, 120–122, 133–137.

15. Rhode, *Justice and Gender,* 4 and *passim*. Rhode does not distinguish between the accommodation and acceptance perspectives within what she terms the disadvantage framework.

16. Scales, "Towards a Feminist Jurisprudence," 435; Scales abandons accommodationism in favor of MacKinnon's dominance perspective in "The Emergence of Feminist Jurisprudence: An Essay," *Yale Law Journal* 95 (1986): 1373–1403. Law, "Rethinking Sex and the Constitution," 1031. Kay, "Models of Equality"; and idem, "Equality and Difference: The Case of Pregnancy," *Berkeley Women's Law Journal* 1(1985): 1–38; for a more detailed discussion of Kay's episodic approach in the employment context, see chapter 5, above. Kay also applies episodic analysis in the family context, where she uses it to address the social consequences of reproductive difference; "Equality and Difference: A Perspective on No-Fault Divorce and Its Aftermath," *University of Cincinnati Law Review* 56(1987): 1–90. It may be that Kay's position fits more easily within the acceptance category, discussed below. For other accommodationist contributions to the debate over pregnancy disability legislation, see Linda J. Krieger and Patricia N. Cooney, "The Miller-Wohl Controversy: Equal Treatment, Positive Action and the Meaning of Women's Equality," *Golden Gate University Law Review* 13, no. 3 (Summer 1983): 513–572 (discussed above in chap. 4); and Nancy E. Dowd, "Maternity Leave: Taking Sex Differences into Account," *Fordham Law Review* 54(1986): 699–765.

17. California Federal Savings and Loan Association v. Guerra, 479 U.S. 272, 290 (1987). Littleton suggests the Supreme Court used an acceptance rather than an accommodation analysis; "Reconstructing Sexual Equality," 1299; see also Martha Minow, *Making All the Difference: Inclusion,*

Exclusion, and American Law (Ithaca, N.Y.: Cornell University Press, 1990), 58–59, 87–88.

18. Christine Littleton, "Equality across Difference: A Place for Rights Discourse?" *Wisconsin Women's Law Journal* 3(1987): 189–212, esp. 193; idem, "Reconstructing Sexual Equality," 1313, 1329–1330; see also idem, "Equality and Feminist Legal Theory," *University of Pittsburgh Law Review* 48 (1987): 1043–1059. Littleton earlier described the acceptance theory as one that reconstructed equality as affirmation of women's difference, but withdrew the term as too celebratory; see "Reconstructing Sexual Equality," 1297 n.99.

19. For the CREW brief, written by Littleton, see chapter 5, above. Finley, "Transcending Equality Theory," 1181–1182.

20. Littleton, "Reconstructing Sexual Equality," 1330–1331.

21. See the works cited in chapter 6, notes 2 and 3, above.

22. Finley, "Transcending Equality Theory," 1158, 1164. Katheleen Lahey, ". . . Until Women Themselves Have Told All That They Have to Tell . . . ," *Osgoode Hall Law Journal* 23(1985): 519–541, esp. 535.

23. Barbara A. Brown, Thomas I. Emerson, Gail Falk, and Ann E. Freedman, "The Equal Rights Amendment: A Constitutional Basis for Equal Rights for Women," *Yale Law Journal* 80(1971): 871–986, esp. 894; Law, "Rethinking Sex and the Constitution," 975–977, 1009 n.204. Martha Minow discusses the dualism of traditional American jurisprudence in *Making All the Difference*, chaps. 4 and 5.

24. I am here focusing on what Michele Barrett distinguishes as experiential diversity; see "The Concept of 'Difference,' " *Feminist Review* 26(1987): 28–41. For an extended discussion of how silence about diversity can mask and perpetuate privilege, see Elizabeth V. Spelman, *Inessential Woman: Problems of Exclusion in Feminist Thought* (Boston: Beacon Press, 1988). The point is not new. It was, for example, an important theme in the civil rights movement of the 1960s; in written form I first encountered such analyses in the discussions of identity offered by James Baldwin, Lillian Smith, and Frantz Fanon. For the rediscovery of diversity by feminist scholars in the 1980s, see Lise Vogel, "Telling Tales: Historians of Our Own Lives," *Journal of Women's History* 2(1991): 89–101.

25. Carol Gilligan, *In a Different Voice: Psychological Theory and Women's Development* (Cambridge: Harvard University Press, 1982). For a typical application of Gilligan, see Finley, "Transcending Equality Theory." For critiques of the influence of Gilligan within feminist legal scholarship, see Kathleen Daly, "Criminal Justice Ideologies and Practices in Different Voices: Some Feminist Questions about Justice," *International Journal of the Sociology of Law* 17(1989): 1–18; and Joan C. Williams, "Deconstructing Gender," *Michigan Law Review* 87 (1989): 797–845.

26. Frances M. Beale, "Double Jeopardy: To Be Black and Female," *New Generation* 51(1969): 23–28; frequently anthologized, for example, in Toni Cade, ed., *The Black Woman: An Anthology* (New York: New American Library, 1970), 90–100. Patricia Hill Collins discusses the term black feminist

thought in *Black Feminist Thought: Knowledge, Consciousness, and the Politics of Empowerment* (Boston: Unwin Hyman, 1990), chap. 2.

27. For early critiques of the parallelism of the additive model, mostly but not entirely by women of color, see, for example, Elizabeth M. Almquist, "Untangling the Effects of Race and Sex: The Disadvantaged Status of Black Women," *Social Science Quarterly* 56(1975): 129–142; Hazel Carby, "White Women Listen! Black Feminism and the Boundaries of Sisterhood," in *The Empire Strikes Back: Race and Racism in 70s Britain*, ed. Centre for Contemporary Cultural Studies (London: Hutchinson, 1982), 212–235; Gloria Joseph, "The Incompatible Menage à Trois: Marxism, Feminism, and Racism," in *Women and Revolution: A Discussion of the Unhappy Marriage of Marxism and Feminism*, ed. Lydia Sargent (Boston: South End, 1981), 91–108; Margaret A. Simons, "Racism and Feminism: A Schism in the Sisterhood," *Feminist Studies* 5(1979): 384–401; Elizabeth V. Spelman, "Theories of Race and Gender: The Erasure of Black Women," *Quest* 5, no. 4 (1982): 36–62; Lise Vogel, "Correspondence: Two Views of 'The Class Roots of Feminism,' " *Monthly Review* 28, no. 9 (1977): 52–60. Deborah K. King summarizes the development of the additive model in "Multiple Jeopardy, Multiple Consciousness: The Context of a Black Feminist Ideology," *Signs* 14(1988–1989): 42–72, esp. 46–47; see also Rose M. Brewer, "Black Women and Feminist Sociology: The Emerging Perspective," *American Sociologist*, Spring 1989, 57–70.

28. King, "Multiple Jeopardy," 49; Aida Hurtado, "Relating to Privilege: Seduction and Rejection in the Subordination of White Women and Women of Color," *Signs* 14(1988–1989): 833–855, esp. 845; Karen Brodkin Sacks, "Toward a Unified Theory of Class, Race, and Gender," *American Ethnologist* 16(1989): 534–550, esp. 542; Collins, *Black Feminist Thought*, 222. See also Chandra Talpede Mohanty, Ann Russo, and Lourdes Torres, eds., *Third World Women and the Politics of Feminism* (Bloomington: Indiana University Press, 1991); and Gloria Anzaldúa, ed., *Making Face, Making Soul/ Haciendo Caras: Creative and Critical Perspectives by Women of Color* (San Francisco: Aunt Lute Foundation Books, 1990).

29. For bibliographical overviews of socialist-feminist theory, see Lise Vogel, "Feminist Scholarship: The Impact of Marxism," in *The Left Academy*, ed. Bertell Ollman and Edward Vernoff (New York: Praeger, 1986), 3: 1–34; Sacks, "Toward a Unified Theory of Class, Race, and Gender."

30. Linda Gordon, "The New Feminist Scholarship on the Welfare State," in *Women, the State, and Welfare*, ed. Linda Gordon (Madison: University of Wisconsin Press, 1990), 9–35, esp. 30; Hazel V. Carby, "The Politics of Difference," *Ms. Magazine*, September/October 1990, 84–85. See also Linda Gordon, "On 'Difference,' " *Genders* 10(1991): 91–111; and the commentaries on Michele Barrett and Mary McIntosh, "Ethnocentrism and Socialist-Feminist Theory," *Feminist Review* 20(June 1985): 23–47, in *Feminist Review*, nos. 22 and 23.

31. Iris Marion Young discusses the problem of groups in *Justice and the Politics of Difference* (Princeton: Princeton University Press, 1990), chap. 2. For

a sympathetic critique of Young's analysis, see Chantal Mouffe, "Feminism, Citizenship, and Radical Democratic Politics," in *Feminists Theorize the Political*, ed. Judith Butler and Joan W. Scott (New York: Routledge, 1992), 369–384.

32. Minow, *Making All the Difference*.

10. Different but Not Unequal

1. Judith Stacey, "Are Feminists Afraid to Leave Home? The Challenge of Conservative Pro-family Feminism," in *What Is Feminism*, ed. Juliet Mitchell and Ann Oakley (New York: Pantheon Books, 1986), 184–237.
2. Martha Fineman, for example, ends her important critique of divorce reform on this note: "The rhetoric of equality is too easily appropriated and utilized to gain support for antifeminist measures. Equality rhetoric is a rhetoric that belongs both to no one, and to everyone. For this reason alone, it would seem time to abandon equality." Martha Albertson Fineman, *The Illusion of Equality: The Rhetoric and Reality of Divorce Reform* (Chicago: University of Chicago Press, 1991), 190.
3. Carol Smart, *Feminism and the Power of Law* (New York: Routledge, 1989).
4. I borrow the term differential consideration from Mary Segers, who used it in a different sense in her pioneering discussion of equality policies: "Equality, Public Policy and Relevant Sex Differences," *Polity* 11(1979): 319–339.
5. Roslyn L. Feldberg, "Comparable Worth: Toward Theory and Practice in the United States," *Signs* 10 (1984–1985): 311–328, esp. 328. For a spectrum of views on comparable worth, see Johanna Brenner, "Feminist Political Discourses: Radical versus Liberal Approaches to the Feminization of Poverty and Comparable Worth," *Gender and Society* 1(1987): 447–465; Ronnie Steinberg, "Radical Challenges in a Liberal World: The Mixed Success of Comparable Worth," *Gender and Society* 1(1987): 466–475; Linda M. Blum, "Possibilities and Limits of the Comparable Worth Movement," *Gender and Society* 1(1987): 380–399; Alice Kessler-Harris, "The Just Price, the Free Market, and the Value of Women," *Feminist Studies* 14(1988): 235–250; Sara Evans and Barbara Nelson, *Wage Justice: Comparable Worth and the Paradox of Technocratic Reform* (Chicago: University of Chicago Press, 1989); Joan Acker, *Doing Comparable Worth: Gender, Class, and Pay Equity* (Philadelphia: Temple University Press, 1989).
6. As discussed above in chapter 7, the specifics of family and medical leave legislation vary. Nadine Taub was influential in broadening the notion of caretaking leave; see her "From Parental Leaves to Nurturing Leaves," *New York University Review of Law and Social Change* 13, no 2 (1984–1985): 381–405.

Index